Global Climate Change

NEW HORIZONS IN ENVIRONMENTAL ECONOMICS

Series Editors: Wallace E. Oates, *Professor of Economics, University of Maryland, USA* and Henk Folmer, *Professor of General Economics, Wageningen University and Professor of Environmental Economics, Tilburg University, The Netherlands*

This important series is designed to make a significant contribution to the development of the principles and practices of environmental economics. It includes both theoretical and empirical work. International in scope, it addresses issues of current and future concern in both East and West and in developed and developing countries.

The main purpose of the series is to create a forum for the publication of high quality work and to show how economic analysis can make a contribution to understanding and resolving the environmental problems confronting the world in the twenty-first century.

Recent titles in the series include:

Global Climate Change

The Science, Economics and Politics

Edited by
James M. Griffin

Professor of Economics and Public Policy
George Bush School of Government and Public Service
Texas A&M University

NEW HORIZONS IN ENVIRONMENTAL ECONOMICS

BUSH SERIES IN THE ECONOMICS OF PUBLIC POLICY

Edward Elgar
Cheltenham, UK • Northampton, MA, USA

Published by
Edward Elgar Publishing Limited
Glensanda House
Montpellier Parade
Cheltenham
Glos GL50 1UA
UK

Edward Elgar Publishing, Inc.
136 West Street
Suite 202
Northampton
Massachusetts 01060
USA

A catalogue record for this book
is available from the British Library

Library of Congress Cataloguing in Publication Data
Global climate change : the science, economics, and politics / edited by James M. Griffin.
     p. cm. — (Bush School series in the economics of public policy ; v. 4) (New horizons in environmental economics)
     Includes index.
     1. Climatic changes. I. Griffin, James M., 1944– II. Series. III. Series: New horizons in environmental economics

    QC981.8.C65 G59 2003
    363.738'745—dc21

                             2002029476

ISBN 1 84376 190 4

Typeset by Manton Typesetters, Louth, Lincolnshire, UK.
Printed and bound in Great Britain by MPG Books Ltd, Bodmin, Cornwall.

Volume IV in the Bush School Series in
the Economics of Public Policy

Edited by James M. Griffin

Corporate Sponsors of the Series and Bush Advisory Board Members

Contents

Figures

Tables

Contributors

Robert L. Bradley, Jr., is President of the Institute for Energy Research, Houston, TX, and adjunct scholar of the Cato Institute. He was formerly Director of Public Policy Analysis at the Enron Corporation.

James A. Edmonds is Chief Scientist and Technical Leader of Economic Programs at the Pacific Northwest National Laboratory in College Park, Maryland. He has written several monographs on climate change, including *Global Energy: Assessing the Future* (?), and is the lead author on his specialty for the IPCC's TAR Report (2001).

Lawrence H. Goulder is Professor of Economics at the Institute for International Studies at Stanford University, Palo Alto, CA, a University Fellow at Resources for the Future, and a Research Associate at the National Bureau of Economic Research.

James M. Griffin is Professor of Economics and Public Policy in the George Bush School of Government and Public Service, and holder of the Bob Bullock Chair at Texas A&M University, College Station, TX.

Lennart Hjalmarssen is Chair in the Department of Economics and Finance, Goteborg University, Sweden.

Brian Hurd is an Assistant Professor in the Department of Agricultural Economics and Agricultural Business at New Mexico State University in Las Cruces, New Mexico.

Jeffrey K. Lazo is a Senior Associate of Stratus Consulting, in Boulder, Colorado.

Alan S. Manne is Professor Emeritus of Operations Research at Stanford University, Palo Alto, CA, a Fellow of the Econometric Society, a Fellow of the American Academy of Arts and Sciences, and a Fellow of the National Academy of Engineering.

Robert Mendelsohn is the Edwin Weyerhaeuser Davis Professor at the Yale School of Forestry and Environmental Studies, Yale, New Haven, CT. He is the author of 'The Impact of Global Warming on Agriculture: A Ricardian Analysis' in the *American Economic Review* (**84**, pp. 753–71).

Gerald R. North is Distinguished Professor of Meteorology and Head of the Department of Atmospheric Sciences at Texas A&M University, College Station, TX, a Fellow of the American Meteorology Society and a Fellow of the American Association for the Advancement of Science.

Paul Portney is the President of Resources for the Future, Washington, DC.

Ronald D. Sands is Senior Economist at the Pacific Northwest National Laboratory in College Park, Maryland.

William H. Schlesinger is Dean of the Nicholas School of the Environment and Earth Sciences and James B. Duke Professor of Biogeochemistry at Duke University, Durham, NC. He is a member of the Committee on Global Climate Change Research of the National Academy of Sciences, and directs the Free Air Carbon Dioxide Enrichment Experiment in the Duke Forest. He is the author of *Biogeochemistry: An Analysis of Global Change* (Academic Press, 1997).

Joel B. Smith is Vice President of Stratus Consulting in Boulder, Colorado, and was formerly Deputy Director of the Climate Change Division of the Environmental Protection Agency. He has examined climate change impacts for a variety of organizations including the World Bank and the International Institute for Applied Systems Analysis, and is convening lead author on his specialty for the IPCC's TAR report (2001).

David G. Victor is the Robert W. Johnson, Jr., Senior Fellow for Science and Technology at the Council on Foreign Relations in New York. He is also Senior Fellow and Director of the Program on Energy and Sustainable Development at the Institute for International Studies, Stanford University, Palo Alto, CA. A political scientist, he is the author of numerous articles on international environmental law and three books, including *The Collapse of the Kyoto Protocol and the Struggle to Slow Global Warming* (Princeton University Press, 2001).

John P. Weyant is the Director of the Energy Modeling Forum at Stanford University, Palo Alto, CA.

1. Introduction: the many dimensions of the climate change issue

James M. Griffin

1 THE MOTHER OF ALL PROBLEMS?

Global climate change has been described as the 'mother' of all problems. This rhetoric suggests that apocalyptic events will unfold as humanity marches blindly forward demanding more and more autos, jet travel, and air-conditioned homes. Once having crossed over the precipice, there will be no returning to that earlier world. The Earth's atmosphere will have been irreversibly violated and humans must forever reap the consequences of their profligate lifestyle.

Whether or not this alarmist view is correct is open to debate. But in another sense, we can agree that as an *intellectual* exercise, climate change appears to be the 'mother' of all problems because of it complexity. Anyone who has attempted to understand the carbon cycle, the climatological interactions of CO_2 in the atmosphere, the effects of climate change on market and non-market activities, the technological options to abate carbon emissions, or how a market-based trading system of CO_2 permits might work usually comes away frustrated and hopelessly bewildered. The available literature is little help as it is often written by specialists to other specialists within the same discipline. Even the specialists may feel frustrated because it is not enough to know the science underlying the carbon cycle, for example. Climate change brings together the disciplines of botany, climatology, biology, atmospheric and oceanic chemistry, glaciology, systems modeling, cloud physics, statistics, economics, and political science. It seems impossible for any one person to achieve proficiency in all these areas.

Do not despair. Even though global climate change may appear hopelessly complex, it does not follow that the lay person cannot understand in a general way the various issues from which reasonable policy prescriptions follow. Nor does it follow that the policy arena must be ceded to the specialists. The specialists may be thoroughly versed in their own narrow area of the global climate change equation, but it is only one aspect. Paradoxically, they may be too deep in the forest to see the trees. For you the lay person with a healthy respect for what you do not know, yours may be the reward of a clear view of the choices before us and the uncertainties on which they hinge. This volume is written for you.

Precisely, because the climate change issue cuts across so many academic disciplines, this volume consists of chapters by eminent scholars who are specialists in their unique area of the overall climate change equation, and it is organized around the following eight 'big picture' questions:

- Chapter 2: What is the linkage between fossil fuel consumption and carbon dioxide (CO_2) concentrations in the atmosphere?
- Chapter 3: What is the relationship between CO_2 concentrations and global warming?
- Chapter 4: Is the principal tool of economic analysis, benefit–cost analysis, adequate for prescribing policy recommendations for global climate change?
- Chapter 5: In a business-as-usual world, what are the damages from global warming on the types of market activities included in GDP?
- Chapter 6: In a business-as-usual world, what are the most significant non-market effects of climate change?
- Chapter 7: What are the mitigation costs of various policies and what technologies are available to significantly reduce CO_2 emissions?
- Chapter 8: What does cost–benefit analysis tell us about how vigorously we should be working to reduce CO_2 emissions?
- Chapter 9: What policy options are likely to lead to cooperative efforts to reduce carbon emissions in a world with independent nation states whose compliance is voluntary?

The last and final question not listed above is the fundamental question, 'What actions are best taken now versus later?'. Each of you will hopefully have reached your own conclusions after reading our experts' answers to the above eight questions.

Chapter 10 is entitled, 'Five letters to the President', and summarizes the policy advice of five close observers to the climate change debate. One might ask, 'But why interject the President of the United States?'. Interestingly, just one week prior to the conference on 6 April 2001, the above papers were presented at a conference on 'Global Climate Change: The Science, Economics and Politics' at the Bush Presidential Conference Center, Texas A&M University, President George W. Bush announced his rejection of the Kyoto Protocol, proclaiming it was not in the nation's interests. To the surprise of the White House, this announcement unleashed a maelstrom of criticism in Europe.

President Bush's rejection of the Kyoto Protocol suddenly thrusts him onto the world stage and calls for his leadership in shaping a new policy that is realistic and workable. Over the ensuing months, President Bush has no doubt received many briefings from numerous experts. Our distinguished group of generalists were told to assume that they had been granted ten minutes in which to brief President Bush on global climate change policy. You will enjoy reading their points of view and comparing them against what you gleaned from the preceding eight 'big picture' questions. Most interestingly, you will enjoy comparing their advice with President Bush's latest plan calling for voluntary reductions of carbon emissions.

Each of the eight 'big picture' questions listed above is addressed in the subsequent eight chapters by a noted specialist in that area. In selecting specialists on each of these topics, a conscious effort was made to select those who would present the mainstream view of the specialists working on that particular issue. Each contributor was asked to present the 'prevailing wisdom' on their particular question. Of course, to the extent that their own views differed from the 'prevailing wisdom', they were at liberty to note these differences.

Why Focus on the 'Prevailing Wisdom'?

Why focus on the prevailing wisdom rather than surveying the full range of opinions since today's prevailing wisdom is often tomorrow's mistaken theories? One only needs to look at the range of oil price projections for the year 2000 made during the heyday of the OPEC (Organization of Petroleum-Exporting Countries) cartel's success in the early 1980s to gain a healthy skepticism for the prevailing wisdom. The widely accepted oil price forecasts for the year 2000 called for $100 per barrel (see International Energy Workshop, 1984) – four times actual prices. A cynic might point out that global climate change research is an industry in itself. The cynic might even ask, 'Why would we expect researchers whose funding depends on a crisis to tell us anything different?'. Besides economic self-interest in the form of research grants, academics are not immune from the type of 'herding' tendencies so apparent on Wall Street.

Academics, like other humans, are not immune from incentives or from the herding mentality. But here the effects are much more subtle than those alluded to by the cynic's view. By their nature, researchers want to work on substantive problems. Consequently, researchers with strong Bayesian beliefs that climate change represents a serious problem are more often attracted to the field than those viewing it as a non-problem. While they do not blindly follow the mainstream view, acceptance by one's peers is also a vital concern. In sum, there does exist the potential for biased and highly misleading policy prescriptions emanating from the prevailing wisdom.

The justification for following the prevailing wisdom rests on three grounds. First, even though there may exist selection bias in the researchers studying the problem and herding tendencies, in both the physical and social sciences, scientific methods require the verification and validation of results. Moreover, even for untested theories, the peer review process in the major journals offers a strong quality control device. Fortunately, in academics there is a free market for ideas that ensures that science will ultimately get it right. Second, it would be impractical to survey the wide range of opinions that might exist on each of the above eight topics. The reader would be left totally confused and unable to judge the credibility of the voluminous facts presented. When confronted with widely conflicting opinions, it is human nature to do nothing. In this case, inaction could be very dangerous since it may be many years before the uncertainty is reduced on many of these topics. By then, largely irreversible damage to the atmosphere may have occurred. Third, surveying the prevailing wisdom on each of these eight critical ingredients in the global climate change equation is an extremely valuable logical exercise – far preferable to simply surveying some group of 'experts', who reflect the vantage of their own narrow specialty. In principle, looking at the prevailing wisdom for all eight questions must form the basis for current climate change policy. Of course, we cannot view today's policy prescriptions as fixed immutably in stone. It will surely evolve as new information alters the prevailing wisdom. In any event, the prevailing wisdom must be the starting point for current policy.

2   BACKGROUND INFORMATION

Why the Emphasis on CO_2?

Before jumping head first into Chapter 2 with discussions of the carbon cycle, it is important to acquire some background facts that will prove helpful throughout the volume. The focus in this volume is the role of carbon dioxide (CO_2) as a determinant of global warming. Carbon dioxide is a greenhouse gas that regulates the rate at which the planet can radiate heat energy back to space. Greenhouse gases are transparent to incoming solar radiation, but largely opaque to the passage of infrared radiation back out into space. In effect, these gases form a type of greenhouse that traps solar heat near the earth's surface, causing global warming and other climate changes. Besides CO_2, other greenhouse gases include halocarbons, nitrous oxide, methane, tropospheric ozone, and water vapor. Most of these greenhouse gases occur naturally and are essential for providing temperate conditions under which life on earth is possible. In effect, the earth comes equipped with its own naturally occurring greenhouse. So greenhouse gases clearly do not belong on the list of air pollutants like sulfur oxides, particulates and so forth.

Since the Industrial Revolution, human-induced (or anthropogenic) emissions of greenhouse gases have gradually increased the concentrations of greenhouse gases. It is these anthropogenic greenhouse gas emissions that are the concern for global climate change. Traditionally, up until 1950, temperature change was dominated by natural factors such as changes in solar radiation and volcanically produced dust veils. Since then, human-induced factors have emerged as the dominant cause of climate change. Disentangling natural from anthropogenic causes is an inexact science, but several statistics stand out. Wigley (1999) reports approximately a 0.5 degree Celsius or a 0.9 degree Fahrenheit increase in global mean temperature over the 1950–2000 period. Wigley's graph suggests that about three-quarters of radiative forcings are attributable to anthropogenic sources (pp. 10, 15). The remainder is primarily attributable to increased solar activity, a natural phenomenon over which we have no control.

Typically, we focus on CO_2 because it is the greenhouse gas that is thought to have contributed the most to global warming over the last 250 years. Climatologists use the concept of 'forcing' to indicate the warming effect of a particular agent such as a greenhouse gas.[1] This allows us to assess how much warming might be attributed to each of the greenhouse gases. It is estimated that CO_2 has historically accounted for 53 percent of the anthroprogenic forcings associated with greenhouse gases (see IPCC, 2001). The second largest contributor, methane gas, accounts for about 17 percent of the warming. Methane arises from a number of sources such as agriculture, livestock, and land-fill emissions. Tropospheric ozone, the third largest contributor, accounts for 13 percent of greenhouse gases forcings. Tropospheric ozone is linked to the emissions of carbon monoxide, nitrogen oxides and light hydrocarbons. The fourth largest anthropogenic contributor, halocarbons, account for 12 percent of greenhouse gas forcings. (They are linked primarily to emissions of chlorofluorocarbons from freon in air-conditioners and refrigerators, which are now regulated under the Montreal Protocol because of their effects on the Earth's ozone layer. Unfortunately, their replacements – while benign to the ozone layer – are relatively bad greenhouse gases.) Nitrous oxides, which account for the remaining 5 percent, are produced primarily by nitrogen compounds in fertilizers.

One might wonder, 'Why does CO_2 receive so much attention, since other greenhouse gases contribute almost half of the total?'. This question seems even more perplexing if indeed *all* anthropogenic forcings explain roughly three-quarters of the 0.9° F (or 0.5° C) mean temperature increase over the last half-century. The effects attributable to CO_2 seem small and hardly a matter for public policy concern. The explanation is complex, but the prevailing wisdom suggests that the effects of CO_2 concentrations over the next 50 years will not be nearly as inconsequential as in the past.

First, compared to other greenhouse gases, CO_2 is a very long-lived gas, meaning that current CO_2 emissions will persist for several centuries in the atmosphere before atmospheric removal mechanisms purge them. In contrast, methane is estimated to have a lifetime of 12 years.[2] Consequently, emissions of CO_2 remain in the atmosphere, contributing to current forcings, while for methane, its concentrations, and thus forcings, depend critically on recent emissions. Thus for CO_2, past as well as future emissions will have very long-term consequences.

Second, CO_2 promises to provide the bulk of the future growth in greenhouse gas concentrations because of its tie to energy consumption. Except in countries experiencing deforestation, energy consumption from fossil fuels contributes almost all of current CO_2 emissions. For example, in the US, fossil fuels are estimated to account for 98 percent of CO_2 emissions (see Energy Information Administration, 2001). Figure 1.1 shows there is a roughly proportional relationship between economic activity measured in GDP and energy consumption. Low-income countries are associated with low energy consumption and vice versa. In the future, as both underdeveloped and developed nations grow, it is inescapable that energy consumption will grow. For the foreseeable future, fossil fuels will account for the bulk of energy consumption. Table 1.1 ranks the world's 20 largest energy consumers and shows

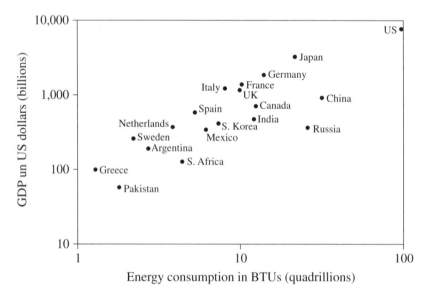

Figure 1.1   Energy use and GDP for selected countries

Table 1.1   Twenty largest energy-consuming nations and their fuel mix (%)

Country	Total energy*	Shares by fuel type			
		Fossil fuel	Nuclear	Hydroelectric	Other
United States	97.1	87.1	8.2	3.6	1.1
China	31.9	92.3	0.5	7.3	0.0
Russia	26.0	89.0	4.7	6.3	0.0
Japan	21.7	80.1	14.5	4.1	1.3
Germany	14.0	85.9	11.6	1.4	1.1
Canada	12.5	65.7	6.1	27.6	0.6
India	12.2	91.9	1.1	6.9	0.1
France	10.3	57.4	35.5	6.8	0.2
United Kingdom	9.9	86.9	11.7	0.6	0.9
Brazil	8.5	59.0	0.5	39.3	1.3
Italy	8.0	92.3	0.0	6.1	1.5
Korea, South	7.4	86.1	13.3	0.6	0.0
Ukraine	6.4	86.1	11.4	2.5	0.0
Mexico	6.1	91.1	1.6	5.5	1.8
Spain	5.2	83.4	11.0	4.8	0.8
Australia	4.7	95.8	0.0	3.5	0.7
Iran	4.7	98.4	0.0	1.6	0.0
South Africa	4.4	96.9	2.9	0.2	0.0
Saudi Arabia	4.3	100.0	0.0	0.0	0.0
Poland	3.8	98.7	0.0	1.1	0.2

Note: * In 10^{15} BTU in 1999.

Source: US Energy Information Administration (1999).

the mix of fuels attributed to fossil fuels, hydroelectric, nuclear, and other energy forms. Typically, fossil fuels account for around 90 percent of total energy consumption. Even in France, which relies heavily on nuclear power for electricity generation, fossil fuels account for 57 percent of total energy requirements. Hydroelectric power is limited primarily by suitable sites and thus has very limited potential for expansion in the industrialized nations. Only in water-rich countries like Brazil does the share of hydroelectric energy approach 40 percent. Solar, biomass, and other miscellaneous energy sources account for less than 2 percent in all of the countries surveyed. This latter statistic is striking because of all the public efforts to jump start alternative energy sources during the energy crises of the 1970s. These alternative energy sources remain uncompetitive with lower-cost fossil fuels. Nuclear energy tends to be more costly than fossil fuels; furthermore, public opposition to nuclear power remains strong throughout much of the developed world. Thus it seems inescapable that for the foreseeable future, fossil fuels will continue to provide the backbone of world energy supplies. In contrast, other greenhouse gases such as methane and nitrous oxides emissions are closely linked to agriculture, which seems likely to expand more slowly as population growth slows. Thus as a fraction of greenhouse gases, CO_2 is estimated to account for three-quarters of future greenhouse gas forcings (see IPCC, 2001).

Third, in the past the temperature effects of the growth in CO_2 via fossil fuels appear to have been substantially offset by increased sulfate aerosols, which tend to have a cooling effect. In the past, sulfur oxide emissions from high sulfur coal and fuel oil grew basically at the same rate as all fossil fuels. Interestingly, the resulting sulfur oxides have just the opposite effects of CO_2-producing global cooling. Paradoxically, the increased CO_2 concentrations from fossil fuels were substantially counteracted by concentrations of sulfur oxides. This may help explain why anthropogenic effects on global mean temperature appear 'small' during the last 50 years. In recent years, environmental efforts have substantially reduced sulfur oxide emissions because of their detrimental health and agricultural effects. These policies have switched the mix of fossil fuels to those with low sulfur content, like natural gas. Now suddenly, the counterbalancing effects of sulfur oxides are no longer as strong. The full impact of the CO_2 concentrations on temperature could then be realized as fossil-fuel consumption expands with worldwide economic activity.

Fourth, some would point to the creation and preservation of carbon sinks, such as forests that absorb CO_2, as a major policy alternative to direct CO_2 abatement. They might claim that by increasing carbon sinks, this might enable the continued growth of CO_2 and the fossil fuels linked to it. But this is not a viable long-run strategy. Surely in the past, the destruction of tropical rain forests destroyed huge carbon sinks which have contributed to global warming in the past half-century. Nevertheless, a ban on the destruction of tropical rain forests or even massive reforestation programs cannot enable carbon sinks to grow fast enough to offset the rapid growth of fossil fuels (see Schlesinger, Chapter 2). The carbon cycle is a very complex phenomenon as explained by Schlesinger. Carbon sinks have in the past absorbed about half of CO_2 emissions (see IPCC, 2001), but the capacity of the system to accommodate larger doses of CO_2 is limited. The limited capacity of carbon sinks means that *incremental* emissions of CO_2 are likely to move directly to the atmosphere, contributing much more directly to future greenhouse gases.

The Important Distinction between CO_2 Emissions and CO_2 Concentration

Having zeroed in on CO_2 as the primary greenhouse gas, scientists typically focus on the following two questions: (i) How long will it take before CO_2 concentration in the atmosphere double? and (ii) What climate changes will result from this doubling of CO_2 concentration? The reader will note that the above two questions center on CO_2 *concentration*, not CO_2 *emissions*. There is a vital difference. CO_2 concentration is a stock concept measuring the amount of CO_2 present in the atmosphere at a given time. CO_2 emissions is a flow concept, measuring the additions of CO_2 to the atmosphere over a given time period. Current CO_2 concentration is governed by the following perpetual inventory equation:

$$CO_2 \text{ Concentration}_t = CO_2 \text{ Concentration}_{t-1} + CO_2 \text{ Emissions}_t - CO_2 \text{ Absorption}_t. \quad (1.1)$$

Once emitted, CO_2 emissions enter the atmosphere raising CO_2 concentrations in period t from the concentrations reached in period $t-1$. CO_2 absorption is proportional to total concentrations, but the rate of absorption is very slow. Thus CO_2 is a 'long-lived gas'. Critically, CO_2 emissions in any period have a relatively small impact on CO_2 concentrations, yet cumulatively over 50 or 100 years, the CO_2 concentrations depend critically on the cumulative sum of past net CO_2 emissions. For example, CO_2 concentrations in the atmosphere are approximately 370 parts per million (ppm). Most recently, CO_2 emissions less absorption are estimated to raise concentrations by only 1.5 (see IPCC, 2001). For example, concentrations might rise from 370 to 371.5 in a year. A key statistic to remember is that CO_2 concentrations in the atmosphere have risen from 280 ppm at the time of the Industrial Revolution to approximately 370 ppm today.

This simple inventory equation explains why global warming is such a potentially serious long-term problem. As explained by Schlesinger in Chapter 2, CO_2 absorption is dependent on the limited capacities of oceans and forests to absorb increased CO_2 concentrations. Consequently, CO_2 emissions remain suspended in the atmosphere for periods as long as several centuries.[3] Society cannot instantaneously adjust CO_2 concentrations and thereby turn up or down the temperature thermostat. Instead, society faces the choice of reducing CO_2 emissions in year t. This cutback will only be meaningful if followed up by subsequent cuts in future periods, since a single, one-shot reduction in any one year will have a minimal impact on total concentrations. While policy makers must tinker with the rate of CO_2 *emissions*, scientists concerned with climate change focus on CO_2 *concentrations* and their effect on climate. Since emission cutbacks in the present are costly and meaningful only if continued in the future, there is a great temptation for policy makers to do nothing, especially since the benefits fall primarily in the future.

Factors Influencing Future CO_2 Emission Rates

It is useful to review the factors that determine total CO_2 emissions from fossil fuels, since together with the carbon cycle (operating through CO_2 absorption in equation (1.1)) they determine the rate of net CO_2 emissions entering the atmosphere. Even under a 'business-as-usual' scenario, the researcher must project future energy demands, separating fossil fuels from non-fossil fuels, and finally identifying individual fossil fuels.

Unfortunately, researchers cannot forecast individual fuel consumption for the next 100 years without making a number of assumptions and specifying a number of key empirical relationships. First, one must develop forecasts of aggregate energy demand for a particular country or region, which necessarily involves quantifying the four determinants of energy demand: (i) population growth, (ii) GDP per capita growth, (iii) energy/non-energy substitution possibilities and (iv) the rate of energy-saving technical change. This visualization of demand postulates that energy demand is directly tied to the underlying population base and its rate of GDP growth. Thus economic activity is seen as the primary driver of energy consumption, whether fed by a growing population and/or by rising per capita incomes. The energy crisis of the 1970s has taught us that there exists the possibility of altering the amount of energy in a dollar's worth of GDP because of either price-induced substitution responses or technical change of an energy-saving nature. Price-induced substitution responses simply reflect the fact that as energy prices increase *vis-à-vis* capital, labor, and material prices, it is possible to substitute other inputs for energy. Also, the energy price increases of the 1970s set in motion a powerful longer-term response – energy-saving technical change. Technological advances have made it possible to produce the same output with substantially less energy use. For illustrative purposes, Figure 1.2 shows the combined effects of price-induced substitution responses and energy-saving technical change as it shows that the energy input per dollar of GDP has fallen substantially since 1970. Figure 1.2 also shows the real price of energy with its meteoric rise in the 1970s and early 1980s followed by a long period of declining real prices. Notice that the sharply rising real prices in this early period triggered price-induced substitution reponses that persisted well into the 1990s. Initially, the response to higher prices was small.

Next, it is necessary to dis-aggregate total energy consumption into fossil and non-fossil fuels and then to split fossil fuels between coal, petroleum, and natural gas. In the first instance, one must identify the price-induced

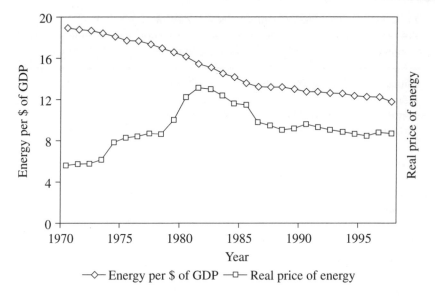

Figure 1.2   Energy input per dollar of GDP versus real price of energy

substitution responses between fossil and non-fossil energy. In the second instance, relative fossil fuel prices shape long-term fuel choices, so it is important to model these substitution responses as well. An important and often forgotten point is that not all fossil fuels are created equal. A million btu (British thermal unit) of coal results in 77 percent more CO_2 than a million btu of natural gas. Petroleum involves 39 percent more CO_2 than a million btu of natural gas (Energy Information Adminstration, 1999). As shown in Table 1.2, the mix of fossil fuels differs considerably across countries. These differences may not seem large, but consider the following example: if China employed the same mix of fossil fuels as the Netherlands, its CO_2 emissions would be reduced by 30 percent. Of course, the Netherlands utilize very little coal and large quantities of natural gas. In contrast, almost two-thirds of China's fossil fuels are attributable to coal.

Additionally, technological change can also significantly alter the mix of fuels. For example, in the absence of technological change, environmental restrictions on sulfur oxide emissions would have effectively eliminated coal from the generation of electricity in the US. Stack gas scrubbers enabled these gases to be captured and converted to elemental sulfur, enabling coal to remain a viable competitor in the electricity generation market. Another example includes combined-cycle electricity generation technology resulting in very fuel-efficient use of natural gas.

Table 1.2   Mix of fossil fuels for selected countries (%)

Country	Coal	Petroleum	Natural gas
China	66.5	30.1	3.4
India	56.1	36.2	7.8
Turkey	32.4	49.1	18.5
Germany	27.1	48.2	24.7
United States	26.5	46.3	27.2
Korea, South	22.7	66.8	10.5
Japan	19.1	65.0	15.9
Russia	17.8	21.5	60.7
Canada	17.3	45.1	37.6
Spain	17.3	69.1	13.6
Belgium	15.1	57.0	27.9
Brazil	11.5	83.5	5.1
Sweden	10.4	85.9	3.7
France	9.6	66.7	23.7
Netherlands	8.4	48.9	42.6
Italy	6.6	58.5	34.9
Norway	6.6	68.0	25.4
Mexico	4.3	72.1	23.6
Argentina	1.9	44.7	53.4

Source: US Energy Information Administration (1999).

But What Is the Scope for Deferring the Date at which CO_2 Concentrations Double?

Envisage a researcher carefully constructing energy supply–demand balances by country, aggregating them to the world level, translating them into CO_2 emissions, and ultimately arriving at CO_2 concentrations. For example, the IPCC (2001) presents a business-as-usual scenario predicting the doubling of CO_2 concentrations over current levels by 2100. Is the date 2100 cast in stone when CO_2 concentrations reach 740 ppm? Obviously, not. We are not being propelled forward by forces beyond our control. There are two factors that can alter our dates with destiny, perhaps pushing off the doubling date indefinitely. First, the price mechanism is a powerful mechanism to alter long-term CO_2 emissions. Admittedly, in the short run, substitution responses are quite limited because fuel choices are largely dictated by the stock of energy-consuming equipment, but in the long run, impressive substitution responses exist. These substitution responses include first the substitution of low-CO_2

fossil fuels, like natural gas, for high-CO_2 fossil fuels like coal. Next, there is the substitution response between fossil and non-fossil fuels. Finally, there is the energy/non-energy substitution mechanism. The second major factor is technological change which can manifest itself in a variety of ways from cheap methods of CO_2 sequestration, greater fuel efficiencies, or clean alternative energy sources. Again, in the short term, the technological frontier is essentially fixed. But over long periods of time, breakthroughs in basic research and development (R&D) can find commercialization and then after diffusion of the new technology, can profoundly reshape the energy landscape. One only needs to compare energy uses in 1900 with those in 2000 to see the effects of new technologies. In sum, both technology and the price mechanism hold great promises in affecting CO_2 emissions 20, 30, or 50 years from now and ultimately to defer significantly or even indefinitely the date at which CO_2 emissions double. But these adjustments will not be costless. They will not occur quickly, and they will not occur automatically.

What Is the Policy Framework around which to Fashion a CO_2 Abatement Strategy?

The fact that the doubling date for CO_2 emissions can be altered tells us that we have choices. Putting aside for the moment the serious issue of obtaining international cooperation to control CO_2 emissions, it is useful to ask the question what path of CO_2 emissions should an enlightened despot choose. But before our enlightened despot can choose a path for world CO_2 emissions, he/she must ask what is the criterion for preferring one path over another? Traditionally, economics has held forth benefit–cost analysis as the preferred framework to answer this question. The idea is straightforward – maximize the present value (*PV*) of benefits (*B*) less costs (*C*) as follows:

$$PV = \text{maximize}\left(B_0 - C_0 + \frac{B_1 - C_1}{1+r} + \ldots + \frac{B_n - C_n}{(1+r)^n} \right). \qquad (1.2)$$

For each time period starting in the current period 0, one computes benefits less costs and discounts the difference at the social discount rate, *r*. The benefits are computed as the market and non-market value accruing in each period from the particular CO_2 emission path chosen. Costs are the additional costs society incurs by reducing CO_2 emissions. The latter can include the higher costs of non-fossil fuels, the costs of CO_2 sequestration, and so forth. For each separate path of CO_2 emissions over time, one can compute the present value. From a policy perspective, traditional economic analysis prescribes choosing the emission path that maximizes the present value of benefits less costs.

This framework treats the whole world as a single entity measuring benefits and costs across all regions. Clearly, there may be large distributional effects with some industrialized regions incurring large CO_2 abatement costs while low-latitude, undeveloped regions may be the primary beneficiaries. In principle, our enlightened despot is not supposed to be influenced by these distributional effects. The benevolent despot knows that by maximizing the present value of benefits less costs, he/she will produce the largest economic surpluses with which to compensate loser regions.

The problem of selecting the optimal path of CO_2 emissions depends critically on what social discount rate, r to apply.[4] The reason for this is that programs which would significantly reduce today's CO_2 emissions will produce high values for C_0 in equation (1.2) with very little current offsetting benefits, B_0. Instead, the benefits will be primarily realized in the distant future. But when future benefits are discounted at rate r, they receive a much lower value in equation (1.2). For example $1.00 in benefits 50 years from now is worth only 3.4 cents today if a 7 percent discount rate is used. Alternatively, using a 2 percent social discount rate, the present value of the same dollar is worth 37.2 cents – almost 11 times more than at a 7 percent rate!

In most applications, discount rates in the 5–7 percent range would be routinely applied since these would reflect current real rates of return. But such rates would make many proposed abatement strategies yield a negative present value. To those calling for immediate large-scale emission reductions, cost–benefit analysis is an anathema to be thrown out or altered dramatically. For example, some argue that a lower social discount rate of say 2 percent should be applied, pointing out that future generations, who will be the primary beneficiaries of current emission reductions, are not present to register their preferences. In Chapter 4, Goulder reviews this contentious issue as well as a number of other arguments that have been raised against using benefit–cost analysis.

What Are the Benefits (B_i) in Equation (1.2)?

In order to compute the benefits, B_i, in equation (1.2) it is necessary to perform the following calculation: compare two paths of CO_2 emissions – one corresponding to the policy resulting in lower CO_2 emissions and the other corresponding to business-as-usual emissions. Then using equation (1.1), compute the implications of these two paths for CO_2 concentrations. The result is two separate paths of CO_2 concentrations related to the two emission paths. Since climate change is linked to CO_2 concentrations (and not the emissions in any one year), it is the *difference* in the two CO_2 concentration paths that determine the change in temperature and thus the benefits from CO_2 abatement in any given period. Even if the policy calls for substantial permanent reductions in emissions, implying substantial differences in the two emission paths, the corresponding two CO_2 concentration paths will show little differences in the near term and widening differentials over time. This explains why the near-term benefits from CO_2 abatement will necessarily be small. But over time, as the two concentration paths diverge, the benefits can become large.

Paradoxically, we use the term 'damages' to result from global warming, while we use the term 'benefits' to refer to *damages avoided* by having lower CO_2 concentrations. Both terms appear on opposite sides of the same coin. In effect, the reduction of CO_2 emissions results in damages avoided – or benefits. Invariably, the policy question arises, 'Will the incremental damages foregone (or benefits) exceed the costs of abating CO_2?'.

Two chapters focus on the benefits resulting from a lower CO_2 emission path. In Chapter 5, Mendelsohn takes the range of temperature increases discussed by North in Chapter 3 and asks what are the benefits resulting from lower temperatures as they relate to market-related activities normally recorded in GDP. Mendelsohn estimates the loss in GDP resulting from a 2.5°C warming and from a 5°C warming. Knowing the damage effects associated with these temperature increases, allows one to compute the benefits, B_i, of avoiding such an increase, which is a key input to the cost–benefit equation (1.2).

An important advancement of Mendelsohn's work is that he attempts to incorporate adaptation into his analysis. For example, global warming in agriculture will make a particular geographic region no longer suitable for growing traditional crops. Does one compute the value of the lost production of the traditional crop as the damage from global warming? Or does one consider that farmers typically adapt by selecting another crop more suitable for warmer weather? By including adaptation, the damage would be much less – the difference in returns from the two crops. Clearly, society will adapt to climate change, not only in agriculture, but in a multitude of other dimensions. Mendelsohn and other researchers in the area face a tremendously complex problem, but efforts are underway to determine the scope of these responses. Perhaps the most fascinating aspect of Mendelsohn's work is the finding of a hill-shaped damage function. Particularly for higher latitudes, modest temperature increases may even be beneficial, implying a movement up the hill. But beyond some level of warming, increasing temperature results in damages. In contrast, warm climates are already on the down side of the hill. Any further warming results unambiguously in damages. In the aggregate, as a percent of worldwide GDP, he concludes that these effects appear small.

Yet another element of benefits from CO_2 abatement are the non-market effects. A whole host of environmental and aesthetic qualities routinely enter the individual's utility even though these goods are not traded and do not comprise part of GDP. For example, climate change may affect recreational uses of vast areas. While the loss may not be recorded in GDP, the asset value of a region can be severely reduced. Yet another example, climate change may increase water temperature, killing huge areas on coral reefs in the Pacific Ocean. Valuing such losses is a daunting task; yet to assume they are negligible is not acceptable to most students of the subject. Smith, Lazo, and Hurd in Chapter 6 tackle this tough problem. Interestingly, it would appear that non-market damages from warming (or the benefits from lowering CO_2 concentrations) are potentially much greater than the market-related damages surveyed by Mendelsohn. Indeed, a vigorous program to reduce CO_2 emissions appears to depend critically on these non-market effects being large.

What Are the Costs in Equation (1.2)?

For any CO_2 emission path, economic efficiency dictates that we choose the least-cost abatement strategy. As Edmonds and Sands emphasize in Chapter 7, there is a long list of various methods to either abate CO_2 directly or to reduce it through increased carbon sinks and carbon sequestration technologies. As mentioned earlier, the price mechanism is a powerful source for long-term reductions in CO_2 emissions. A carbon tax or transferable pollution permits will put a 'price' on CO_2 which will unleash a variety of substitution responses such as energy/non-energy substitution, non-fossil fuels for fossil fuels, and low-carbon fossil fuels for high-carbon fossil fuels. Putting a price on carbon could also encourage the technological advances that have even greater potential for alleviating the problem. While creating incentives for the development of cost-effective responses is central, it is still useful to ask the following question: 'Given existing technologies and their costs of CO_2 abatement and given existing substitution possibilities, what are the least-cost methods for achieving various levels of emissions?'.

Edmonds and Sands review the data and offer some interesting findings in Chapter 7. For example, they compare the costs of various carbon sequestration technologies as well as hydrogen produced by fuel cells. Their results are central to filling in the C_i in equation (1.2). It is important to remember that obtaining large CO_2 emission reductions in the near term will be extremely costly. Given the fixity of the energy-consuming capital stock , it is preferable to link major changes to the turnover of this capital stock. Over the longer term, the costs of achieving a given percentage reduction in CO_2 emissions fall sharply. Even though long-term abatement costs are much lower, there is the tough question of how do we set in motion forces today that will guarantee these long-term responses and at the same time avoid unnecessarily high abatement costs in the present.

But What Is the Answer when We Solve the Benefit–Cost Equation (1.2)?

Even though the cost–benefit paradigm embedded in equation (1.2) gives us a clear framework within which to solve the problem of what CO_2 emission path is optimal, mathematically implementing it is fraught with practical difficulties. For example, even though the global mean temperature increase may be 2.5°C for a doubling of CO_2 concentrations, North (Chapter 3) notes that temperature increases will vary significantly by region with higher latitudes experiencing greater increases *vis-à-vis* equatorial areas. Night-time temperature increases seem likely to exceed daytime temperatures. Also, some areas will be more vulnerable to rising sea levels than others. This calls for a benefit–cost analysis that is finely dis-aggregated. Besides the computational complexity, the manpower and data requirements for such a modeling exercise are enormous. In response, modeling efforts have taken two paths. The first attempts to provide considerable geographic detail and to embed the best available benefit and cost estimates for each region. These models are called integrated assessment models. Yet another modeling approach is to use highly aggregated, simplified models. These models, like an impressionist painting, focus on representing the key relationships. Moreover, they have the advantage that one person can easily understand its properties and test its sensitivities to key parametric assumptions.

In Chapter 8, Alan Manne uses a model of this latter sort to answer the key question of what cost–benefit analysis tells us. Manne adopts an intertemporal model in which time is represented by decades. The mathematical problem he solves is the maximization of the utility of consumption where CO_2 concentrations enter his model by reducing GDP. Manne assumes that corresponding to a 2.5°C warming is a loss in market and non-market value equivalent to 1 percent of GDP. This assumption implies considerably higher damages than Mendelsohn's estimates for market losses. This of course, leaves considerable scope for the type of non-market effects surveyed in Chapter 6 by Smith, Lazo, and Hurd. The key conclusion from Manne's model is that an optimal policy would call for a moderate carbon tax of approximately \$10 to \$12/ton, but with the tax rising significantly over time – reaching \$60 per ton by 2050. Manne's results are of critical importance because of its moderation. For example, a carbon tax of \$12/ton would raise the price of gasoline by about 3 cents per gallon. He rejects doing nothing, but also rejects other proposals which could result in carbon taxes of 5 or 10 times that magnitude.

What Happens when We Throw International Politics into the Mix?

Manne's calculation of the optimal tax an enlightened despot would select is an interesting intellectual exercise, but convincing some 200+ nations in the world to voluntarily reduce CO_2 emissions throws us squarely into the world of international politics with its own set of constraints. Suddenly, the question shifts from what is economically optimal to what is politically achievable. Reaching an international consensus is complicated by a number of inescapable impediments. First, the damages from global warming will be quite unevenly distributed around the globe. Mendelsohn's finding of a hill-shaped damage response suggests that higher-latitude countries will initially benefit from moderate temperature increases. In contrast, lower-latitude regions, which tend to be the poorer, least-developed countries, will experience damages, even for small temperature increases. Yet another factor complicating the situation is that undeveloped nations in already hot climate regions face many more pressing problems than climate change. Consequently, they appear unlikely to cooperate in any abatement programs.

Not only will the benefits from reduced CO_2 concentrations be spread quite unevenly across the globe, but the costs of abatement will be spread quite unevenly as well. High-benefit regions rarely match high-abatement-cost regions. To achieve voluntary compliance, one would like each country to find it individually advantageous to reduce CO_2 emissions. But this is unlikely to occur except where high abatement costs are matched by high benefits. Instead, we observe a world where the primary beneficiaries of lower CO_2 concentrations are the poorer countries located in more temperate regions. While these countries will be the primary beneficiaries, they too will suffer the greatest damages from global warming.

Even if all countries' economic interests were mutually aligned, game theory suggests that each country's best response is to 'not cooperate' with some worldwide agreement to reduce CO_2 emissions. The prediction is that many will choose to be 'free riders'. By opting out of any agreement, the individual country avoids higher energy prices and becomes a low-cost producer *vis-à-vis* other complying nations. Furthermore, participation by any one country would not significantly affect worldwide CO_2 concentrations.[5] In sum, pursuing one's own economic interests suggest strong incentives for non-compliance. Can these be overcome? If so, what are the best mechanisms for dealing with climate change? In Chapter 9, David Victor tackles these important questions, looking at a variety of policy options. These policy options include carbon taxes, tradeable emission permits, a hybrid approach, and a pure technology approach. Victor's discussion, cast in the light of political realities, greatly enriches our understanding of the role political factors will play.

Table 1.3   Twenty largest emitters of CO_2 from fossil fuels

Country	CO_2 emissions*
United States	1519.9
China	668.7
Russia	400.1
Japan	306.7
India	243.3
Germany	229.9
United Kingdom	152.4
Canada	150.9
Italy	121.3
France	108.6
Korea, South	107.5
Ukraine	104.3
Mexico	100.6
South Africa	99.5
Australia	93.9
Brazil	88.9
Poland	84.5
Iran	84.3
Spain	81.6
Saudi Arabia	73.9

Note: * Millions of metric tons carbon equivalent from fossil fuels.

 Source: US Energy Information Administration (1999).

First, Victor offers his answer to the question of whether full compliance should be a necessary condition for proceeding with a policy of emission abatement. He recognizes that certain countries, such as China and India, are unlikely to participate initially. Table 1.3 ranks the various countries according to their estimated CO_2 emissions in 1999. Note that China and India rank second and fifth, respectively, despite their relatively low per capita incomes. Victor feels that to require compliance by such developing nations as a precondition for any cooperative action, would vitiate any hope of a cooperative policy. At the same time, countries below China and India on Table 1.3 would likely find it galling that these two large carbon emitters would be exempted.

Victor examines the difficulties of various control mechanisms. While most economists might favor a global carbon tax, Victor recognizes the difficulties of obtaining worldwide agreements on a common tax. Quantitative limits, such as those pegged to 1990 emissions for each country, as in the Kyoto Protocol, have the advantage of giving each country a well-defined target – in this case a ceiling below which it must reduce its CO_2 emissions. But since some countries can reach their targets at low cost, while others will face much higher costs, the overall costs of compliance can be reduced by encouraging the trading of emission permits. In effect, under a tradeable permits scheme, each country is granted CO_2 emission permits equal to its target. Countries who do not use all of their emission permits can sell them to other countries who find it too expensive to reach their target. In effect, emission permits would be a traded good, like other commodities. In fact, for sulfur-oxide emissions from power plants in the US, a vigorous market for emission permits already exists. This market seems to function well and offers promise for dealing with CO_2 emissions.

As Victor notes, the implementation of such policies raises a number of problems such as the initial distribution of the permits and policing compliance. Each nation need not receive emission permits equal to its target. Rather, all that is required is that the number of permits issued equal total emissions across all countries. The initial allocation of emission permits could be a powerful tool to buy the participation of hesitant countries or to compensate certain poor countries who will be particularly disadvantaged by climate change. Yet another important issue Victor considers is policing compliance and ensuring that emission permits are valid. It is clear that this is an important detail that has been swept under the rug.

Yet another major difficulty with setting arbitrary limits on CO_2 emissions and issuing only a fixed quantity of permits, is that the price of emission permits may fluctuate widely. Just as wholesale electricity prices in California reached phenomenal highs as demand bumped up against a fixed capacity, there is the possibility that many of the world's large industrial powers might find themselves emitting CO_2 beyond their countries' target and the supply of unused permits might be quite small. In this situation, the price of emission permits could skyrocket far beyond the levels of the carbon tax calculated by Manne in Chapter 8. Skyrocketing emission permits would in turn bid up the price of non-fossil fuels and low-carbon fossil fuels like natural gas, which would in turn send cost shock waves throughout the economy. The result could be akin to the energy crisis of the 1970s with a return to stagflation – high inflation and the stagnation of economic growth. In the end, the damage to the world economy could be pronounced for all the achievement of an arbitrary level of CO_2 emissions. Alternatively, had targets been set a few percent lower, the price of emission permits might have remained at reasonable levels without any deleterious macroeconomic effects. The problem, of course, is that the targets have been set many years earlier by mutual agreement and cannot be adequately forecasted many years into the future. One solution, Victor suggests, would enable additional permits to be issued when the price of permits reaches a certain ceiling. This would in effect, introduce a safety valve that would set a cap on the price of emission permits. During periods when additional permits would be sold, the system would behave analogously to a carbon tax with the tax proceeds going to the agency issuing the permits.

Yet another alternative Victor considers is a technological approach aimed at developing low-cost, non-fossil fuels or other technologies resulting in sharply lower CO_2 emissions. The advantage of the purely technological approach is twofold. First, it does not require a cooperative approach for its success. The US and any other interested nations can simply fund such an initiative. Second, by focusing entirely on new low-cost technologies, the world economy would avoid the short-term macroeconomic dislocation associated with rising fuel prices, whether from a carbon tax or tradeable permits. Presumably, when commercial alternatives to existing fossil fuels are developed, they would simply displace existing fossil-fuel technologies and energy prices would fall, rather than rise significantly. Consumers would benefit and so would the environment. As Victor points out, the drawback to sole reliance on technology is that it does not utilize the price mechanism to induce substitution responses such as non-energy for energy, non-fossil for fossil fuels, and low-carbon for high-carbon fossil fuels. Without increases in the fossil-fuel prices paid by consumers, these new technologies must compete as today against cheap fossil fuels. Higher fossil-fuel prices – induced by carbon taxes, tradeable permits, or a hybrid approach – will make it easier for new clean energy sources to compete and accelerate the diffusion of the new technologies.

3 ORGANIZATION OF THE MONOGRAPH

As noted above, the monograph is organized around eight basic questions, drawing upon experts in each of the respective fields to provide answers. Chapter 2 by William H. Schlesinger examines the carbon cycle and explains how CO_2 emissions ultimately find their way into the atmosphere. Schlesinger provides a key input to the remainder of the volume – the projected date at which CO_2 concentrations reach twice their current levels assuming a business-as-usual policy. William Schlesinger is particularly suited to address these issues; he is a specialist in bio-chemistry and directs the Free Air Carbon Dioxide Enrichment experiment in the Duke Forest – a project that aims to understand how an entire forest ecosystem will respond to growth in elevated CO_2.

Global climate change

In Chapter 3, Gerald R. North, an atmospheric physicist, examines the links connecting CO_2 emissions, concentration, and temperature change. Specifically, North takes the projected doubling of CO_2 concentration projected by Schlesinger and translates it into temperature and sea-level responses. At Texas A&M, he leads a research group building global climate models and simulating altered climates, and routinely applies estimation theory and statistical techniques to test the ability of these climate models to simulate responses to changes in CO_2.

Chapter 4, by Lawrence H. Goulder, switches from the domain of meteorology to economics to ask whether the economist's conventional tool of policy analysis, benefit–cost analysis, is adequate to deal with this potential 'Mother of all Problems'. Goulder examines the adequacy of cost–benefit analysis as a policy prescription to deal with a problem involving very long-term effects and widely different distributional effects. His previous research exploring the potential to achieve environmental protection at relatively low cost through alternative, market-based policies such as emission taxes and tradeable emissions permits, makes him particularly well-suited to address this important question.

Robert Mendelsohn is the author of Chapter 5, 'Assessing the market damages from climate change'. In effect, he provides estimates of the market-related benefits of engaging in CO_2 abatement. He is a resource economist specializing in the valuation of the effects of climate change. His path-breaking paper in the *American Economic Review* utilizes the notion of Ricardian rents as a measure of the economic loss from climate change in US agriculture and develops procedures to empirically value such changes. These measures include the effects of adaptation as farmers adjust their crops and planting cycles.

In Chapter 6, Joel Smith, Jeffrey Lazo, and Brian Hurd deal with valuing non-market damages from climate change. They are members of Stratus Consulting, a firm specializing in environmental consulting. Smith has a long history with the Climate Change Division of the Environmental Protection Agency, where he was Deputy Director and has examined climate change impacts and adaptation issues for a variety of organizations.

Chapter 7 focuses on quantifying the abatement costs of alternative CO_2 emission strategies. James Edmonds and Ronald Sands are uniquely qualified to bring the latest cost information to fill in the benefit–cost equation. Both are economists by training and have had years of experience in energy and climate modeling.

Alan Manne authors Chapter 8, which seeks to determine what cost–benefit analysis would tell us about the speed and intensity with which we should optimally reduce CO_2 emissions over time. To this task, Manne brings an impressive list of credentials plus the wisdom from many years of modeling experience. He has a unique knack of adapting relatively simple economic models to study energy–economy interactions and more recently climate–energy–economy interactions.

In Chapter 9, David Victor places the policy choices before us in an international political perspective. Victor, a political scientist by training but knowledgeable about climate change technology and economics, addresses his topic with clarity and incisive thought. He is a major policy specialist on climate change, and author of *The Collapse of the Kyoto Protocol and the Struggle to Slow Global Warming*, a monograph released just prior to President's Bush proclamation about the Kyoto Protocol. Interestingly, this monograph is very critical about the flawed nature of the Protocol and calls for a fresh start.

Hopefully, after completing Victor's chapter, you, the reader, will have formed your own policy conclusions. Is global climate change really the 'Mother' of all problems or does it belong further down the list after AIDS or world hunger or whatever? Of course, none of us can definitively answer this question at this point in time, but we can form opinions about its likely future importance. Should we adopt a wait and see attitude or should we embark immediately on a program to wean the world economy from fossil fuels? In between these extremes, are there low-cost options that will make a real difference in the future? These are the exact questions that President Bush will wrestle with as he attempts to move beyond Kyoto.

Chapter 10, 'Five letters to the President', comprises letters written by three round table discussants and two other participants of the conference. The group consisted of Dr Lennart Hjalmarsson, a noted Swedish economist who was the architect of electricity deregulation in Sweden, Dr Paul Portney, the President of Resources for the Future – an organization with a long tradition of excellent research in natural resources, Dr John Weyant, Director of the Energy Modeling Forum at Stanford University, Dr Rob Bradley, a self-described 'climate change skeptic' and former Director of Public Policy Analysis at the Enron Corporation, and Dr James Edmonds of the Pacific Northwest National Laboratory and coauthor of Chapter 7. These letters are very interesting because of the diversity of opinions offered. It is against this backdrop that the President must fashion US climate change policy and provide world leadership. Since these letters are representative of the types of advice President Bush has received, imagine yourself in the Oval Office, wrestling with this topic. Whose advice will you follow and how will you explain it to the American public?

NOTES

1. It is useful to think of the forcing associated with a particular gas as the factor that translates a given concentration of the gas into a temperature effect. Different greenhouse gases have different forcing coefficients.
2. For a comparison of atmospheric lifetimes of the different greenhouse gases, see IPCC. 2001, p. 47.
3. IPCC (2001) estimate that several centuries after CO_2 emissions occur, about a quarter is still present in the atmosphere, suggesting a very small, but non-zero depreciation rate.
4. Since equation (1.2) is usually expressed in real or inflation-adjusted dollars, the social discount rate should also be expressed in real terms, meaning it will be significantly below nominal interest rates.
5. Except perhaps the United States and a few other large CO_2 emitters.

REFERENCES

Energy Information Administration (EIA) (1999), *International Energy Annual 1999*, Washington, DC: EIA.

Energy Information Administration (EIA) (2001), *Emissions of Greenhouse Gases in the United States 2000: Carbon Dioxide Emissions*, Washington, DC: EIA.

'International Energy Workshop: A Summary of the 1983 Poll Responses' (1984), *The Energy Journal*, **5** (1): 45–64.

IPCC (2001), *Climate Change 2001: Contributions of Working Group I to the Third Assessment Report on Climate Change*, edited by J.T. Houghton et al., London: Cambridge University Press.

Wigley, Tom M.L. (1999), 'The Science of Climate Change: Global and U.S. Perspectives', Arlington, VA: Pew Center on Global Climate Change.

2. The carbon cycle: human perturbations and potential management options

William H. Schlesinger

1 INTRODUCTION

A variety of gases, including water vapor (H_2O), carbon dioxide (CO_2), methane (CH_4) and nitrous oxide (N_2O), add to the radiative forcing of Earth's atmosphere, meaning that they absorb certain wavelengths of infrared radiation (heat) that is leaving the Earth and thus raise the temperature of the atmosphere. Since glass has the same effect on the loss of heat from a greenhouse, these gases are known as 'greenhouse' gases. It is fortunate that these gases are found in the atmosphere; without its natural greenhouse effect, the Earth's temperature would be below freezing, and all waters on its surface would be frozen. However, for the past 100 years or so, the concentrations of CO_2, CH_4 and N_2O in the atmosphere have been rising as a result of human activities. An increase in the radiative forcing of Earth's atmosphere is destined to cause large and rapid changes in climate, disrupting both human society and natural ecosystems.

Relative to a molecule of CO_2, the greenhouse warming potential of each molecule of methane and nitrous oxide added to Earth's atmosphere is about 25 times and 200 times greater, respectively. Nonetheless, most attention has focused on CO_2 because it will contribute more than half of the increase in radiative forcing during the next 100 years, it has a long residence time in the atmosphere-ocean system on Earth, and the major cause of its increase in the atmosphere, fossil-fuel combustion, is well known and potentially subject to regulation (Reilly et al. 1999).

In an attempt to understand the changing chemistry of the Earth's surface – that is, its biogeochemistry – scientists try to understand what controls the movements of gases in and out of the atmosphere and to estimate a global budget for each gas that cycles through the atmosphere. For the carbon cycle, biogeochemists assess the emissions of CO_2 to Earth's atmosphere relative to the natural processes that add or remove CO_2 to/from that reservoir, allowing us to forecast atmospheric CO_2 concentrations and the human impact on future climate. In this, our job is far from complete: while biogeochemists have a good estimate of worldwide fossil-fuel emissions, we have highly conflicting views about whether the biosphere – especially forests and soils – is now a source or sink for atmospheric CO_2.

The most recent budget for atmospheric CO_2 prepared by the Intergovernmental Panel on Climate Change (IPCC, 2000) contains an unknown sink (or fate) for CO_2 that amounts to about 30 percent of estimated annual emissions (Table 2.1). In the face of such uncertainty, policy makers will certainly demand a better accounting by biogeochemists before taking serious actions to reduce fossil-fuel emissions globally. We also need to know how the terms in this equation will change in the future. What will happen, for instance, if fossil-fuel combustion increases to 15 PgC/yr?[1] Most oceanographers see a diminishing marginal uptake of CO_2 by the oceans (Archer, 1995), so that ocean uptake is not likely to exceed 5 PgC/yr. If forests constitute the unknown 'residual' term in the equation, then undisturbed forests now perform a great service to society, and their preservation should be ensured. Looking to the future, we need to know if forests will function more efficiently to take up CO_2 in the face of higher concentrations of CO_2 and warmer temperatures in Earth's atmosphere. Thus, studies of forest growth are now intimately tied to questions of public policy and global biogeochemistry.

Table 2.1   Atmospheric budget for CO_2, 1989–1998 (units of PgC/yr)

Fossil-fuel emissions		Deforestation		Atmospheric increase		Ocean uptake		Residual
6.3	+	1.6	=	3.3	+	2.3	+	2.3

Source: IPCC (2000).

2   THE GLOBAL CARBON CYCLE

The concentration of CO_2 is controlled by a variety of processes that add and subtract CO_2 to/from the atmosphere. Nearly all of these processes are cyclic – for example, the removal of CO_2 by plant photosynthesis,

$$CO_2 + H_2O \rightarrow CH_2O + O_2, \tag{2.1}$$

is balanced by the return of CO_2 and the consumption of oxygen (O_2) when plant tissues burn or decompose:

$$CH_2O + O_2 \rightarrow CO_2 + H_2O. \tag{2.2}$$

It is important to recognize that the global carbon cycle consists of a variety of such cyclic processes operating at different rates and different time-scales. The cycles are overlaid on one another, each contributing to the overall, global biogeochemical cycle of carbon.

The most basic cycle, often called the carbonate-silicate subcycle, is driven by the reaction of atmospheric CO_2 with the Earth's crust in the process of rock weathering. Since this reaction would occur on a lifeless Earth, it is a component of the *abiotic* carbon cycle on Earth (Figure 2.1). Rock weathering transfers CO_2 to the world's oceans, via rivers, in the form of bicarbonate (HCO_3^-). Bicarbonate is eventually removed from seawater by the deposition of calcium carbonate (limestone, or $CaCO_3$), which is added to the Earth's crust. When the Earth's crust undergoes subduction and metamorphism, CO_2 is returned to the atmosphere in volcanic emanations. The presence of life on Earth has increased the rate of some of these processes (for example, witness the deposition of marine carbonate by oysters), but this portion of the global carbon cycle appears to have turned slowly for nearly all of geologic time. Very few marine sediments are more than 150 million years old (Smith and Sandwell, 1997). Presumably, the carbon content of older sediments has been returned to the atmosphere.

Each year, the amount of carbon moving in the carbonate-silicate cycle is relatively small: volcanic emissions are currently estimated between 0.02 and 0.05 PgC/yr (Williams et al., 1992; Bickle, 1994), annual riverflow of HCO_3^- is 0.40 PgC/yr (Suchet and Probst, 1995), and the formation of $CaCO_3$ carries about 0.38 PgC/yr to ocean sediments (Milliman, 1993). It would take nearly 3,000 years for rock weathering to remove the current pool of CO_2 from the atmosphere in the absence of emissions from other sources. The geologic record shows periods when volcanic emissions greatly exceeded the rate that CO_2 could react with the Earth's crust, and high levels of CO_2 built up in the atmosphere (Owen and Rea, 1985). However, for all intents and purposes, this subcycle now appears reasonably well balanced, and there is no credible evidence that the current buildup of CO_2 in Earth's atmosphere can be attributed to recent, unusually high levels of volcanic activity or to lower rates of rock weathering.

Another component of the abiotic cycle of carbon derives from the presence of liquid water at the Earth's surface. Any time that CO_2 rises in Earth's atmosphere, a greater amount will dissolve in water, in the following reaction:

$$CO_2 + H_2O \rightarrow H^+ + HCO_3^- \rightarrow H_2CO_3. \tag{2.3}$$

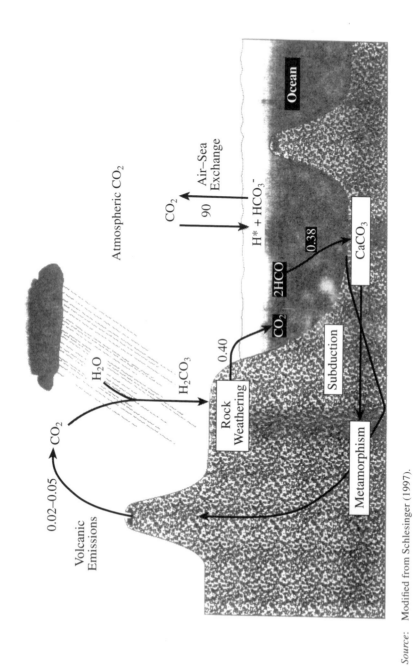

Source: Modified from Schlesinger (1997).

Figure 2.1   Abiotic processes contributing to the global carbon cycle of present-day Earth

28

The reaction is mediated by Henry's Law, which describes the distribution of any gas, with significant solubility, between the gaseous and liquid phases in a closed system. Played out at the global level, Henry's Law means that the oceans act to buffer changes in atmospheric CO_2 concentration. As the concentration has risen owing to industrial emissions during the past 150 years, a significant fraction of the CO_2 that might otherwise be in the atmosphere has dissolved in ocean waters. Indeed, we can document the oceanic uptake of CO_2 by comparing sequential measurements taken at the same locale during the past few decades (Quay et al., 1992; Peng et al., 1998). The total uptake of CO_2 by the oceans is determined by the downward mixing of surface waters into the deep sea, in a global pattern known as the thermohaline circulation (Broecker 1997). Marine biogeochemists are fairly confident, that as a result of rising CO_2 concentrations in Earth's atmosphere, the net uptake of CO_2 by the world's oceans is about 2 PgC/yr – about 20 times more than estimates of enhanced consumption of atmospheric CO_2 by rock weathering (Andrews and Schlesinger, 2001). However, they are also fairly confident that the uptake of CO_2 by the oceans will not increase in proportion to the future anticipated increase of CO_2 in the atmosphere (Archer 1995).

In contrast to the abiotic cycle, the *biotic* carbon cycle stems directly from the presence of life on Earth (Figure 2.2). On land and in the sea, photosynthetic organisms remove CO_2 from the atmosphere, using it to form organic matter (equation (2.1)). Globally, the annual production of new plant tissues is known as *net primary production*, which is estimated to capture 105 PgC/yr – with 54 percent occurring on land and the rest in the sea (Field et al., 1998).

The mean residence time for a molecule of CO_2 in Earth's atmosphere – about 5 years – is largely determined by the uptake of carbon in photosynthesis. The well-known annual oscillations of CO_2 concentration in Earth's atmosphere occur because a large fraction of global photosynthesis occurs in regions with seasonal climate – that is, where plants grow only during the summer. As a result of their uptake of CO_2, marine phytoplankton maintain an undersaturated CO_2 concentration in the ocean's surface waters, which enhances the marine uptake of CO_2 from the atmosphere. However, most of the CO_2 removed from the atmosphere by photosynthesis is not captured for long, because dead organic matter decomposes rapidly in soils and seawater. The long-term accumulation of carbon in undecomposed materials in soils is about 0.4 PgC/yr (Schlesinger 1990), while the storage of carbon in marine sediments is only about 0.1 PgC/yr (Berner, 1982).[2]

By establishing *bio*geochemistry, life on Earth has stimulated the movement of CO_2 to and from the atmosphere (Schlesinger, 1997). Through geologic time, the products of photosynthesis have added a huge amount of organic matter to the Earth's crust ($\approx$15,600,000 PgC). Nevertheless, the current rate

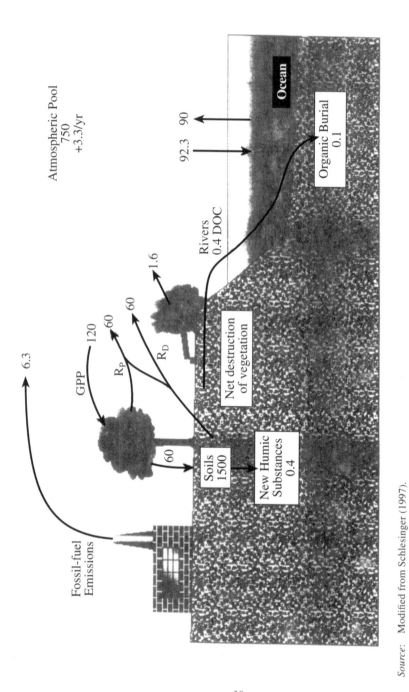

Source: Modified from Schlesinger (1997).

Figure 2.2   Biotic and anthropogenic processes contributing to the global carbon cycle of present-day Earth

of carbon storage in sediments is rather small – not unlike the rates through most of geologic time (Garrels and Lerman, 1981).

3   PAST VARIATIONS IN ATMOSPHERIC CO_2

One way to gain perspective about the potential future trajectory for atmospheric CO_2 is to examine the geologic record of its concentration in the past. How high has the CO_2 concentration been in the past? How fast did it reach past high levels? Do past fluctuations offer any insight about how effective the various subcycles of the global carbon cycle will be in buffering future fluctuations in atmospheric CO_2?

There is good reason to believe, and some supporting geologic evidence, that the concentration of CO_2 in Earth's atmosphere in the distant past was much higher than today. Persistent high concentrations of CO_2 are likely to have characterized Earth's history before the evolution of land plants, which subsequently greatly increased the consumption of CO_2 by rock weathering (Berner, 1998; Moulton et al., 2000). High concentrations of CO_2 in Earth's early history may have been instrumental in maintaining Earth's temperature above the freezing point of water at a time when the Sun's luminosity was significantly lower than today.

Despite such high levels of CO_2 during the Earth's 'deep' geologic past, studies of marine sediments indicate that atmospheric CO_2 has remained in a narrow range between 100 and 400 ppm[3] over the past 20 million years (Pearson and Palmer, 2000). Bubbles of air trapped in layers of the Antarctic ice pack show concentrations in the range of 180 to 290 ppm over the past 420,000 years (Petit et al., 1999), with low values associated with glacial epochs and higher values during warmer, interglacial periods. Small variations, between 230 and 290 ppm, since the end of the last glacial epoch (10,000 years ago) suggest short-term temporal imbalances in the global carbon cycle (Indermuhle et al., 1999), with fluctuations in the amount of forest biomass partially responsible for changes in atmospheric CO_2. During the past 2000 years, concentrations of CO_2 have remained between 270 and 290 ppm, except since the Industrial Revolution (Barnola et al., 1995). The rise in CO_2 during the past 150 years appears to be associated with global warming (Mann et al., 1998; Crowley, 2000), and the most current IPCC (2001) projections are for levels reaching 550 ppm in 2050 and > 700 ppm by 2100 (Figure 2.3).

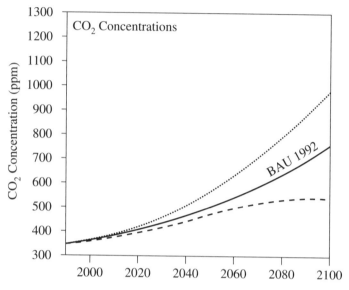

Source: IPCC (2001).

Figure 2.3 *CO_2 emissions projected from fossil-fuel combustion, showing high, low and business-as-usual (BAU) scenarios*

4 HUMAN PERTURBATIONS OF THE GLOBAL CARBON CYCLE

Each year, humans extract more than 6 Pg of organic carbon from the Earth's crust (oil, coal, and natural gas) and convert it to CO_2 that is added to the atmosphere. The IPCC (2001) 'business-as-usual' scenario predicts CO_2 emissions will rise to 15 PgC/yr by the year 2050, largely due to increases in fossil-fuel combustion (Figure 2.4). Our impact on the global carbon cycle may appear small compared to some of the natural transfers, such as decomposition, that also add (or subtract) CO_2 to the atmosphere (Figure 2.2), but it is important to recognize that photosynthesis and de-composition are naturally occurring, counterbalancing processes that produce no large net source or sink of atmospheric CO_2 on an annual basis. In contrast, with fossil-fuel combustion, humans remove organic carbon from the Earth's crust at a rate more than 100 times greater than the storage of organic carbon in newly-formed marine sediments. We must count on Henry's Law and changes in the activity of the biosphere to buffer any changes in atmospheric CO_2 concentration.

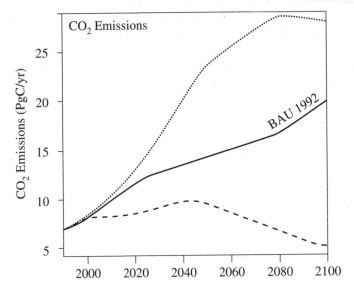

IPCC (2001).

*Figure 2.4   Atmospheric CO_2 concentrations resulting from emissions
scenarios outlined in Figure 2.3*

Forest destruction, largely deforestation in the tropics, is also thought to be a net source of atmospheric CO_2, although the exact magnitude is most uncertain. Melillo et al. (1996) estimate a release of 1.2 to 2.3 PgC/yr as CO_2 from global tropical deforestation in the 1990s; however, Houghton et al. (2000) report a net release of only 0.2 PgC/yr from the Brazilian Amazon, where tropical deforestation rates are thought to be among the highest globally. Regrowth of vegetation on deforested lands and lands abandoned from agriculture may account for the discrepancy. We can hope that the improving long-term satellite record of forest cover in the tropics will allow us to refine our estimates of deforestation rates (Skole and Tucker, 1993).

The carbon balance of forests must consider changes in the temperate zone that may offset (or augment) changes that are occurring in the tropics. Using an inverse model[4] of atmospheric CO_2 concentrations, Tans et al. (1990) suggested that the northern temperate latitudes were a net sink for carbon, largely as a result of the regrowth of forests on abandoned agricultural lands. Similar conclusions derive from other inverse modeling studies (Denning et al., 1995; Ciais et al., 1995), and Fan et al. (1998) estimated that the sink in North America was as large as 1.7 ± 0.5 PgC/yr between 1988 and 1992. Battle et al. (2000) postulate a net global uptake of carbon by forests at

1.4 ± 0.8 PgC/yr – that is, the uptake in the northern latitudes more than compensated for all the losses from tropical deforestation. Their results are consistent with studies of changes in atmospheric O_2 (Keeling et al. 1996). The results of inverse modeling studies imply that the net emission from tropical deforestation has been overestimated (Ciais et al., 2000).

By themselves, inverse modeling studies would seem to identify the residual term in Table 2.1 and to resolve the atmospheric CO_2 budget; however, estimates of actual changes in the carbon storage on land fall far short of the values predicted by such models. In a global analysis of forest greenness using satellite remote sensing, Potter (1999) found that deforestation was a source of 1.44 PgC/yr to the atmosphere, of which 0.29 PgC/yr accumulated in regrowth, for a net release of 1.15 PgC/yr from the terrestrial biosphere. Earlier, Dixon et al. (1994a) calculated a net source of 0.9 ± 0.2 PgC/yr from an inventory of world forests. Post and Kwon (2000) concluded that the rate of soil carbon accumulation as a result of reforestation and afforestation globally (0.16 PgC/yr) also falls short of the 'missing sink' of carbon on land. So as we enter the twenty-first century, we have highly conflicting views about whether the world's forests are waxing or waning in their extent and carbon storage!

Examining historical forest inventories, Houghton et al. (1999) find an accumulation of 0.037 PgC/yr in US forests during the 1980s, postulating a maximal upper limit for carbon storage at 0.35 PgC/yr if a variety of other processes, including greater carbon storage in soils, are included. Alternative estimates indicate a net accumulation of 0.17 PgC/yr in eastern US forests (Brown and Schroeder, 1999), 0.2 PgC/yr in all US forests (Birdsey et al., 1993), and <0.5 PgC/yr in all of North America's forests (Chen et al., 2000) – similar to the North American sink determined by inverse modeling (Ciais et al., 2000). A recent workshop convened to reconcile the inverse-modeling and inventory studies agreed that there was a sink of 0.30 to 0.58 PgC/yr in the United States during the 1980s (Pacala et al., 2001).

In the face of losses of carbon from tropical forests and only a small sink in North America, we must postulate huge, recent increases in the carbon uptake and storage in Siberian forests, for which the driving mechanism is unclear. Kolchugina and Vinton (1993) estimate a net sink of 0.49 PgC/yr in forests and their soils of the former Soviet Union, but most alternative estimates are lower. Shepashenko et al. (1998) calculate a net loss of carbon from Siberian forests in recent decades.

5   PROSPECTS FOR THE FUTURE

Changes in forest biomass and soil carbon storage have certainly affected atmospheric CO_2 concentrations in the past, and there is some indication that year-to-year variability in the accumulation of CO_2 in the atmosphere is affected by changes in the activity of the terrestrial biosphere (Bousquet et al. 2000; Houghton 2000). Despite the wide disparity between inverse-model and inventory estimates of forest carbon storage, there is no doubt that the growth of atmospheric CO_2 concentrations would be even greater if it were not for forest regrowth in the temperate zone. Nevertheless, while these forests grow, CO_2 concentrations continue to rise. Can we expect, or orchestrate, more uptake by terrestrial ecosystems in the future?

The carbon uptake by forests is determined by their total area, as well as factors that affect the rate of carbon accumulation per unit of area, including forest age. Total area is affected by human land-use decisions as well as increases in the spatial extent of forests, as determined by a warmer climate (Myneni et al. 1997). Changes in local carbon uptake are determined by climate, CO_2 fertilization, and the enhanced deposition of nitrogen from regional air pollution. Young forests show the most rapid carbon uptake, with the rate of carbon sequestration decreasing with time (Chapman et al. 1975; Schiffman and Johnson 1989). Separate studies using biogeochemical modeling (Schimel et al. 2000) and an analysis of historical forest inventory (Caspersen et al. 2000) agree that changes in land use dominate the current net uptake of carbon by US forests.

Keeling (1993) notes that the increasing amplitude of the annual oscillation of atmospheric CO_2 must mean that some process has stimulated the biosphere – presumably via increased rates of photosynthesis. However, there are several indications that the stimulation of photosynthesis by CO_2 fertilization, while widely observed in short-term experiments (Curtis and Wang 1998), does not result in large increases in plant mass, when the exposure is long term and plants can acclimatize to the higher CO_2 levels (Hattenschwiler et al. 1997; Idso 1999). The initial 25 per cent growth response in a young (15–year-old) stand of loblolly pine in the Duke Forest Free Air CO_2 Enrichment (FACE) experiment dropped below statistical significance during the fourth year of exposure, apparently owing to nutrient deficiencies in the soil (DeLucia et al. 1999; Oren et al. 2001). Large increases in the rate of root respiration and decomposition minimize changes in the pool of carbon in soil organic matter, despite greater inputs of dead plant materials to the soil (Schlesinger and Lichter 2001).

Increased deposition of nitrogen from the atmosphere should also stimulate the growth and carbon content of forests (Holland et al. 1997). However, the growth enhancement from nitrogen deposition may simply allow forests to attain maximum biomass more rapidly, rather than at higher final values. Excessive nitrogen deposition is often a cause of acid rain, leading to soil acidifications that can reduce forest growth. Simultaneous exposure to other air pollutants, such as ozone, may also explain the relatively low growth enhancements in forests of the eastern US (Caspersen et al. 2000).

Estimates of the N-derived sink also need to be discounted to the extent that emitted nitrogen falls on non-forested lands (Townsend et al. 1996; Asner et al. 1997). Furthermore, only a fraction of the added inputs of nitrogen accumulates in vegetation, where C/N ratios are high and carbon storage is most efficient (Nadelhoffer et al. 1999; Schlesinger and Andrews 2000). Abiotic processes can add nitrogen to soil organic matter, lowering its C/N ratio without adding significantly to soil carbon storage (Johnson et al. 2000). Accounting for many of these effects, Townsend et al. (1996) estimate the N-derived sink at 0.44 to 0.74 PgC/yr.

Without explicit management to enhance carbon storage on land, reforestation of abandoned agricultural land is the most plausible cause of a carbon sink in the terrestrial biosphere, both now and in the foreseeable future. A large amount of land in the eastern US has reverted to forest since agricultural abandonment in the past century (Hart 1968; Delcourt and Harris 1980). These lands now support growing forests, which are accumulating carbon dioxide from the atmosphere. While reforestation of these lands may be helpful in mediating the rise of atmospheric CO_2 concentrations, it offers no long-term solution to the greenhouse-warming problem. It would require reforestation of all the once-forested land on Earth, including that now used for agriculture or covered by urban areas, to store 6 PgC/yr – the amount emitted each year from fossil-fuel combustion (Vitousek 1991).

The IPCC (2000) panel on *Land Use, Land-Use Change and Forestry* evaluated the potential for direct human intervention to enhance the storage of carbon in forests and soils, concluding that a significant potential exists to mediate the rise of CO_2 in Earth's atmosphere. However, many of the recommended management procedures, including afforestation and intensification of agricultural management, need careful scrutiny to ensure that the costs associated with the practice do not exceed the benefits or credits received for incremental carbon storage. The afforestation of marginal lands is likely to require especially large inputs of energy in planting, irrigation, and fertilization of young trees (Dixon et al. 1994b). Turhollow and Perlack (1991) calculate an energy ratio (that is, energy in biomass grown/energy input) of 16 for hybrid poplar grown for biomass energy in Tennessee. Amortizing the initial cost to establish forestry plantations over a 50–year rotation, the cost of carbon sequestration ranges from $1 to $69 per metric ton, with a median value of $13 (Dixon et al. 1994b). However, the rate of carbon storage in forests declines as they mature, so 'the only way by which reforestation programs can continue to sequester carbon over the long term is if they transition into programs to produce commercial biomass fuels' (Edmonds and Sands, Chapter 7 this volume) – that is, we must replace fossil fuel with biomass energy.

Implementation of reduced and conservation tillage practices in agriculture appears to offer a consistent net benefit by enhancing soil carbon storage (Kern and Johnson 1993; Robertson et al. 2000; West and Marland, in review); however, greater use of nitrogen fertilizer often does not (Schlesinger 2000). The release of CO_2 by pumping irrigation water also greatly exceeds the enhanced carbon storage found in irrigated agricultural soils (Schlesinger 2000). Wildly positive forecasts (for example, 0.4–0.8 PgC/yr) have been made for the potential to increase carbon storage in agricultural soils (Lal 2001), but reality is not nearly so sanguine. Pacala et al. (2001) estimate that the carbon storage in cropland soils of the US was only 0 to 0.04 Pg/yr during the 1980s. Kern and Johnson (1993) estimated that immediate implementation of conservation tillage on all US farmland with this potential would provide a sink (<0.015 PgC/yr) accounting for only about 1 percent of the fossil-fuel emissions in the US at today's levels. Substantial areas are already in conservation tillage regimes (Uri 1999), for which the net carbon sequestration potential is estimated at 0.0003 PgC/yr (Uri 2000). Moreover, similar to the pattern of carbon storage during forest regrowth, storage in soils is finite, and the rate will diminish with time (Schlesinger 1990).

6 WARMING

If the Earth's temperature rises due to the greenhouse effect, we can expect soils to be warmer, especially at high latitudes. Except in some deserts, the rate of decomposition in soils increases with increasing temperature – as seen both in compilations of literature values (Raich and Schlesinger 1992) and nearly all studies that have imposed experimental warming (Rustad et al. 2001). The increase in soil respiration[5] doubles with a 10°C rise in temperature – that is, the Q_{10} of the relationship is about 2.0 (Kirschbaum 1995; Palmer-Winkler et al. 1996; Kätterer et al. 1998). The greatest response is found in samples of surface detritus and in soils from cold climates (Lloyd and Taylor 1994). Nearly all models of global climate change predict a loss of carbon from soils as a result of global warming (Schimel et al. 1994; McGuire et al. 1995).

As a result of cold, water-logged conditions, organic matter accumulates in boreal and tundra soils (Harden et al. 1997; Trumbore and Harden 1997). Radiocarbon measurements indicate limited turnover, but nearly all the organic matter is found in labile fractions that will be easily decomposed should the climate warm (Chapman and Thurlow 1998,; Lindroth et al. 1998). In the tundra, melting of permafrost and concomitant lowering of the water table may lead to a large increase in decomposition (Billings et al. 1983; Moore and Knowles 1989). Indeed, Oechel et al. (1993, 1995) found evidence of a large loss of soil organic matter in tundra habitats as a result of recent climatic warming in Alaska, and Goulden et al. (1998) found a significant loss of carbon from soils during several warm years that caused an early spring thaw in a boreal forest of Manitoba. Recent measurements of European forests show greater respiration, and lower net uptake, by forests at high latitudes, perhaps as a result of climatic warming during the past several decades (Valentini et al. 2000). In response to global warming, large losses of CO_2 from boreal forest and tundra soils could reinforce the greenhouse-warming of Earth's atmosphere (Woodwell 1995).

7 CONCLUSIONS

The IPCC (2001) offers a number of scenarios that predict the future course of atmospheric CO_2 concentrations (Figure 2.3). The business-as-usual scenario shows emissions rising to 15 PgC/yr and atmospheric concentrations rising to 550 ppm by the year 2050. Even the most rigorous abatement scenarios show concentrations of >500 ppm in the year 2100, nearly all scenarios show emissions >10 PgC/yr in the year 2050 (Figure 2.4), dwarfing even the most optimistic predictions for enhanced carbon storage in the terrestrial biosphere. Thus, if we are serious about preventing climate change, I see no alternative but to cut emissions, substantially and immediately. Alternative suggestions simply divert our attention from this problem, and precious time is lost in our attempt to control the emissions of this gas, which will otherwise take centuries for natural processes to remove from Earth's atmosphere.

NOTES

1. 1 PgC = 10^{15} gC = 1 gigaton (GtC) = 1 billion metric tons of carbon.
2. It is curious to note that the annual storage of carbon in marine sediments is less than the carbon delivered to the oceans by rivers (Schlesinger and Melack 1981), so that decomposition in the oceans appears to consume all marine production, plus a large fraction of the annual riverine transport. Thus, the oceans act as a net heterotrophic system (Smith and MacKenzie 1987).
3. 1 ppm = 1 part per million = 1 μl l^{-1} = 0.0001%.
4. Inverse models predict the atmospheric CO_2 concentration based on the latitudinal distribution of fossil-fuel emissions and ocean uptake. Any difference between the predicted and observed concentrations is taken to result from sources or sinks in the land biosphere.

5. Soil respiration is the release of CO_2 from the soil surface, which is an index of decomposition (Schlesinger 1977).

REFERENCES

Andrews, J.A. and W.H. Schlesinger (2001), 'Soil CO_2 dynamics, acidification, and chemical weathering in a temperate forest with experimental CO_2 enrichment', *Global Biogeochemical Cycles* **15**: 149–62.

Archer, D. (1995), 'Upper ocean physics as relevant to ecosystem dynamics: a tutorial', *Ecological Applications* **5**: 724–39.

Asner, G.P., T.R. Seastedt and A.R. Townsend (1997), 'The decoupling of terrestrial carbon and nitrogen cycles', *BioScience* **47**: 226–34.

Barnola, J.M., M. Anklin, J. Porcheron, D. Raynaud, J. Schwander and B. Stauffer (1995), 'CO_2 evolution during the last millennium as recorded by Antarctic and Greenland ice', *Tellus* **47B**: 264–72.

Battle, M., M.L. Bender, P.P. Tans, J.W.C. White, J.T. Ellis, T. Conway and R.J. Francey (2000), 'Global carbon sinks and their variability inferred from atmospheric O_2 and $\delta^{13}C$', *Science* **287**: 2467–70.

Berner, R.A. (1982), 'Burial of organic carbon and pyrite sulfur in the modern ocean: its geochemical and environmental significance', *American Journal of Science* **282**: 451–73.

Berner, R.A. (1998), 'The carbon cycle and CO_2 over Phanerozoic time: the role of land plants', *Philosophical Transactions of the Royal Society of London* **353B**: 75–82.

Bickle, M.J. (1994), 'The role of metamorphic decarbonation reactions in returning strontium to the silicate sediment mass', *Nature* **367**: 699–704.

Billings, W.D., J.O. Luken, D.A. Mortensen and K.M. Peterson (1983), 'Increasing atmospheric carbon dioxide: possible effects on arctic tundra', *Oecologia* **58**: 286–9.

Birdsey, R.A., A.J. Plantinga and L.S. Heath (1993), 'Past and prospective carbon storage in United States forests', *Forest Ecology and Management* **58**: 33–40.

Bousquet, P., P. Peylin, P. Ciais, C. Le Quere, P. Friedlingstein and P.P. Tans (2000), 'Regional changes in carbon dioxide fluxes of land and oceans since 1980', *Science* **290**: 1342–6.

Broecker, W.S. (1997), 'Thermohaline circulation, the Achilles heel of our climate system: will man-made CO_2 upset the current balance', *Science* **278**: 1582–8.

Brown, S.L. and P.E. Schroeder (1999), 'Spatial patterns of aboveground production and mortality of woody biomass for eastern U.S. forests', *Ecological Applications* **9**: 968–80.

Caspersen, J.P., S.W. Pacala, J.C. Jenkins, G.C. Hurtt, P.R. Moorcroft and R.A. Birdsey (2000), 'Contributions of land-use history to carbon accumulation in U.S. forests', *Science* **290**: 1148–51.

Chapman, S.B., J. Hibble and C.R. Rafarel (1975), 'Net aerial production by *Calluna vulgaris* on lowland heath in Britain', *Journal of Ecology* **63**: 233–58.

Chapman, S.J. and M. Thurlow (1998), 'Peat respiration at low temperatures', *Soil Biology and Biochemistry* **30**: 1013–21.

Chen, J., W. Chen, J. Liu, J. Cihlar and S. Gray (2000), 'Annual carbon balance of Canada's forests during 1895–1996', *Global Biogeochemical Cycles* **14**: 839–49.

Ciais, P., P. Peylin and P. Bousquet (2000), 'Regional biospheric carbon fluxes as inferred from atmospheric CO_2 measurements', *Ecological Applications* **10**: 1574–89.

Ciais, P., P.P. Tans, M. Trolier, J.W.C. White and R.J. Francey (1995), 'A large northern hemisphere terrestrial CO_2 sink indicated by the $^{13}C/^{12}C$ ratio of atmospheric CO_2', *Science* **269**: 1098–102.

Crowley, T.J. (2000), 'Causes of climate change over the past 1000 years', *Science* **289**: 270–77.

Curtis, P.S. and X. Wang (1998), 'A meta-analysis of elevated CO_2 effects on woody plant mass, form, and physiology', *Oecologia* **113**: 299–313.

Delcourt, H.R. and W.F. Harris (1980), 'Carbon budget of the southeastern U.S. biota: analysis of historical change in trend from source to sink', *Science* **210**: 321–3.

DeLucia, E.H., J.G.Hamilton, S.L. Naidu, R.B.Thomas, J.A.Andrews, A. Finzi, M. Lavine, R. Matamala, J.E. Mohan, G.R. Hendrey and W.H. Schlesinger (1999), 'Net primary production of a forest ecosystem under experimental CO_2 enrichment', *Science* **284**: 1177–9.

Denning, A.S., I.Y. Fung and D. Randall (1995), 'Latitudinal gradient of atmospheric CO_2 due to seasonal exchange with land biota', *Nature* **376**: 240–43.

Dixon, R.K., S. Brown, R. Houghton, A.M. Solomon, M.C. Trexler and J. Wisniewski (1994a), 'Carbon pools and flux of global forest ecosystems', *Science* **263**: 185–90.

Dixon, R.K., J.K. Winjum, K.J. Andrasko, J.J. Lee and P.E. Schroeder (1994b), 'Integrated land-use systems: assessment of promising agroforest and alternative land-use practices to enhance carbon conservation and sequestration', *Climatic Change* **27**: 71–92.

Fan, S., M. Gloor, J. Mahlman, S. Pacala, J. Sarmiento, T. Takahashi and P. Tans (1998), 'A large terrestrial carbon sink in North America implied by atmospheric and oceanic carbon dioxide data and models', *Science* **282**: 442–6.

Field, C.B., M.J. Behrenfeld, J.T. Randerson and P. Falkowski (1998), 'Primary production of the biosphere: integrating terrestrial and oceanic components', *Science* **281**: 237–40.

Goulden, M.L., S.C. Wofsy, J.W. Harden, S.E. Trumbore, P.M. Crill, S.T. Gower, T. Fries, B.C. Daube, S.-M. Fan, D.J. Sutton, A. Bazzaz and J.W. Munger (1998), 'Sensitivity of boreal forest carbon balance to soil thaw', *Science* **279**: 214–17.

Harden, J.W., K.P. O'Neill, S.E. Trumbore, H. Veldhuis and B.J. Stocks (1997), 'Moss and soil contributions to the annual net carbon flux of a maturing boreal forest', *Journal of Geophysical Research* **102**: 28805–16.

Hart, J.F. (1968), 'Loss and abandonment of cleared farm land in the eastern United States', *Annals of the Association of American Geographers* **58**: 417–40.

Hattenschwiler, S., F. Miglietta, A. Raschi and C. Korner (1997), 'Thirty years of *in situ* tree growth under elevated CO_2: a model for future forest responses?', *Global Change Biology* **3**: 463–71.

Holland, E.A., B.H. Braswell, J.-F. Lamarque, A. Townsend, J. Sulzman, J.-F. Muller, F. Dentener, G. Brasseur, H. Levy, J.E. Penner and G.-J. Roelofs (1997), 'Variations in predicted spatial distribution of atmospheric nitrogen deposition and their impact on carbon uptake by terrestrial ecosystems', *Journal of Geophysical Research* **102**: 15849–66.

Houghton, R.A. (2000), 'International variability in the global carbon cycle', *Journal of Geophysical Research* **105**: 20121–30.

Houghton, R.A., J.L. Hackler and K.T. Lawrence (1999), 'The U.S. carbon budget: contributions from land-use change', *Science* **285**: 574–8.

Houghton, R.A., D.L. Skole, C.A. Nobre, J.L. Hackler, K.T. Lawrence and W.H. Chomentowski (2000), 'Annual fluxes of carbon from deforestation and regrowth in the Brazilian Amazon', *Nature* **403**: 301–4.

Idso S.B. (1999), 'The long-term response of trees to atmospheric CO_2 enrichment', *Global Change Biology* **5**: 493–5.

IPCC (Intergovernmental Panel on Climate Change) (2000), *Land Use, Land-Use Change and Forestry*, Cambridge University Press, Cambridge.

IPCC (Intergovernmental Panel on Climate Change) (2001), *Working Group One, Third Assessment Report*, Cambridge University Press, Cambridge.

Indermuhle, A., T.F. Stocker, F. Joos, H. Fischer, H.J. Smith, M. Wahlen, B. Deck, D. Mastroianni, J. Tschumi, T. Blunier, R. Meyer and B. Stauffer (1999), 'Holocene carbon-cycle dynamics based on CO_2 trapped in ice at Taylor Dome, Antarctica', *Nature* **398**: 121–6.

Johnson, D.W., W. Cheng and I.C. Burke (2000), 'Biotic and abiotic nitrogen retention in a variety of forest soils', *Soil Science Society of America Journal* **64**: 1503–14.

Kätterer, T., M. Reichstein, O. Andren, and A. Lomander (1998), 'Temperature dependence of organic matter decomposition: a critical review using literature data analyzed with different models', *Biology and Fertility of Soils* **27**: 258–62.

Keeling, C.D. (1993), 'Global observations of atmospheric CO_2', in M. Heimann (ed.), *The Global Carbon Cycle*, Springer-Verlag, New York, pp. 1–29.

Keeling, R.F., S.C. Piper and M. Heimann (1996), 'Global and hemispheric CO_2 sinks deduced from changes in atmospheric O_2 concentration', *Nature* **381**: 218–21.

Kern, J.S. and M.G. Johnson (1993), 'Conservation tillage impacts on national soil and atmospheric carbon levels', *Soil Science Society of America Journal* **57**: 200–210.

Kirschbaum, M.U.F. (1995), 'The temperature dependence of soil organic matter decomposition and the effect of global warming on soil organic C storage', *Soil Biology and Biochemistry* **27**: 753–60.

Kolghugina, T.P. and T.S. Vinton (1993), 'Carbon-sources and sinks in forest biomes of the former Soviet Union', *Global Biogeochemical Cycles* **7**: 291–304.

Lal, R. (2001), 'World cropland soils as a source or sink for atmospheric carbon', *Advances in Agronomy* **71**: 145–91.

Lindroth, A., A. Grelle and A.-S. Moren (1998), 'Long-term measurements of boreal forest carbon balance reveal large temperature sensitivity', *Global Change Biology* **4**: 443–50.

Lloyd, J. and J.A. Taylor (1994), 'On the temperature dependence of soil respiration', *Functional Ecology* **8**: 315–23.

Mann, M.E., R.S. Bradley and M.K. Hughes (1998), 'Global-scale temperature patterns and climate forcing over the past six centuries', *Nature* **392**: 779–87.

McGuire, A.D., J.M. Melillo, D.W. Kicklighter and L.A. Joyce (1995), 'Equilibrium responses of soil carbon to climate change: empirical and process-based esimates', *Journal of Biogeography* **22**: 785–96.

Melillo, J.M., R.A. Houghton, D.W. Kicklighter and A.D. McGuire (1996), 'Tropical deforestation and the global carbon budget', *Annual Review of Energy and Environment* **21**: 293–310.

Milliman, J.D. (1993), 'Production and accumulation of calcium carbonate in the ocean; budget of a nonsteady state', *Global Biogeochemical Cycles* **7**: 927–57.

Moore, T.R. and R. Knowles (1989), 'The influence of water table levels on methane and carbon dioxide emissions from peatland soils', *Canadian Journal of Soil Science* **69**: 33–8.

Moulton, K.L., J. West and R.A. Berner (2000), 'Solute flux and mineral mass balance approaches to the quantification of plant effects on silicate weathering', *American Journal of Science* **300**: 539–70.

Myneni, R.B., C.D. Keeling, C.J. Tucker, G. Astar and R.R. Nemani (1997), 'Increased plant growth in the northern high latitudes from 1981 to 1991', *Nature* **386**: 698–702.

Nadelhoffer, K.J., B.A. Emmett, P. Gundersen, O.J. Kjonaas, C.J. Koopmans, P. Schleppi, A. Tietema and R.F. Wright (1999), 'Nitrogen deposition makes a minor contribution to carbon sequestration in temperate forests', *Nature* **398**: 145–8.

Oechel, W.C., S.J. Hastings, C. Vourlitis, M. Jenkins, G. Riechers and N. Grulke (1993), 'Recent change of arctic tundra ecosystems from a net carbon sink to a source', *Nature* **361**: 520–23.

Oechel, W.C., G.L. Vourlitis, S.J. Hastings and S.A.Bochkarev (1995), 'Change in arctic CO_2 flux over two decades: effects of climate change at Barrow, Alaska', *Ecological Applications* **5**: 846–55.

Oren, R., D.S. Ellsworth, K.H. Johnson, N. Phillips, B.E. Ewqers, C. Maier, K.V.R. Schafer, H. McCarthy, G. Hendrey, S.G. McNulty and G.G. Katul (2001), 'Soil fertility limits carbon sequestration by forest ecosystems in a CO_2-enriched atmosphere', *Nature* **411**: 469–72.

Owen, R.M. and D.K. Rea (1985), 'Sea-floor hydrothermal activity links climate to tectonics: the Eocene carbon dioxide greenhouse', *Science* **227**: 166–9.

Pacala, S.W., G.C. Hurtt, D. Baker, P. Peylin, R.A. Houghton, R.A. Birdsey, L. Heath, E.T. Sundquist, R.F. Stallard, P. Ciais, P. Moorcroft, J.P. Caspersen, E. Shevliakova, B. Moore, G. Kohlmaier, E. Holland, M. Gloor, M.E. Harmon, S.-M. Fan, J.L. Sarmiento, C.L. Goodale, D. Schimel and C.B. Field (2001), 'Consistent land- and atmosphere-based U.S. carbon sink estimates', *Science* **292**: 2316–20.

Palmer-Winkler, J., R.S. Cherry and W.H. Schlesinger (1996), 'The Q_{10} relationship of microbial respiration in a temperate forest soil', *Soil Biology and Biochemistry* **28**: 1067–72.

Pearson, P.N. and M.R. Palmer (2000), 'Atmospheric carbon dioxide concentrations over the past 60 million years', *Nature* **406**: 695–9.

Peng, T.-H., R. Wanninkhof, J.L. Bullister, R.A. Feely and T. Takahashi (1998), 'Quantification of decadal anthropogenic CO_2 uptake in the ocean based on dissolved inorganic carbon measurements', *Nature* **396**: 560–63.

Petit, J.R., J. Jouzel, D. Raynaud, N.I. Barkov, J.-M. Barnola, I. Basile, M. Bender, J. Chappellaz, M. Davis, G. Delaygue, M. Delmotte, V.M. Kotlyakov, M. Legrand, V.Y. Lipenkov, C. Lorius, L. Pepin, C. Ritz, E. Saltzman and M. Stievenard (1999), 'Climate and atmospheric history of the past 420,000 years from the Vostok ice core, Antarctica', *Nature* **399**: 429–36.

Post, W.M. and K.C. Kwon (2000), 'Soil carbon sequestration and land-use change; processes and potential', *Global Change Biology* **6**: 317–27.

Potter, C.S. (1999), 'Terrestrial biomass and the effects of deforestation on the global carbon cycle', *BioScience* **49**: 769–78.

Quay, P.D., B. Tilbrook and C.S. Wong (1992), 'Oceanic uptake of fossil fuel CO_2: carbon-13 evidence', *Science* **256**: 74–9.

Raich, J.W. and W.H. Schlesinger (1992), 'The global carbon dioxide flux in soil respiration and its relationship to vegetation and climate', *Tellus* **44B**: 81–99.

Reilly, J., R. Prinn, J. Harnisch, J. Fitzmaurice, H. Jacoby, D. Kicklighter, J. Melillo, P. Stone, A. Sokolov and C. Wang (1999), 'Multi-gas assessment of the Kyoto Protocol', *Nature* **401**: 549–55.

Robertson, G.P., E.A. Paul and R.R. Harwood (2000), 'Greenhouse gases in intensive agriculture: contributions of individual gases to the radiative forcing of the atmosphere', *Science* **289**: 1922–5.

Rustad, L.E., J.L. Campbell, G.M. Marion, R.J. Norby, M.J. Mitchell, A.E. Hartley, J.H. C. Cornelissen and J. Gurevitch (2001), 'A meta-analysis of the response of soil respiration, net nitrogen mineralization, and aboveground plant growth to experimental ecosystem warming', *Oecologia* **126**: 543–62.

Schiffman, P.N. and W.C. Johnson (1989), 'Phytomass and detrital carbon storage during forest regrowth in the southeastern United States piedmont', *Canadian Journal of Forest Research* **19**: 69–78.

Schimel, D.S., B.H. Braswell, E.A. Holland, R. McKeown, D.S. Ojima, T.H. Painter, W.J. Parton and A.R. Townsend (1994), 'Climatic, edaphic, and biotic controls over storage and turnover of carbon in soils', *Global Biogeochem Cycles* **8**: 279–93.

Schimel, D., J. Melillo, H. Tian, A.D. McGuire, D. Kicklighter, T. Kittel, N. Rosenbloom, S. Running, P. Thornton, D. Ojima, W. Parton, R. Kelly, M. Sykes, R. Neilson and B. Rizzo (2000), 'Contribution of increasing CO_2 and climate to carbon storage by ecosystems in the United States', *Science* **287**: 2004–6.

Schlesinger, W.H. (1977), 'Carbon balance in terrestrial detritus', *Annual Review of Ecology and Systematics* **8**: 51–81.

Schlesinger, W.H. (1990), 'Evidence from chronosequence studies for a low carbon-storage potential of soils', *Nature* **348**: 232–4.

Schlesinger, W.H. (1997), *Biogeochemistry: An Analysis of Global Change*, 2nd edn, Academic Press, San Diego.

Schlesinger, W.H. (2000), 'Carbon sequestration in soils: some cautions amidst optimism', *Agriculture, Ecosystems and Environment* **82**: 121–7.

Schlesinger, W.H. and J.A. Andrews (2000), 'Soil respiration and the global carbon cycle', *Biogeochemistry* **48**: 7–20.

Schlesinger, W.H. and J. Lichter (2001), 'Limited carbon storage in soil and litter of experimental forest plots under increased atmospheric CO_2', *Nature* **411**: 466–9.

Schlesinger, W.H. and J.M. Melack (1981), 'Transport of organic carbon in the world's rivers', *Tellus* **33**: 172–87.

Shepashenko, D., A. Shvidenko and S. Nilsson (1998), 'Phytomass (live biomass) and carbon of Siberian forests', *Biomass and Bioenergy* **14**: 21–31.

Skole, D. and C. Tucker (1993), 'Tropical deforestation and habitat fragmentation in the Amazon: satellite data from 1978 to 1988', *Science* **260**: 1905–10.

Smith, S.V. and F.T. MacKenzie (1987), 'The ocean as a net heterotrophic system: implications from the carbon biogeochemical cycle', *Global Biogeochemical Cycles* **1**: 187–98.

Smith, W.H.F. and D.T. Sandwell (1997), 'Global sea floor topography from satellite altimetry and ship depth soundings', *Science* **277**: 1956–62.

Suchet, P.A. and J.L. Probst (1995), 'A global model for present-day atmospheric/soil CO_2 consumption by chemical erosion of continental rocks (GEM-CO_2)', *Tellus* **47B**: 273–80.

Tans, P.P., I.Y. Fung and T. Takahashi (1990), 'Observational constraints on the global atmospheric CO_2 budget', *Science* **247**: 1431–8.

Townsend, A.R., B.H. Braswell, E.A. Holland and J.E. Penner (1996), 'Spatial and temporal patterns in terrestrial carbon storage due to deposition of fossil fuel nitrogen', *Ecological Applications* **6**: 806–14.

Trumbore, S.E. and J.W. Harden (1997), 'Accumulation and turnover of carbon in organic and mineral soils of the BOREAS northern study area', *Journal of Geophysical Research* **102**: 28817–30.

Turhollow, A.F. and R.D. Perlack (1991), 'Emissions of CO_2 from energy crop production', *Biomass and Bioenergy* **1**: 129–35.

Uri, N.D. (1999), 'Factors affecting the use of conservation tillage in the United States', *Water, Air and Soil Pollution* **116**: 621–38.

Uri, N.D. (2000), 'Conservation practices in US agriculture and their implication for global climate change', *Science of the Total Enviornment* **256**: 23–38.

Valentini, R., G. Matteucci, A.J. Dolmann, E.-D. Schulze, C. Rebmann, E.J. Moors, A. Granier, P. Gross, N.O. Jensen, K. Pilegaard, A. Lindroth, A. Grelle, C. Bernhofer, T. Grunwald, M. Wubinet, R. Ceulemans, A.S. Kowalski, T. Vesala, U. Rannik, P. Berbigier, D. Loustau, J. Guomundsson, H. Thorgeirson, A. Ibrom, K. Morganstern, R. Clement, J. Moncrieff, L. Montagnani, S. Minerbi and P.J. Jarvis (2000), 'Respiration as a main determinant of carbon balance in European forests', *Nature* **404**: 861–5.

Vitousek, P.M. (1991), 'Can planted forests counteract increasing atmospheric carbon dioxide?', *Journal of Environmental Quality* **20**: 348–54.

West, T.O. and G. Marland (in review), 'Carbon sequestration, carbon emissions, and net carbon flux in agriculture: a comparison of tillage practices', *Agriculture, Ecosystems and Enviroment*.

Williams, S.N., S.J. Schaefer, M.L. Calvache and D. Lopez (1992), 'Global carbon dioxide emission to the atmosphere by volcanoes', *Geochimica et Cosmochimica Acta* **56**: 1765–70.

Woodwell, G.M. (1995), 'Biotic feedbacks from the warming of the Earth', in G.M. Woodwell and F.T. MacKenzie (eds), *Biotic Feedbacks in the Global Climate System*, Oxford University Press, Oxford, pp. 3–21.

3. Climate change over the next century

Gerald R. North*

1   INTRODUCTION: WHAT ARE CLIMATE AND CLIMATE CHANGE?

The purpose of this chapter is to summarize the latest information available about the changes of climate expected over the next century given various scenarios of external anthropogenic perturbations (climatologists call these 'forcings') of the climate system. The chapter begins with a short introduction to climate with some definitions of terms and the kinds of tools used in the forecast of future climates. Important throughout is the concern for the uncertainties that creep in at every stage of the calculation/prediction process.

Weather Versus Climate

Climate is a statistical summary of weather. Such a summary can help describe what is expected in a given instance in a probabilistic sense. It is sometimes stated that 'Climate is what you expect, weather is what you get'. I also like the baseball maxim that 'it is better to be lucky than good'. Each adage describes in its way the difference between the probabilistic statement and the outcome of an individual event. But it is conceivable that the probability distribution function describing the phenomenon is not fixed in time but changes because of external influences. For instance, the mean of the distribution might shift slowly toward higher values, or perhaps the variance or spread of outcomes (dispersion) broadens over time. When we say climate changes we mean that the *distribution* of weather outcomes changes systematically. When we encounter a strange or anomalous weather pattern (or sequence of patterns), we want to know whether that outcome is merely a rare event drawn from the old fixed distribution or whether the distribution itself has changed. This is the key question in establishing whether 'global warming' has occurred from the physical scientist's point of view: is the global scale warming experienced over the last century due to some external agent or is it simply a rare event in the long history of natural weather fluctuations?

In principle, if there is no external perturbation to the system – such as might be induced by a change in atmospheric greenhouse gas concentration – the climatological probability distribution would be steady over millennia. To what extent is the past century's warming rare, and if so does humankind have anything to do with it?

Past Climates and Greenhouse Effect

The Earth's climate has changed significantly over geologic time (Crowley and North, 1991). Seventy million years ago the planet was much warmer and more moist than today and the biota of that time were accordingly very different. It is estimated that carbon dioxide concentrations in the atmosphere were many times those of today – a possible mechanism for that warm period. Beginning a few tens of millions of years ago the continental land masses gradually moved to a configuration that was conducive to the formation of large continental ice sheets on Greenland and Antarctica. During the last few million years these ice sheets have expanded and contracted with a remarkably simple pattern in time. Analysis of the composition of frequency components along with an understanding of celestial mechanics led paleoclimatologists to conclude that the waxing and waning of the great ice sheets was being controlled by the changes in Earth's orbital elements: eccentricity of the elliptical orbit, wiggles of the tilt angle of the spin axis with respect to the orbital plane and a precession of the perihelion of the elliptical orbit.

Weather variables (for example, annual averages of surface temperature at a set of stations) act somewhat like random variables (for example, outcomes of drawings from a fixed probability distribution). The outcomes of these annual averages are correlated with one another if the stations are closer than a few thousand kilometers. There is also a correlation in time of the values recorded from a given station. This temporal or *serial correlation* can lead us into confusion because we may not always be dealing with statistically independent information. When we go to apply statistical tests for significance we must take this serial correlation into account, otherwise we will be overestimating the number of independent samples and therefore draw erroneous conclusions. For example, if an annual average is strongly correlated with the year before, the two readings are highly redundant and little new information is added by the new reading. If we are trying to estimate the mean and other parameters associated with the histogram we might be fooled and not collect enough annual averages to make a precise enough estimate. In global climatology this is a serious challenge, since the variability of the global average temperature has contained in it very long time-scales (serial correlation over very long periods), making it difficult from our limited record of instrumental data to establish what the 'normal' climate is.

As the weather variables evolve over history they fill out a histogram which constitutes an estimate of the underlying probability distribution. This kind of fluctuation of the weather variables occurs even in the absence of climate change. We call this kind of variability for a fixed climate *natural variability*. The large spatial scales (for example, global averages) fill out their probability distribution very slowly, typically over a period of decades (or even longer for oceanic variables).

Understanding of climate has undergone a revolution since the mid-1970s. This revolution followed the invention of the numerical weather forecast and the introduction of global observing systems. The numerical weather forecast followed quickly on the heels of the development of the digital computer in the 1950s. The procedure of formulating a forecast involved solving the equations of motion of the atmosphere forward in time given the initial conditions (from the point of view of classical mechanics this is like predicting the trajectory of a projectile from its initial position and velocity vector). Day in, day out forecasts and the ensuing experience (data collecting, analysis, and modeling) along with faster computers with ever greater storage capacity improved weather forecasts steadily over the last half-century.

Numerical Simulation of Climate

The atmosphere and oceans consist of fluid elements that are accelerated and thereby having themselves continually relocated; as they move, these masses of gas or liquid expand and contract, cool and warm, and trace species carried along in fluid parcels may undergo physical and chemical transformations. Clouds can form creating a medium that absorbs or reflects visible and/or infrared radiation, precipitation falls out of the parcels, evaporation and condensation occur, radiant energy warms and cools the air or water. These fluid elements are accelerated by forces exerted on them in accord with Newton's Second Law. Mathematically this system is governed by a set of coupled nonlinear partial differential equations. To obtain an approximate solution to the equations one partitions the sphere into a grid with horizontal resolution of between a hundred and a thousand kilometers (450 to 45,000 boxes) depending on available computing resources. Of course, there are processes at smaller scales than this such as individual storms and fronts – these have to be neglected or taken into account on some kind of statistical or average basis (a process known as *parameterization* by modelers). Similarly in the vertical one partitions the atmospheric mass into 10 to 100 layers. The partitioning leads to 4500 to 4.5 million cells each of which can be thought of as an accounting center with about ten variables (for example, temperature, wind components, humidity and so on). The oceans have to be partitioned similarly but to a finer horizontal resolution since important eddy processes occur at scales near or below 100 km in size (for example, Gulf Stream meanderings). Taken altogether this is a problem of such magnitude as to choke the world's fastest computers.

A short history of climate modeling is important to the understanding of its current state of evolution. In the 1970s the first atmospheric general circulation models (AGCMs) were adapted to this problem by running short (a few years long) simulations in which only the atmosphere participated (oceans and land surfaces were passive). In fact, the atmosphere was simulated with mean annual solar conditions (no seasons) and the surface was treated in a very crude fashion akin to a thin swampy layer. By the mid-1980s the surface was more realistically treated and a mixed layer of the ocean (top 100 meters) was added. With these additions the seasonal cycle could be simulated. In order to simulate climate it was necessary to run about 15 years of simulation to generate a system whose seasonal statistics were periodic and so on, 15 years being the time for the oceanic mixed layer to come to its seasonally varying steady state. To simulate 15 years with this simple AGCM took months of computer time on state-of-the-art computers. During the 1980s there were numerous experiments with doubling carbon dioxide and changing the solar constant from one value to another, typically 1 percent. It was not possible to examine time-dependent changes in carbon dioxide until the mid-1990s when coupled ocean/atmosphere models (AOGCMs) came into being.

In parallel with the development of the atmospheric model was the development of the ocean general circulation model (OGCM). Finally, the two were coupled together in the AOGCM. This coupling was not without problems since the two subsystems have vastly different time-scales of adjustment (weeks for the atmosphere compared to years or even centuries for the deep oceans) and some subtle processes in the exchanges between the two were not modeled well enough in the first implementations. For example, precipitation is notoriously difficult to model at fine scales and yet this is important in ocean circulation, since the injection of fresh water at the surface changes the buoyancy characteristics of the ocean and can affect overturning. A patch-up called *flux adjustment* was the dominant paradigm for half a decade. In flux adjustment certain exchanges of moisture, momentum and so on, from the atmosphere to the ocean were inserted in an *ad hoc* way to make the coupled system stabilize and also agree with the seasonal climatology. It is only in the last few years that the flux adjustment schemes have been eliminated and with their removal a major criticism of the coupled models was neutralized.

The 1990s also witnessed the introduction of many more sophisticated processes in the form of land and biological processes. Also more carefully formulated subsystems treating sea and land-based ice were introduced or improved upon. In addition, most modern models were able to include sulfate aerosols (the tiny particles produced in most combustion and that are suspended in the reflecting and/or absorbing sunlight). This last meant that these tiny particles that are carried by the winds and removed by rainfall or slow sedimentation from the air could be traced in the models. The sulfate aerosol is important in climate because it is thought to play a role in reflecting sunlight back into space before it can be used in heating the ground and surrounding air. In other words, sulfate aerosols are a cooling agent acting against the greenhouse effect. Less well understood is the possibility of some of the aerosols acting as sunlight absorbers (so-called black soot effect); this would warm the neighboring air, counteracting some of the cooling due to reflection of light back to space. As will be seen later, the size of these and related effects due to aerosol interactions remains a serious problem in climate change research. Finally, the most modern models are now including some details of atmospheric chemistry and in particular aspects of the carbon cycle.

Problems with Climate Modeling

Aside from the sheer mass of the problem of keeping track of so many variables without erring, there are other formidable problems in the simulation of climate. The main problems relate to the way the subgrid scale processes are incorporated into the numerical formulation. As stated in the last section even at a horizontal resolution of 100 km, there are significant processes that occur at even smaller scales. For example, the formation of cloud is usually at smaller scales and clouds play an important role in the heating/cooling budget of an individual grid cell. Similarly, updrafts in tropical convection systems are no larger than a few kilometers in diameter. The secret of what goes on in these tiny shafts has a lot to do with the distribution of water and cirrus cloud over all of the tropics (which form about half the Earth's surface area).

It would not matter about these small features except that they tend to accumulate with the same sign leading to global-scale residuals. The most important of these is the *global feedback mechanism*. Consider a thought experiment in which the sun's brightness is increased. The planet's temperature will increase as a primary response to the increased heating. But other things in the system respond as well. In particular, one might expect the amount of water vapor to increase in the atmosphere of the warmer planet because evaporation rates have a strong temperature dependence. But water vapor is a greenhouse gas and its increased concentration will lead to an even warmer planet. This mechanism is thought to amplify the temperature response to any external perturbation by as much as a factor of two. It is an example of a positive feedback mechanism – the so-called *water vapor feedback*. There are numerous feedback mechanisms that have been proposed, some of which have proven innocuous and some have endured scrutiny over the years of testing and probing. Some of these include the ice-reflectivity feedback, which says that warming the planet makes the ice sheets contract, which in turn makes the planet less reflective to solar heating. This feedback mechanism is positive and may amplify the greenhouse effect a few tens of percent. Clouds are generally thought to be a positive feedback mechanism, but even the sign of cloud feedback is problematic because testing such a hypothesis with real data is so difficult.

The feedback mechanisms often operate at subgrid scales. They are built into the numerical models with great care but always including some empirical (really adjustable) parameters or 'fudge factors'. The greatest problem now in climate modeling is to find the right values of these adjustable parameters such that the simulated present climate is consistent with all available data. Unfortunately, there are always more values to fix than there are data to determine them. In other words, the suite of adjustable parameters is not unique and this lack of uniqueness leads different models to have different climate sensitivities to external forcings (that is, different future climates for a given societal scenario).

2   WHAT CAUSES CLIMATE TO CHANGE?

If the climate system were closed with no external changes in the conditions that govern it, the temperature and other fields would fluctuate because of the non-linearities in the governing processes (chaotic system) – leading to the natural variability of weather discussed earlier. But on the whole the probability distributions are presumably steady over time. However, some outside agents can be introduced that can change the mean temperature of the planet even according to the most elementary considerations. Some of these agents are clearly anthropogenic, for example the famous greenhouse effect, which occurs when the concentration of greenhouse gases (CO_2, CH_4, N_2O, tropospheric O_3 (the troposphere is the part of the atmosphere which is rather well mixed and is usually below about 12 km – the altitude of jet plane flight) and so on) is increased. Other external forcings comprise anthropogenic aerosols including those from sulfates, soot particles from biomass burning and mineral dust. Stratospheric ozone depletion actually causes a slight cooling. Figure 3.1 shows the accumulated energetic perturbations (watts/square meter) estimated from these sources in changing the climate over the last 250 years. The estimates depend on a number of assumptions ranging from source strengths and locations to approximations to the radiative effects of the differ-

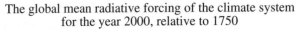

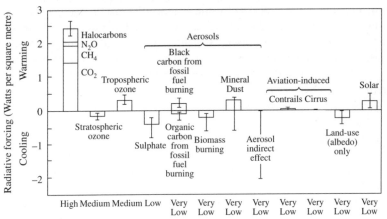

Note: The descriptors along the baseline of the graphic indicate the level of confidence in the magnitude of the result above it. The vertical lines indicate a rough estimate of the standard error in the estimate.

Source: IPCC (2001).

Figure 3.1 Forcings in Wm⁻² for various agents thought to have induced climate change since 1750

ent agents. Once the source strengths are known, atmospheric models can disperse the pollutants into their distributions over the globe.

Figure 3.1 indicates that the greenhouse effect has directly contributed roughly 2.4 Wm^{-2} to the warming over the last 250 years. Feedback effects might amplify or diminish this perturbation perhaps by a factor of two.

3   THE IPCC PROCESS

The Intergovernmental Panel on Climate Change (IPCC) is an international group of scientists organized by and reporting to the United Nations. The IPCC is charged with the responsibility of reporting every five years to the public through publication of the results of research on climate change over the previous five years. The first report was published in 1990 (First Assessment Report, FAR), the Second Assessment Report (SAR) was published in 1996 and the Third Assessment Report (TAR) was published and released by

Cambridge University Press in August 2001. The IPCC does not itself conduct research, but simply gathers and reports research carried out by scientists from all nations. The process of gathering the information that goes into each assessment report is conducted over a period of a few years prior to publication. Literally hundreds of scientists gather in numerous meetings around the world to address individual aspects of the problem and they eventually arrive at a draft of the final document whose length is over a thousand pages. After drafts of the chapters are written, they are distributed to hundreds of other scientists for anonymous reviews. The final product represents (in my opinion) the most up-to-date and accurate thinking on the problem at the moment. It is not perfect, but there does not seem to be a better way to do this enormous and rather tiring job. There are separately available summaries for policymakers – these summaries are more controversial since they inevitably represent a selection of material from the report that could be construed as being influenced by political considerations.

The next section presents a condensed version of the Policymakers' Summary of the TAR.

Summary of the Third Assessment Report (TAR)

The globe is warming

Perhaps the most important finding is that data show rather convincingly that the Earth has been warming rapidly over the last century. The instrumental record is more certain than it was five years ago, and it indicates that the global average temperature is up by about 0.6°C over the last century. The 1990s are the warmest decade of the last century with 1998 the warmest on record. The instrumental record of global average temperature is shown in Panel (a) of Figure 3.2. Going beyond the thermometric instrumental record, several groups have analyzed new proxy data from ice cores and other sources suggesting that the twentieth century is unique in its abrupt warming compared to other centuries during the last millennium. Panel (b) of Figure 3.2 shows the record of the last millennium using proxy data which include evidence from tree rings and ice cores. Over the last few decades where upper air data are available, there are indications that air temperature has increased significantly throughout the lowest eight kilometers of the atmosphere. Snow- and ice-covered areas have been significantly decreasing. Sea level has increased by 0.1 to 0.2 meters. Heavy precipitation events may have increased in middle latitudes. At the same time some variables have not changed significantly, such as the frequency of occurrence of Atlantic hurricanes.

Variations of the Earth's surface temperature for:

(a) the past 140 years

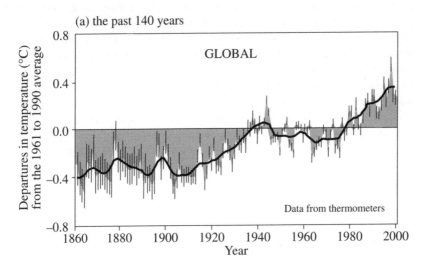

(b) the past 1,000 years

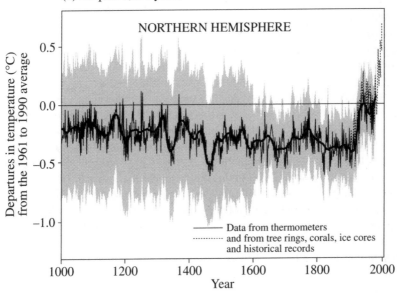

Source: IPCC (2001).

Figure 3.2   *(a) Instrumental record of global average surface temperatures over the last 140 years. (b) Estimate of the global average temperature for the last 1000 years (based upon a combination of proxy data)*

Greenhouse gases are increasing

Greenhouse gas concentrations are up. For example, carbon dioxide is up 31 percent since the beginning of the Industrial Revolution, taken here to be 1750. About three-quarters of this increase is thought to be attributable to fossil-fuel burning, but other sources include clearing of land (burning or decay of felled trees leads to carbon dioxide emission) and various industrial processes – in particular, the cement industry. The rate of increase of carbon dioxide is slightly variable from 0.9 to 2.8 ppm (parts per million) per year. Methane (CH_4) has increased 151 percent over this same period and about half of this is presumed to be anthropogenic. Nitrous oxide is up 17 percent. The chlorofluorocarbons (CFCs, from spray cans and refrigerants) have increased enormously, but their rate has dropped in the last few years due to the Montreal Protocol.

Aerosols and natural forcings

Aerosols have been increasing over this period due to human activities. These particulates can cause changes in climate in several ways. Most are the sulfate aerosols that come from fossil-fuel burning. For the most part these should cause a cooling effect on the atmosphere because they reflect solar radiation back to space before it can heat the surface. Some soot-like aerosols come from biomass burning and these can have a mixed effect, both reflecting solar radiation back to space and absorbing sunlight that then heats the surrounding air. Finally, aerosols can modify the formation of clouds; this is called the *indirect aerosol effect* and is currently rather poorly understood, although some models purport to include it, albeit crudely.

Some other natural forcings include volcanic eruptions capable of spreading a veil of aerosols in the stratosphere (the stratosphere is the 30-kilometer layer of air above the troposphere – it is very stable and stratified in laminar-like layers and does not exchange air or other matter readily with the troposphere), screening out sunlight. The volcanic aerosols (mostly of the sulfate variety) tend to remain in the stratosphere for a year or two, then fall out. The climatic effect can be quite dramatic. For example, after the eruption of Mt. Pinatubo in 1991, the globe cooled temporarily by nearly 1°C, but the anomaly in global surface temperature was washed out in a matter of a few years. Hence, volcanic activity can lead to punctuated coolings of rather large magnitude lasting for a few years each. When bunched together they can cause a prolonged cooling of the global average temperature.

Other natural forcings include the effects of solar variability. It is now well established from satellite observations that the total radiation from the sun has a variation following the nearly periodic 11-year solar cycle. The amplitude of this cycle is about 0.1 percent in luminosity and attempts have been made to detect this very faint signal in the climate system response with mixed but somewhat optimistic results (North and Wu, 2001). Theoretically, the sun has been increasing its luminosity over the century, but the most popular theories indicate that this stimulus to global warming may be only a small fraction of that expected by the greenhouse effect. I take the theory of a brightening sun to be rather speculative at this point, since there are virtually no observations and the theory is so far not compelling.

Climate model confidence has increased

There is a general feeling in the climate research community that our confidence in climate models has improved over the last five years. For example, there has been a much better appreciation of the many processes involved in climate and climate change. A number of new observing programs and special experiments have collected and analyzed data over this period and much new data have come from satellite observing systems such as the Tropical Rainfall Measuring Mission (Kummerow et al., 2000). Our ability to simulate the present seasonal cycle and such features as El Nino has increased significantly. In addition, there have been some successful simulations of past climates. Even with this increase in our confidence, climate models still exhibit a plus/minus 50 percent range of uncertainty in their prediction of the response of the global average temperature due to a doubling of CO_2.

Evidence for attribution

There has been considerable activity over the last five years in the area of detecting climate response signals and therefore our ability to attribute most of the response over the last 50 and 100 years to various inducing agents, including greenhouse gases, anthropogenic aerosols, volcanic activity and solar variation. There are three steps in the detection process:

1. The detection and attribution results require climate model simulations lasting thousands of years to establish the level and patterns of natural variability ('noise' in this application).
2. Then an *ensemble* of climate model runs with prescribed forcings is used to establish the expected responses or signal patterns.
3. One then passes the data through this detection program and comes up with an estimate of the signal strengths in the data and their statistical uncertainty.

The results from several groups are consistently showing that the greenhouse gas signal is very significant at better than the 95 percent confidence level and so is that for the volcanic responses. The results are significant for the aerosol contribution only over the last 50 years. Solar cycle response is still marginal at about the 75 percent confidence level (in addition to the IPCC TAR report, see North and Wu, 2001).

Human activities will continue through the twenty-first century

The adjustment times in the earth/atmosphere system for different green-house gases differ. In particular, it is important to realize that the time for adjustment of the atmospheric concentration of CO_2 and N_2O is hundreds of years. This means that after quickly pumping an overload of CO_2 into the air it will take some two hundred years for the atmosphere system to adjust itself back to its normal equilibrium level for this gas. The same holds for N_2O. On the other hand, it has been pointed out that methane has a much faster equilibration time and taking action on reducing methane emissions is likely to have a quick response and might be part of an important greenhouse reduction strategy (Hansen et al., 2000).

Temperatures and sea level are to rise

Because of the long adjustment times for the greenhouse gases and because of the long response times of some of the slower components of the system (for example, deep layers of the world oceans and continental ice sheets). These slowly responding parts of the system take a long time to 'catch up' with the current radiation balance or imbalance. These components will cause the system to lag behind the current imbalance but in turn when and if we make a change in our greenhouse gas emission rates, they will lag behind in responding to this and warming may well continue for hundreds of years. In fact, the sea level would surely continue rising as the excess heat spreads throughout the oceans and causes thermal expansion leading to sea-level rise.

More understanding needed

Finally the report suggests that additional research is needed to gain a more complete understanding of the system. I will not elaborate here, but it is clear that more and faster computers are essential and the continued deployment of global observing systems that can provide data that can be used to confront and adjust the models. In addition, there need to be many more process studies of such components as the cloud and water vapor processes.

Scenarios of Future Climate Forcings

As a part of the IPCC process a Special Report on Emission Scenarios (SRES) has been issued (available at www.ipcc.ch). The idea behind this report was to provide a wide range of scenarios for the next century built upon various detailed assumptions about population change, cultural shifts which embody different approaches to energy production and emission schemes. The SRES scenarios include all the known relevant greenhouse gases: carbon dioxide (CO_2), methane (CH_4), nitrous oxide (N_2O) and a few other trace gases such as certain sulfur compounds and the chlorofluorocarbons.

The SRES scenarios forming several categories will be briefly outlined here. The scenarios are grouped into 'storylines'. In each storyline are a group of families. The first storyline, denoted A1, describes:

> A future world of very rapid economic growth, global population that peaks in mid-century and declines thereafter, and the rapid introduction of new and more efficient technologies. Major underlying themes are convergence among regions, capacity building, and increased cultural and social interactions, with a substantial reduction in regional differences in per capita income. The A1 scenario family develops into three groups that describe alternative directions of technological change in the energy system. The three A1 groups are distinguished by their technological emphasis: fossil intensive (A1F1), non-fossil energy sources (A1T), or a balance across all sources (A1B).

There are other storylines (B1, B2, ...) that need not be elaborated upon here, since the reader can consult the original SRES document. Suffice it to say that the 40 different scenarios cover a rather wide range of conceivable world behaviors that might occur over the next century. These emission scenarios as a function of time are illustrated in Figure 3.3.

Figure 3.4 shows the concentrations of CO_2 based upon the emission scenarios combined with a carbon cycle model. Figure 3.5 takes this a step further to the actual forcings in Wm^{-2}. As indicated in Figure 3.5, the main contribution to warming over the next century is expected to come from increases in the concentration of CO_2.

An important caution expressed in the SRES is that the distribution across different scenarios does not represent any kind of statistical distribution in the probabilistic sense. There is no reason to think that the peak or even the mean across this distribution is in any sense a 'most likely' or an indicator of any other form of central tendency. The range of different emissions scenarios is just that – the range of emission time series based upon a set of reasonable but obviously highly uncertain assumptions.

Note that all the emission scenarios for carbon dioxide are in amounts emitted, not in the amount left behind in the atmosphere. But taking the fraction of carbon dioxide stored in the atmosphere to be a fixed fraction (roughly three-quarters) we see that in the fossil-fuel emission chart a doubling (from now) might be expected to occur some time in mid-century. It would not be unreasonable to assume (but with considerable uncertainty) that the contribution from land use is roughly fixed.

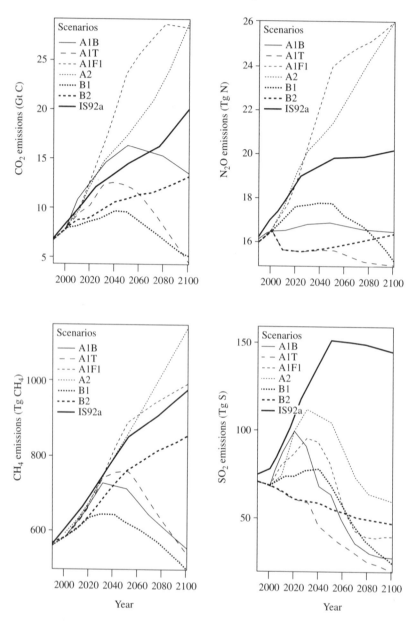

Source: IPCC (2001).

Figure 3.3   Different emission scenarios from the SRES, including CO₂, CH₄, N₂O and SO₂

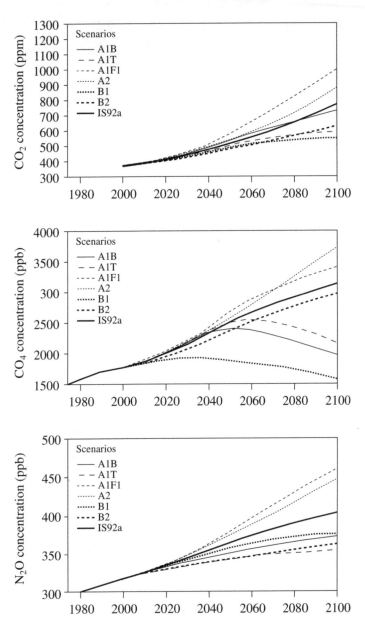

Source: IPCC (2001).

Figure 3.4   Modeled concentration of CO$_2$ based upon the SRES emission scenarios

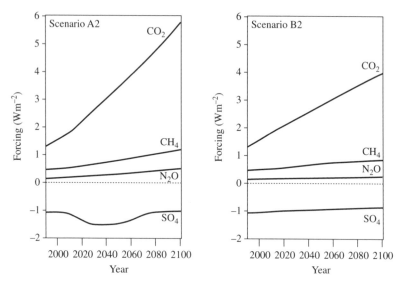

Source: IPCC (2001).

Figure 3.5   *Forcings in Wm⁻² for the emissions scenarios and modeled
concentrations depicted in Figures 3.3 and 3.4*

4   CLIMATE RESPONSES TO FUTURE FORCINGS

In response to the emissions scenarios presented in the previous section,
climate modelers have made runs with these driving forces as stimuli for
climate response over the next century.

Global Results for Temperature and Precipitation

Global results are often presented for future climate scenarios. A serious question posed by the policymaker is: why present global results if we are only
interested in what happens locally? There are several important scientific reasons for the climatologist to present first the global average result. The first is
related to data. Collecting and reliably analyzing data over the past century is
difficult because of natural variability (leading to a lack of representativeness
of the spatially sampled temperature data) and measurement error (not just
random error but biases such as the 'urban heat island effect' – for discussions
see any of the IPCC Reports). With respect to natural variability there are a
finite number (roughly 64) of statistically independent regions over the Earth

for the surface temperature field. This means we can place a gauge in each of these independent 'boxes' and average them together to form an estimate of the global mean whose standard error is the standard deviation of the local measurement divided by about eight. Hence, averaging the independent boxes together reduces the error due to the contribution due to natural variability and therefore provides a better estimate of the global change signal.

The second reason is theoretical. The driving force (greenhouse effect or solar) for climate change is primarily at the global scale. If the system response were linear we might expect the response to be primarily at the global scale. Hence, the climate response signal from greenhouse gas increases is mainly at the global scale with small geographical departures due to localized feedback mechanisms such as polar icecap responses. While the climate system is hardly linear, many numerical experiments with models suggest that to a good first approximation the global average has this simplifying property. Another related reason is that models tend to develop more error in the form of bias at smaller scales. This suggests that averaging over large spatial areas might eliminate some model error just as it does in the case of observational error.

But of course we do need answers at the regional level for detailed policy analysis. Models are unreliable in most instances at the regional level as can be seen from the differences in predictions from the different models. Some of these differences will be discussed as the results are presented in the next subsection. As a general rule, surface temperature can be more reliably computed from models than precipitation.

Given the emission scenarios and modeled concentrations from the last section we are in position to insert these inputs into the models and return future climate responses. In general we would like to conduct a group of runs with the same forcings and other boundary conditions to form a statistical ensemble. This is necessary to average out the effects of natural variability (and random error, too). There are many climate models operating around the world. Those that were chosen for this particular study were the one at the United Kingdom Meteorological Office (UKMO) and the one at the Max Planck Institute (MPI) in Hamburg. These are among the most sophisticated in the world and reasonably represent typical climate model results. A discussion of uncertainties will be presented later.

Figure 3.6 presents a view of the projected global average temperatures over the next century. The figure shows that over all the ensemble of emission scenarios and over the envelope of simulations the global average temperature change for the next century might reasonably be expected to fall in the range of 1.8 and 6.0°C.

The final global graphic in Figure 3.7 is the sea-level rise expected from the emission scenarios. This result comes from a combination of a simplified

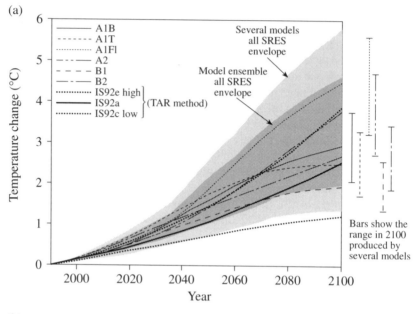

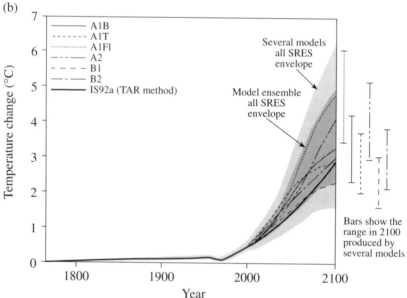

Source: IPCC (2001).

Figure 3.6   Modeled responses in the global average temperature by the Hadley Centre Model and an envelope of other models for a representative group of emission scenarios

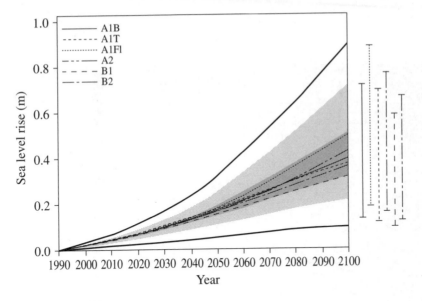

Source: IPCC (2001).

Figure 3.7   *Sea-level rise based upon a simplified model of ocean volume and estimates of land ice volume and extent from AOGCMs*

model of ocean volume but driven by AOGCM simulated estimates of land ice volume.

Regional Results of Simulations

Climate models produce detailed maps of the changes in surface temperature and precipitation as a function of position over the globe. Figure 3.8 shows a difference map of the mean temperature and range (across an ensemble of models) of the expected temperatures between the present and an average of the projected climate in years 2071–2100. In the figure we can see an amplification of the warming toward the poles. In addition there is a small tendency for land surfaces to lead the ocean surfaces in the warming. These are the main features of the regional warming expected. The IPCC TAR also presents a similar picture for precipitation. Most of the precipitation changes are in the tropics. But in my opinion the precipitation change estimates at the regional level are well beyond the capabilities of today's climate models and will not be presented here.

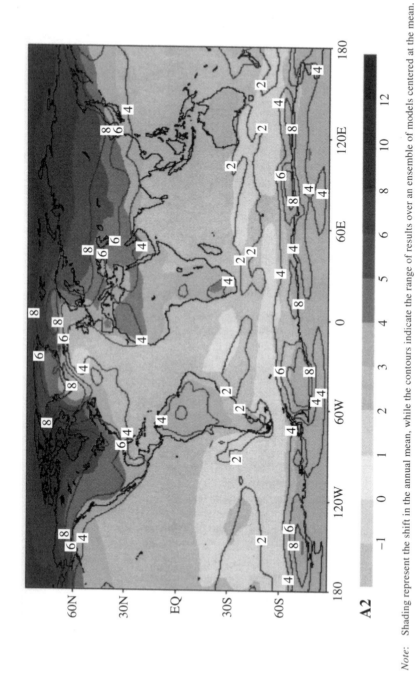

Note: Shading represent the shift in the annual mean, while the contours indicate the range of results over an ensemble of models centered at the mean.

Source: IPCC (2001).

Figure 3.8 Regional surface temperature differences from the present to the 2071–2100 average

5 SUMMARY, CONCLUSIONS ABOUT CLIMATE PROJECTIONS

The IPCC framework and the coupled atmosphere/ocean general circulation model seem as satisfactory as any at present to develop scenarios of forcings and the resulting future climates based upon estimates of emissions of greenhouse gases and land use over the next century. A large number of numerical simulation models have been developed around the world for this purpose, and there is some agreement among them, but it is hardly perfect. A reasonable uncertainty figure on the global average temperature change over the next century to use is plus/minus 50 percent given a particular emission scenario. However, it must be admitted that the plus/minus 50 percent figure is based not upon any realistic assessment of error considering the underlying physical factors but rather it is a kind of envelope of responses by the several (few tens at most) different climate models around the world.

A serious problem with the procedure used so far is the lack of an objective error model for assessment of the numerical simulations. Currently the only method of assessing the uncertainty is to compare one model's result to that of the others, forming an envelope of scenario responses. Such a procedure is fraught with danger because of the tendency for political considerations to enter.

NOTE

* *Acknowledgement* All the figures in this chapter were taken from the IPCC Report listed in the references. The author is grateful for the opportunity to participate in the IPCC process and to have access to the findings prior to formal publication.

REFERENCES

Crowley, T.J. and G.R. North (1991), *Paleoclimatology*, Oxford University Press, New York.
Hansen, J., M. Sato, R. Ruedy, A. Lacis and V. Oinas (2000), 'Global warming in the twenty-first century: an alternative scenario', *Proceedings of the National Academy of Sciences*, **97**, 9875–80.
IPCC (1990), Climate Change: The IPCC Scientific Assessment, edited by J.T. Houghton et al., London: Cambridge University Press.
IPCC (1996), Climate Change 1995: Impacts, Adaptation and Mitigation of Climate Change: Second Assessment Report on Climate Change, edited by R.T. Watson et al., London: Cambridge University Press.
IPCC (2001), Climate Change 2001: Contribution of Working Group I to the Third Assessment Report of Climate Change, edited by J.T. Houghton et al., London: Cambridge University Press.

Kummerow, C., J. Simpson, ..., 23 others, ... and K. Nakamura (2000), 'The status of the Tropical Rainfall Measuring Mission (TRMM) after two years in orbit', *Journal of Applied Meteorology*, **39**, 1965–82.

North, G.R. and Q. Wu (2001), 'Detecting climate signals using space-time EOFs', *Journal of Climate*, **14**, 1839–63.

4. Benefit–cost analysis and climate-change policy

Lawrence H. Goulder*

1 INTRODUCTION

Economics has contributed importantly to the evaluation of potential climate-change policies. One contribution has been to compare the *cost-effectiveness* of different policy alternatives – that is, to compare the cost of meeting a given environmental goal (such as a given reduction in atmospheric concentrations) under different policies. Another contribution is to indicate which nations, industries, income groups, or generations might win or lose under various policies. Thus, economic analysis can help reveal the *distribution of impacts* under different policy alternatives.

A third important contribution is the application of benefit–cost analysis to evaluate policy alternatives. Benefit–cost analysis considers the projected positive and adverse impacts of a proposed policy, imputes values to those impacts, and arrives at an overall measure of the proposal's net benefits. The information from these analyses can help us rank policy alternatives and shape our thinking about what types of policies (if any) should be put in place to combat climate change. Benefit–cost analysis differs from cost-effectiveness analysis in that it considers both the benefits and the costs of a given policy. While cost-effectiveness analysis takes the environmental target as given when it compares policies, benefit–cost analysis can compare policies that involve different environmental consequences. As a result, benefit–cost analysis can be used both to evaluate alternative policy instruments (for example, a carbon tax versus tradeable carbon permits versus energy performance standards) as well as to reveal, for a given instrument, how stringently it should be imposed (for example, how many carbon permits should be issued). Thus it can help in choosing both the policy instrument and the environmental goal or target.

This chapter examines benefit–cost analysis as it is applied to climate-change policy. Section 2 below describes the main elements of a benefit–cost assessment and the underlying principles that dictate how benefits and costs are defined and measured. The ultimate statistic arrived at in a benefit–cost analysis is a policy's efficiency impact or net benefit. The section discusses the relationship between this statistic and social welfare. Section 3 examines two important and controversial issues associated with benefit–cost analysis: the discounting of future benefits and costs, and the application of benefit–cost analysis to situations involving a high degree of uncertainty. While benefit–cost analysis is a powerful tool, it cannot address all relevant dimensions of a policy evaluation. Section 4 examines some of the limitations of benefit–cost analysis – limitations that sometimes are not fully understood or appreciated in policy discussions. The section indicates that other evaluation criteria beyond the net benefits or efficiency change are very important. These other criteria are especially important when policy impacts differ widely across the affected population and when the distribution of income among the affected population is highly uneven. These circumstances apply in the case of climate policy. Section 5 offers general conclusions.

2   ELEMENTS OF BENEFIT–COST ANALYSIS

Scientists have identified a range of biophysical impacts that would stem from an increase in concentrations of greenhouse gases. Many of these potential impacts offer genuine cause for concern. Few onlookers would welcome the rise in sea level, increased severity of storms, or threats to biodiversity that could accompany climate change.

Although the concerns about climate-change impacts are warranted, convincing policymakers that society ought to avert them requires more than pointing out the potential harms. Politicians and much of the general public want to know what sacrifices or costs are involved in policies that would avert climate change. Thus, it is helpful to provide information about the costs as well. Beyond that, it is useful to have a way of comparing a proposed policy's benefits with its costs. A benefit–cost analysis allows for such comparisons by translating benefits and costs into common units.

The Basic Formula

The ultimate statistic from a benefit–cost analysis is a number for the aggregate net benefits from a policy change, relative to the situation without the policy. Let B_i represent the benefits of the policy to individual i, and let C_i represent the costs to that individual. A benefit–cost analysis aggregates these benefits and costs and calculates the excess of benefits over aggregate costs. Thus it focuses on net benefits NB in the aggregate, expressed by:

$$NB = \sum_i (B_i - C_i). \qquad (4.1)$$

The formula is often adapted to situations where the benefits and costs occur at various points in time. Let B_{it} and C_{it} represent the benefit and cost to person i at time t. Assume that the analysis considers the impacts on I individuals (that is, $i = 1, 2, \ldots, I$) and that t ranges from year 0 (the present time) to some future year T. The present value of the net benefit is the net benefit aggregated over individuals and across time:

$$PVNB = \sum_{i=1}^{I} \sum_{t=0}^{T} [(B_{it} - C_{it})/(1+\delta)^t]. \qquad (4.2)$$

The discount rate δ is used to translate future benefits or costs into equivalent benefits or costs in the present. (We shall discuss the rationale for discounting in Section 3 below.) Thus, in the benefit–cost formula, a benefit occurring 20 years in the future and valued at X at that time counts the same as a benefit occurring today that is currently valued at $X/(1 + \delta)^{20}$.

The central focus of climate change policies is to avoid some of the changes in climate and associated damages that would occur under 'business as usual', that is, in the absence of a climate policy. The 'benefit' from a proposed policy is the value of the damages avoided. B_{it} represents the value of the damages that are avoided to individual i in year t. Such benefits might include avoided energy expenditures, to the extent that avoiding climate change reduces energy bills. Or they might involve avoided losses of biodiversity, expressed in dollars that reflect what avoiding these losses is worth to humans. They could also involve the value of avoided losses of human health, to the extent that climate change would increase diseases to humans (such as tropical diseases like malaria). The chapters by Robert Mendelsohn (Chapter 5) and by Joel Smith, Jeffrey Lazo and Brian Hurd (Chapter 6) in this volume identify key potential impacts and indicate estimated values of the damages from these impacts.

The C_{it} denote the costs associated with the policy change. In the context of climate-change policy, there may be some opportunities to reduce emissions of greenhouse gases at no cost – this is the 'no-regrets' circumstance that politicians love. But most studies indicate that large-scale reductions in such emissions will entail costs. Industrialized nations currently are highly dependent on fossil fuels, whose combustion releases carbon dioxide (CO_2) into the atmosphere. Reducing CO_2 emissions generally requires reductions in the use of other fossil fuels, especially coal. Such reductions, in turn, require the adoption of alternative industrial processes that in many cases are more expensive for firms than the existing processes. Advances in knowledge may lead to the discovery of new technologies that allow for cheap reduction with reduced input of fossil fuels, but developing these new technologies often involves a cost as well. Thus, there may be costs of reducing emissions even if the channel for such reductions is a new, 'carbon-free' technology that proves useful for a given industry.

The costs to industry imply some combination of losses of profit or higher prices to consumers, depending on how much of this cost is shifted forward onto consumers through higher prices. Lower profits or higher prices mean a loss of real income. Lower profits imply lower incomes to owners of firms and perhaps managers as well. Higher prices imply that consumers' dollars no longer can buy as many real goods and services: thus consumers' real incomes fall. The costs to industry might also cause reductions in employment, thus lowering incomes to workers. 'Cost' is the overall loss of real income to these various participants in the economy.[1] A detailed discussion of the potential costs of climate change policies is offered in the chapter by Jae Edmonds and Ron Sands in this volume (Chapter 7).

The *PVNB* is a measure of the aggregate net benefits from a policy change. If the *PVNB* is positive, the aggregate benefits outweigh the costs, and in this sense the policy yields an improvement relative to no policy, that is, the status quo. If it is negative, the costs outweigh the benefits, which calls in question the advisability of introducing the policy.

Beyond indicating the change relative to the status quo, the *PVNB* can also help rank a policy with other policy alternatives. The policy with the highest *PVNB* offers the highest aggregate net benefits, and thus appears the most attractive in benefit–cost terms.

Figure 4.1 is a simple diagram to illustrate how net benefits are related to the extent of greenhouse gas reduction. The horizontal axis is the percentage reduction in atmospheric concentrations of greenhouse gases. The diagram simplifies issues dramatically by ignoring the time dimension. In particular, it ignores how the timing of reductions in concentrations affects costs and benefits. In the diagram, both the benefits and the costs rise as atmospheric concentrations are reduced. However, costs ultimately rise faster than benefits. The reduction level R^* is that which maximizes the net benefits. The slopes of the total benefit and total cost curves represent the *marginal* benefits and costs – the change in benefit or cost associated with the next incremental reduction. Net benefits – the distance between the total benefit and total cost curves – are maximized when the marginal benefit equals the marginal cost, that is, when the slopes are the same. Thus, the slopes are the same at the reduction level given by R^*. Any further reduction beyond R^* implies lower net benefits because the additional benefits from the additional reduction would be less than the additional costs. In the diagram, if abatement of greenhouse gases exceeds R^* but falls short of R_0, the net benefits are still positive, but less than the net

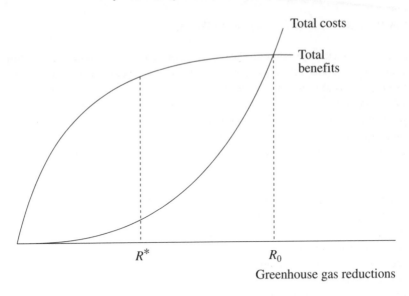

Figure 4.1   Benefits, costs and greenhouse gas reductions

benefits associated with R^*. The net benefits are zero at the point where the reductions reach R_0, and become negative when reductions are larger than R_0.

Sophisticated computer models have been used to fathom the costs and the benefits under various policies involving different levels of reduction of greenhouse gases. For example, the DICE model developed by William Nordhaus calculates the time-profile of CO_2 abatement that maximizes net benefits. Simulations with this model in Nordhaus (1994) indicate that under the optimal (*PVNB*-maximizing) time profile, the *PVNB* is $271 billion in 1989 dollars. This is a large number in absolute terms, though it represents a fairly small fraction (4-100ths of a percent) of the present value of consumption under the status quo or 'business as usual'.

The models need not consider only optimal policies. Several models have been applied to evaluate the abatement profiles called for under real-world policies or programs such as the Kyoto Protocol.[2] According to the DICE model, the Protocol requires more stringent reductions in greenhouse gases than the reductions that would maximize net benefits. Indeed, the model estimates that the Protocol would yield *negative* net benefits by requiring reductions in emissions that involve relatively high costs.

It is also possible to apply these economic models to assess the *cost-effectiveness* of various policy alternatives; that is, to compare the costs of meeting a given environmental target (such as a particular level of concentrations in greenhouse gases) under different types of policies.[3]

Net Benefits, Efficiency, and Social Welfare

How much weight should one give to a benefit–cost assessment in evaluating policy alternatives? To answer this question, it is necessary to have a clear sense as to what is meant by 'net benefits'. These are the sum of the various valuations (positive and negative) that various individuals attach to the impacts of a policy. Clearly this sum is relevant to the evaluation of a policy and deserves attention. Economists define 'efficiency' in terms of the aggregate net benefits of a policy. A policy that yields positive net benefits is described as yielding an *efficiency improvement* relative to the status quo.

For many of us, the fact that a policy offers positive net benefits (an efficiency improvement) gives it some appeal. A source of this appeal is the fact that policies with aggregate net benefits have the *potential* to yield what economists call a *Pareto improvement* – a situation where some people are better off from the policy change, while no one is worse off. Why do positive net benefits imply the potential for a Pareto improvement? If aggregate benefits exceed aggregate costs, the winners could use some of their benefits to fully compensate the losers, and still have something left over. After providing compensation, the winners would still be better off than the status quo (since aggregate benefits exceed aggregate costs), while the would-be losers would be no worse off – they would be fully compensated.

The appeal of any policy that actually brings a Pareto improvement is very strong. Any policy that makes no one worse off, while benefitting at least some, seems unquestionably better than the status quo. However, in practice, the compensation from winners to losers that is necessary to yield a Pareto improvement is rarely carried out. Thus, efficiency-improving policies only offer the *potential* for a Pareto improvement; they do not yield an actual one. If a proposed policy offers only a potential Pareto improvement – that is, if it does not include compensation to prevent anyone from being worse off – it may remain highly attractive, since yielding positive aggregate net benefits is attractive in its own right. But the appeal is not as strong as it would be if the winners compensated all the losers.

Figure 4.2 illustrates the notions of potential and actual Pareto improvements. Consider the utility of two individuals, 1 and 2. The utility frontier in the figure shows the maximum amount of utility to one individual consistent with a given amount of utility to the other individual. Suppose the combination of utilities under the status quo is given by point A in the figure. Now suppose a given policy change leads to the utility combination indicated by point B. As drawn, individual 2 gains from this policy, and individual 1 loses. Suppose the policy passes a benefit–cost test. This means that the value of the gains (in monetary units) to individual 2 exceeds the value of the loss (in monetary units) to individual 1. Hence, passing the benefit–cost test implies

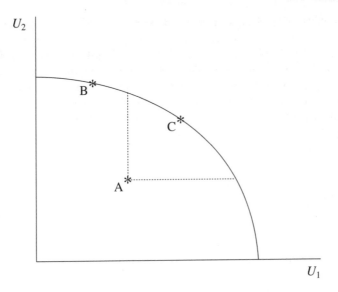

Figure 4.2   Potential versus actual Pareto improvements

that the policy allows a potential Pareto improvement. A lump-sum payment from individual 2 to individual 1 could leave both parties at least as well off as under the status quo, and leave at least one party better off. Point C represents one point that could be reached after a lump-sum payment of this sort.

These considerations suggest that the evaluation of a given proposed policy should account for other features beyond the net benefits obtained from a benefit–cost analysis. Especially when there is no actual Pareto improvement, concerns about equity motivate us to examine the distribution of benefits and costs – who wins and who loses. The distribution of impacts can be measured along various dimensions – across income groups, industries, regions, or time. The *PVNB* statistic provides no information along these lines (although the individuals carrying out a benefit–cost assessment might have obtained this information as part of their analysis. Many people might prefer a policy with slightly lower net benefits to one with greater net benefits if the former policy yielded a more even distribution of impacts. Thus, social welfare involves concerns about distribution (and equity) as well as efficiency.

Other aspects of the policy deserve attention as well. The degree of risk associated with a policy change is usually another relevant consideration. When the uncertainties are significant, it is appropriate to consider the prob-ability distributions for benefits or for the costs. These indicate the benefits or costs under different possible states of the world or scenarios. For example, we can think of a 'benign' scenario as one in which the business-as-usual emissions of greenhouses gases (that is, the emissions occurring in the absence of policies to reduce such emissions) lead to little or no serious changes in climate. A particularly bad scenario is one in which the business-as-usual emissions lead to very dramatic and damaging changes in climate. Other scenarios might lie in between. Suppose that people need to choose between two policies, Policy A and Policy B, where the latter policy is more costly and involves more extensive reductions in greenhouse gas emissions. Suppose also that:

- Policy A yields a higher expected value of net benefits. That is, if one takes a weighted average of the net benefits under the different scenarios (using the probabilities of the different scenarios as weights), this weighted average is higher under Policy A.
- Policy B yields considerably higher protection to humans and thus much higher net benefits in the particularly bad scenarios.

If individuals are risk averse, they might prefer Policy B to Policy A, despite the fact that Policy A has higher net benefits 'on average'. Risk-averse individuals give extra weight to the results under particularly bad scenarios.

A further relevant consideration is political feasibility. A policy with greater chances of passing through political filters might seem more attractive than one that has little chance of doing so, even if the former policy has somewhat lower net benefits.

Thus, while the key product of a benefit–cost analysis – a measure of aggregate net benefits – is a very important element of policy evaluation, it should not be the sole consideration. We shall return to this issue in Section 4.

Defining and Measuring Benefits

Defining benefits

In benefit–cost assessments, both benefit and costs are measured in money units such as dollars. While few people object to measuring costs in these units, some are uneasy about translating biophysical impacts into dollars when assessing benefits. Some critics claim that the very process of putting a dollar value on a change to the environment somehow debases the concern for the environment. To address this issue, it helps to consider closely what is intended in the translation.

The 'benefit' associated with a climate policy is meant to represent what the avoided damage from the policy is worth to people. This worth is sometimes called the *willingness to pay* to avoid the damage. The benefit can also be measured as *required compensation* – what people would have to be paid to be compensated for the damage they would suffer if the climate change occurred.[4]

This can be expressed a bit more formally as follows. Suppose that a person's utility (or well-being) U depends on income, Y, and the level of environmental quality, Q. We can write the person's utility function as $U(Y, E)$, where U is a positive function of both Y and E. Here environmental quality Q is a measure of physical characteristics of the environment. In the case of climate change policy, we can think of Q as measuring how benign the climate is, overall. Suppose that under business as usual there would be changes to the climate that tend to be harmful. Thus, Q would fall to the 'low' value Q_L. Now suppose that a given climate policy would prevent Q from falling so much, so that it would end up at the higher value Q_H. The willingness-to-pay measure of the benefit from avoiding climate change is the change in income, DY, that has the same impact on utility as the reduction in environmental quality from Q_H to Q_L. In this situation, the benefit to the individual (avoided damage) is the change in income ΔY that satisfies:

$$U(Y - \Delta Y, Q_H) = U(Y, Q_L).$$

We can think of this as what the 'improvement' in environmental quality from Q_L to Q_H is worth to a people – even though what is actually involved is the prevention of a reduction in Q, not an improvement.[5] By translating the physical changes in the environment into income-equivalents, we can compare benefits and costs, since costs are measured as changes in income as well.

When economists translate an avoided environmental damage into an equivalent income change, they are effectively considering how much other goods and services would be needed to substitute for a loss of environmental quality and preserve well-being. Income is just a proxy for other goods and services. Dollars or money units are just an intermediary for translating units of environmental quality into equivalent 'other things'. What economists are really aiming to do is to determine the amount of other things that would be psychologically equivalent to the change in environmental quality. A key aspect of this approach is the assumption that 'other things' can be made equivalent to the environmental change – that is, that other things can substitute for environmental quality in providing satisfaction or utility.

Thus a key assumption underlying the economist's valuation of benefits (avoided damages) is that other things are psychologically substitutable for levels of environmental quality. The economist's approach would break down if income could not compensate for changes in environmental quality – if people's psyches just did not work that way, or if no finite amount of money could compensate for the damage to well-being that comes from a loss of environmental quality. In practice, however, people do seem willing to consider trading off income for environmental quality – at least to a degree – and in most cases the willingness to pay for environmental protection (or required compensation for a loss of environmental quality) is not infinite. People usually do not seem to be willing to go to any cost to avoid a deterioration in the environment.[6]

In sum, economists define benefits in terms of what the avoided losses in environmental quality are worth to people. As mentioned earlier, the sum total of these valuations, minus the sum total of costs, ought not to be the sole consideration in evaluating policy options. But this statistic does seem to be an important consideration, one with some normative power.

Measuring benefits

If one accepts the usefulness of valuing benefits this way, there remains the challenge of measuring these benefits – that is, of figuring out what is the willingness to pay to avoid a damage (or what is the required compensation). This is a very difficult enterprise, as the chapters by Mendelsohn and by Smith, Lazo and Hurd in this volume will attest. The reader will find important details on measurement methods in those chapters. Here I shall simply mention the main categories of potential damages, and the categories of methods to measure willingness to pay to avoid them.

Economists divide the potential damages from climate change as stemming from two broad categories of impact: market impacts and non-market impacts. As the name suggests, market impacts are those expressed in a market in some fashion. These include impacts on agricultural productivity (reflected in agricultural profits and land values), on energy requirements (reflected in levels of expenditure on energy), and on coastal infrastructure (reflected in costs of dismantling or relocating structures and equipment – efforts made necessary by sea-level rise).

Non-market impacts tend to be those that are not expressed in markets, or that are expressed in markets only very indirectly. Impacts on the functioning of ecosystems are examples of non-market damages. To the extent that climate change alters or compromises the functioning of ecosystems, these changes are not directly expressed in markets.

Since almost any impact of climate change ultimately has market consequences, the distinction between a market impact and a non-market impact is not always clear cut. For example, various ecosystem impacts (usually categorized as non-market impacts) ultimately have market impacts. In particular, the flood-control or water purification services offered by ecosystems ultimately affect the values of residential properties or the need to devote funds to build water-purification facilities.

The market impacts, as well as some of the non-market impacts, can be valued by examining what people do indeed pay to enjoy the environmental service involved. Thus, for example, the value of increased agricultural productivity can be derived from the amount people pay for increments to agricultural output. This offers an indication of the damage from reduced agricultural productivity, and thus the benefit from avoiding such damage. The chapter by Mendelsohn provides important details on valuation methods, particularly those that apply to market impacts.

For some impacts, there is little evidence of willingness to pay from actual behavior. For example, people attach considerable value to the protection of biodiversity, but this value is primarily an 'existence value' that comes from the intellectual recognition of the existence of various species. Although some of the value of biodiversity might be expressed in market behavior (such as the amounts people are willing to pay for ecotourism or the amounts people contribute to environmental organizations whose mission is to protect wildlife), much of this value is not expressed this way. To assess these values, researchers need to elicit people's valuations through survey techniques such as the contingent valuation method. (See the Smith–Lazo–Hurd chapter for details.)

Over the past thirty years, researchers have made great strides in developing increasingly effective methods for measuring the benefits from environmental policies, including potential climate policies.[7] There have been substantial improvements in the methodologies for both revealed-preference (market-based) valuation methods and stated-preference (interview-based) methods. Nonetheless, this is not an exact science; the estimates of individuals' valuations involve substantial uncertainties. Despite the uncertainties, policy analysts tend to find the information from these studies quite useful in evaluating policy alternatives. We shall return to the issue of uncertainty in the next section.

3   DEALING WITH TIME AND UNCERTAINTY

Discounting

The benefits and costs of climate-change policies extend through time. Atmospheric physics indicates that policies implemented today (affecting global emissions of greenhouse gases) would exert some influence on the climate a century or two from now. To come up with a measure of net benefit, the benefits and costs occurring at different periods of time must somehow be combined. In general, future benefits and costs are discounted – their values are reduced – when they enter the *PVNB* formula (see equation (4.2)). The issue of discounting has generated significant controversy, in considerable part because of misunderstandings as to what underlies the application of the discount rate. This section aims to clarify what is involved.[8]

Rationale for discounting

The main purpose of discounting is to translate future benefits or costs into equivalent units. Recall that a benefit–cost analysis aims to calculate, in money units (for example, dollars), what a person is willing to pay to avoid a damage (in the case of a benefit) or must sacrifice as part of the policy's implementation (in the case of a cost). When benefits and costs occur in the future, one needs to convert the willingness-to-pay or required-sacrifice values into equivalent values in today's dollars. The need for a discount rate stems from the fact that capital is productive: a dollar's worth of resources invested today can be expected to generate more than a dollar's worth of goods and services in the future.[9]

Consider the following example. Suppose that a climate policy, introduced today, would avoid significant damage 80 years from now. Suppose also (for now) that future generations will have the same incomes as today's generations, and that their 'tastes' will be the same – they will have the same concern for the environment or the same distaste for damages from climate change as today's generation does. Finally, suppose that, 80 years from now, the avoided climate damage in that year is worth $200 to someone alive at that time. Thus, the willingness to pay, expressed 80 years from now, is $200. But in today's dollars the willingness to pay is much less. If the market rate of interest is 5 percent, then $4.04 today translates into $200 in 80 years. So, for comparability with today's benefits and costs, we need to convert the $200 into a much smaller value ($200/1.05^{80} = \$4.04$).

Previously we observed that when net benefits are positive, the winners from the policy change in question can compensate the losers and have something left over. Thus, the policy offers a *potential Pareto improvement*. Note that discounting according to the method just described is entirely consistent with this feature. For if the policy involved (with discounting) yields net benefits, the winners could fully compensate the losers. For simplicity, suppose the only benefit was the avoided damage, 80 years ahead, to a single individual 1, and that at that future time it is worth $200 to individual 1 to avoid the damage. Suppose the only *cost* was to individual 2, and that the cost is incurred today and amounts to $3.00. According to the formula, this policy yields a positive *PVNB*. In principle, individual 1 could fully compensate individual 2 by paying that individual $3.00 (for example, through debt policy in which the current generation imposes debt burden on future generations). The payment, in future dollars is $148.68 – less than the $200 benefit. Thus, after compensation is made, individual 1 is better off and individual 2 is no worse off.

In contrast, if the future benefit of $200 were *not* discounted, it is possible to arrive at a policy that appears to offer a positive net benefit, and yet which does not allow for a potential Pareto improvement. If the sign of the *PVNB* calculation is to indicate reliably the presence or absence of a potential Pareto improvement, discounting is essential. (This applies to both benefits and costs.) Thus, compensation property that motivates benefit–cost analysis jus- tifies the use of a discount rate.

Complications

In practice, applying discounting involves complications. One complication is uncertainty: we do not know what the market rate of interest will be each year over the indefinite future. If analysts assume higher interest rates than those that arise, they will discount the future too much. In the climate policy context, this means they will end up underestimating the future benefits from proposed policies. The opposite is the case if they assume interest rates that are too low.[10] We return to the issue of uncertainty below.

Another important issue is intergenerational equity. In the climate policy context, the benefits of climate policy tend to occur in the future, while many of the costs occur in the nearer term. Some people would argue that, even if future benefits are not large enough to offset current costs, current genera- tions nevertheless have an ethical obligation to undertake climate policy. In light of such concerns, one might be tempted to employ a lower discount rate, since this would give greater weight to benefits (and costs) that occur in the distant future.[11]

Intergenerational equity deserves to be a central concern in assessing cli- mate-change policies. That said, it avoids considerable confusion and substantially facilitates policy analysis to keep equity considerations separate from the benefit–cost analysis. Once the interest rate to build in equity con- cerns is altered, the distinction between the potential-Pareto-improvement (efficiency) criterion and other legitimate policy-evaluation criteria such as intergenerational equity is blurred. It then becomes more difficult to ascertain the meaning of a *PVNB* result.[12] Indeed, much more information relevant to intergenerational equity can be obtained by examining directly the benefits and costs to different generations than by considering whether the *PVNB* is positive or negative after some adjustment has been made to the discount rate. Thus it seems better to perform a *PVNB* calculation as a pure efficiency calculation – a calculation of whether gains to winners exceed losses to losers. One can subsequently consider the *PVNB* result along with the very important distributional impacts and related equity implications in arriving at an overall policy appraisal.[13]

Uncertainty

Critics have objected to benefit–cost analysis applied to climate-change policies on the grounds that it tends to obscure uncertainties and related future
risks. The future damages due to climate change, and hence the benefits from
policies to mitigate these damages, are inherently difficult to quantify. From
this observation some critics argue that benefit–cost analysis tends to give a
false sense of certainty about the future and thus to underestimate future risks.

This is a valid argument against the misapplication of benefit–cost analysis, but not against benefit–cost analysis itself. Given the significant
uncertainties, considering only the central or best-guess values for benefits or
costs in a benefit–cost assessment is unsatisfactory. A crucial element of
climate-change policy analysis is to consider the risks of low-probability,
high-consequence events – particularly the events on the 'tail' of the distribution associated with very bad scenarios. Thus, policy analysts should develop
probability distributions, not single numbers, for estimated net benefits (and
their components). Probability distributions provide information that influences the attractiveness of policies.

As mentioned in Section 2 above, the overall appeal of a policy will
usually depend not only on the mean of the net benefit distribution, but also
on its variance. If the public is risk averse, a policy that involves a somewhat
lower mean but provides greater assurance against a very serious negative
climate outcome will be preferred over a policy with a higher mean that
offers less 'insurance'. Thus, the presence of uncertainty does not argue
against benefit–cost analysis *per se*; rather, it argues for a broader application
of benefit–cost analysis – to generate a whole distribution of net benefits,
rather than a single number.[14]

Some analysts claim that the uncertainties are so great that one cannot
come up with probability distributions for the relevant benefits or costs. This
might be regarded as a case of *fundamental* uncertainty. There is some
disagreement among analysts as to what constitutes the best approach in such
cases. Many researchers argue that the best course of action is to ask experts
for their subjective probabilities and to combine this information to generate
probability distributions for different scenarios. Others claim that one can do
little more in such cases than indicate 'here are the benefits or costs *if* this
scenario applies', without claiming any likelihood for any particular scenario.
In my view, researchers always have at least an implicit idea of the likelihood
of a scenario. In the absence of some sense of likelihood, there is no basis for
making any policy decisions, including the decision to stick with the status
quo. Hardly anyone holds a fundamentally agnostic view of this type.[15]

Another option is to focus on cost-effectiveness analysis instead of benefit–cost analysis. As mentioned in the introduction, cost-effectiveness analysis

compares policies in terms of the costs of achieving some specified environmental target. For example, the target could be reaching greenhouse gas concentrations of 550 parts per million in the year 2100 (a lower concentration than would occur under business as usual). This analysis could compare a range of policy instruments (taxes versus mandated technologies versus carbon caps) as well as a range of time profiles for abatement under each instrument. A given policy is more cost-effective than another if it achieves the specified target at lower cost.

Cost-effectiveness analysis avoids the need to deal with uncertainties about benefits. The environmental target is given to the analyst.[16] However, this does not entirely eliminate the need for benefit–cost analysis. Policy analysts, policymakers, and the general public will at some point wish to evaluate or re-evaluate the environmental target, to consider whether it is too stringent, too lax, or about right. This cannot be done without attention to the environmental benefits associated with reaching the target, and thus this gives a major role to benefit–cost analysis. The various benefit–cost analyses of the Kyoto Protocol performed this function in investigating whether the emissions reductions targets under the Protocol were reasonable.

4   LIMITS TO BENEFIT–COST ANALYSIS

Section 2 indicated that benefit–cost analysis does not provide information on all the characteristics of a policy relevant to its contribution to social welfare. This section looks more closely at some of the limitations. Benefit–cost analysis is an extremely powerful and useful tool. But the application of this tool will be most effective if practitioners not only indicate its strengths but also make clear its limitations. Some of the distrust of benefit–cost analysis may derive from economists' not acknowledging fully the limitations of the method.

What Is the Normative Significance of a Potential Pareto Improvement?

Proponents of benefit–cost analysis feel that the scale of efficiency improvements – or the magnitude of the aggregate net benefits – deserve to be a major consideration in evaluating policies. Few people would disagree. The disagreements concern how much weight should be given to a benefit–cost statistic.

Actual versus potential Pareto improvements
Sections 2 and 3 have emphasized the distinction between a potential Pareto improvement and an actual one. It is extremely rare that a proposed policy

will generate an actual Pareto improvement, either directly or via transfers from winners to losers.

For some (for example, Lind, 1999) the value of benefit–cost analysis is significantly reduced in situations where there are no actual Pareto improvements. The point is highly relevant to climate-change policy. The benefits and costs of climate-change policies are very unevenly distributed, and compensation schemes are limited. Hence, at best, climate policies offer only potential Pareto improvements.[17] Lind claims that the potential-Pareto-improvement property has limited normative force, and emphasizes the importance of bringing other normative criteria into the policy assessment. The point seems important, though there is no objective way to determine how much weight should be given the benefit–cost assessment in comparison with other policy criteria.

Do positive net benefits indicate an improvement in utilitarian social welfare?

Another issue relates to the normative appeal of benefit–cost analysis. A claimed attraction of benefit–cost analysis is its connection to social welfare when social welfare is defined in utilitarian terms – that is, as the sum of individual utilities. One might suspect, in particular, that passing a benefit–cost test – and thus offering a potential Pareto improvement – improves social welfare when social welfare is defined this way. If this is the case, then the normative appeal of benefit–cost analysis is as strong as the case for a utilitarian social welfare function.

In fact, however, passing this test does not guarantee an increase in utilitarian welfare. The reason is that benefit–cost analysis compares income-equivalents to changes in utility (the various 'ΔYs' discussed above); it does not compare the changes in utility. Even if the difference in income-equivalents is positive (and the policy passes a benefit–cost test), the differences in the changes in utility may not be.

To see this, suppose that all people have the same utility functions but differ in income. Suppose also that the marginal utility of income is declining, as in Figure 4.3. Now suppose that a given policy just passes a benefit–cost test, with the rich enjoying net benefits and the poor suffering net costs. In Figure 4.3, the changes in utility to the rich and poor are indicated by ΔU_R and ΔU_P, respectively; the equivalent changes in income are indicated by EV_R and EV_P, respectively; (using 'EV' for equivalent variation). Note that this policy passes a benefit–cost test: the rich person's income-equivalent gain (EV_R) exceeds the poor person's income-equivalent loss ($-EV_P$). But the gain in utility to the rich is smaller in absolute terms than the reduction in utility to the poor: $\Delta U_R < -\Delta U_P$. Since the poor have a high marginal utility of income, even a 'small' cost in terms of income-equivalents may imply a large loss of

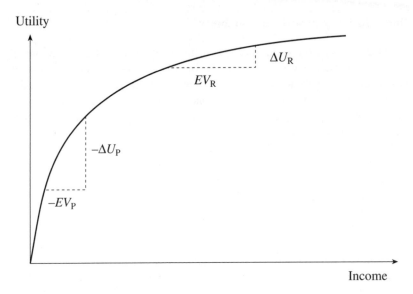

Figure 4.3   Changes in utility versus changes in income-equivalents

utility. Likewise, since the rich have a lower marginal utility of income, a 'large' benefit in terms of income-equivalents may imply a small utility gain.

Thus, even if a policy passes the benefit–cost test, the utility gain to the winners may be smaller than the utility loss to the losers. So, even though benefit–cost analysis has utilitarian underpinnings, passing the benefit–cost test cannot guarantee an improvement in a utilitarian social welfare function. This reinforces the notion that the normative force of benefit–cost analysis is limited when the policy does not produce actual (as opposed to potential) Pareto improvements. The chances that a project passing a benefit–cost test fails to raise utilitarian social welfare are enhanced when there are significant disparities in the incomes of the winners and losers.

As mentioned in Section 3, from one perspective the principal beneficiaries of climate policy are the *poorer* countries. Thus, the problem just mentioned – which involves benefits to the rich – might not seem to apply in the climate-policy context. However, if (as mentioned earlier) one takes the reference point as involving a climate policy, and considers the benefits and costs of *not* implementing a policy, the situation is one where the principal beneficiaries are the rich countries, and the problem just mentioned applies. The relation-ship between net benefits and a utilitarian welfare gain remains somewhat tenuous.

Does Efficiency Ensure Sustainability?

In international policy discussions, many have criticized the economist's attention to efficiency on the grounds that efficiency-improving policies do not ensure sustainability. Even the 'optimal' or efficiency-maximizing policy cannot guarantee sustainability. The concern for sustainability is a particular example of a concern about equity. In this case, the issue is intergenerational equity – fairness to future generations.

There has been more heat than light on this issue. A first step in providing more light is to define 'sustainability', a term that means different things to different people. One definition emphasizes sustaining for the indefinite future a capacity for well-being. To the extent that sustainability is an ethical issue, the latter definition seems most useful. As emphasized by Solow (1992), the current generation's ethical obligation to future generations is to ensure that they can enjoy a quality of life that is at least as high as that which we now enjoy. There is relatively little obligation to sustain particular resources, unless those resources are in some way essential to quality of life. Thus we can define the sustainability condition as the (ethically motivated) requirement that future generations be able to enjoy at least the same living standards (that is, levels of consumption, broadly defined) as the current generation. How does this criterion relate to the criterion of economic efficiency?

Under certain conditions, an efficient growth path will automatically satisfy the sustainability criterion. Then the sustainability criterion is superfluous.[18] The efficiency growth path will satisfy the sustainability criterion if there is technological progress (at all times) and if the elasticity of substitution between exhaustible resources and other productive inputs is greater than one.[19] However, if the elasticity of substitution is less than one, the efficient growth path might not satisfy the sustainability criterion.

Although the empirical work on this issue is far from conclusive, there are reasons to suspect that for several natural resources, the elasticity is indeed less than one. Water and topsoil are good candidate resources. This suggests that long-run analyses need to consider carefully the sustainability issue.

Many climate-change models appear to give fairly optimistic projections in terms of sustainability. Nearly all of the integrated assessment models employed in the Stanford Energy Modeling Forum's recent assessment of benefits and costs of climate-change policies projected rising consumption through time.

Should we therefore conclude that efficient paths will satisfy sustainability after all? Not necessarily. To the extent that these models explicitly consider exhaustible resources, they also tend to have producible backstop resources that are perfect substitutes. In these models, rising consumption is guaranteed so long as there is any technological progress.

The assumption of backstop technologies for every exhaustible resource is a useful starting point, especially in highly aggregated models. But some important phenomena might be overlooked at such a high level of aggregation. There is a need for more disaggregated growth models with considerable detail on exhaustible natural resources, and with close attention to potential limits in substitution opportunities.

This subsection thus indicates a limitation both in the efficiency criterion and in applied models' abilities to assess sustainability. The efficiency criterion cannot offer us assurance of sustainability. It seems important to consider policies' implications in terms of sustainability (or more generally, in terms of the intergenerational distribution of well-being) as well as in terms of efficiency. Current assessments of sustainability are hampered by the fact that existing growth models tend to assume perfect substitution for exhaustible resources. Models with greater detail and closer treatment for substitution potentials will enable researchers to examine sustainability more closely. In more sophisticated models, 'optimal' climate policies could violate the sustainability criterion.

The Measure of Net Benefits Depends on Distribution

A third key issue is that the net benefit statistic can be highly sensitive to the distribution of income or wealth. Efficiency is not entirely separate from distribution. As noted, the net benefits express, in money units, the change in utility from a policy change, and the benefits reflect willingness to pay. But willingness to pay depends on the distribution of income or wealth.

In particular, the distribution of income affects our measure of the benefits from avoiding changes in climate. Current studies[20] indicate that changes in climate would be especially harmful to developing countries. Thus the principal beneficiaries from avoiding climate change are the developing countries. Since per capita incomes in these countries are relatively low, the measure of benefits – the willingness to pay – is lower than would be the case if the countries had higher incomes.

The efficiency calculation can be highly sensitive to distribution. Indeed, a different wealth distribution could reverse the sign of the efficiency calculation. In light of this sensitivity, the efficiency calculation seems to deserve less weight in an overall policy assessment to the extent that the existing distribution of wealth is considered highly inequitable.[21]

This may strike some readers as old news. After all, nearly all respectable 'social welfare functions' include distribution, as well as efficiency, as arguments.[22] True. But the present point is not that distribution deserves consideration as well as efficiency. It is that the efficiency calculus itself is a function of distribution. When we acknowledge this dependence on distribution, we might wish to give somewhat lower weight to the net benefit statistic than we would if it was assumed that the statistic did not depend on distribution.

Some Policies Cannot Be Evaluated with a Benefit–Cost Analysis

A common theme in the previous three subsections is the importance of complementing efficiency calculations with other information that indicates distributional impacts and thereby addresses ethical concerns.

The present subsection raises a different type of issue. It is well known that welfare economics requires exogenous preferences. A stationary utility function is necessary for calculating willingness to pay and obtaining income-equivalents to changes in utility.

The point is not new. But a key implication of this point is not fully appreciated. The assumption of exogenous preferences significantly limits the types of policy interventions that economists can assess. In particular, it reduces the set of climate-change policies that can be evaluated.

Consider the following alternative policies for reducing dependence on fossil fuels. One is a tax on gasoline; the other is a government advertising or 'jawboning' campaign aimed at encouraging people to reduce their consumption of gasoline. The latter program would make the case that reducing use of heating oil is part of one's civic duty. If successful, this latter program works by changing individual's preferences.

Economists have the tools to evaluate the efficiency gain from the tax policy. In Figure 4.4, the gain is represented by the usual shaded efficiency triangle. This represents the environmental gain (A + B) minus the lost consumer surplus (B).

Suppose the government can bring about the identical reduction in heating oil demand through the 'jawboning' policy. This effectively shifts the consumer's demand curve to D'. Unfortunately, economists have no way of measuring the efficiency gain from this policy. Two different sets of preferences are involved, one underlying the original demand curve and one underlying the new one. Economists cannot assess efficiency impacts or changes in consumer surplus here, because preferences have changed. Suppose the administration costs of each policy were exactly the same. Which policy is better? Economic analysis cannot answer the question.

The consequence of this is that economists do not analyze the latter type of policy. Yet the latter policy is important. There are numerous activities – tipping in restaurants, recycling of bottles and cans and so on – that stem from a notion of civic duty, rather than from any economic incentive.[23] Bringing 'energy conservation' into the civic-duty category could signifi-

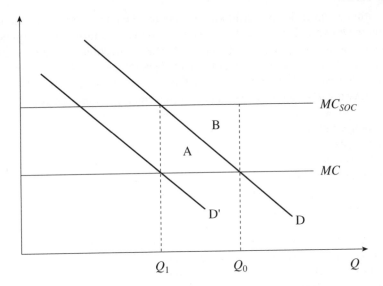

Figure 4.4   Effects of tax and 'jawboning' policies

cantly help reduce emissions of carbon dioxide. But economists have no way of analyzing the welfare implications of such a policy. Economic analysis is capable of assessing policies that restrict behavior (such as legal prohibitions) or that provide incentives to change behavior (such as taxes or subsidies). But policies aimed at changing preferences cannot be handled.

Economics might never be able to evaluate such policies. As long as it cannot, it is constructive for economists to point out the sorts of policies which might significantly address the problem at hand and yet which are not within the domain of economic analysis. Doing so helps put the other policy options on the table, even if they are not susceptible to economic analysis. In addition, this provides an entrée for other disciplines in evaluating policy options. Ethicists, in particular, can help provide clues as to the merits of a jawboning campaign to discourage consumption of home heating oil.[24]

5   CONCLUSIONS

This chapter describes the basic elements of benefit–cost analysis and describes how it can be applied to evaluate climate-change policies. It articulates the underlying principles that dictate how benefits and costs are defined and measured, and discusses difficult issues in the application of such analysis, including aggregation over time (discounting) and attention to uncertainties.

Although the efficiency criterion inherent in a benefit–cost assessment has significant normative implications, the criterion is sometimes misinterpreted and its normative power exaggerated. A chief attraction of a policy that satisfies a benefit–cost test is that it offers the potential for a Pareto improvement. However, policies rarely involve the compensation schemes that would be necessary to generate actual Pareto improvements or even approximations to such improvements. This implies a need to complement a benefit–cost analysis with attention to the distribution of policy gains and losses and other dimensions of impact.

This is especially important in the climate-change policy context because the distribution of climate-change impacts is very uneven across regions, socioeconomic groups, and generations. This raises important concerns about international and intergenerational equity. With regard to intergenerational equity, in particular, it seems important to recognize that policies that generate efficiency gains do not necessarily satisfy a sustainability criterion. However, under most integrated assessment models for climate-change policy analysis, the efficient policies produce growth paths that in fact do satisfy this criterion. This might suggest that, as an empirical matter, efficiency ensures sustainability. However, the benign result from existing models might reflect the fact that the models rule out the 'essentiality' of exhaustible resources by assuming perfect substitution of these resources via backstop technologies. Future models that consider more closely the possibilities of limited substitution (perhaps with great disaggregation) would offer a better understanding of whether meeting the sustainability criterion requires a departure from the efficient path.

The chapter shows that benefit–cost analysis cannot be applied to all potentially useful policies. Many significant policies – especially ones that would lead to changed preferences – cannot be evaluated on efficiency grounds. Economists can perform a useful function by acknowledging that these other policies exist and inviting other social scientists to shed light on their potential virtues.

Notwithstanding its limitations, benefit–cost analysis is a powerful and important tool for policy evaluation, and the efficiency criterion has substantial normative significance. The efficiency or net benefit properties of policies are crucial considerations in assessing policy alternatives, although other properties of features of policies deserve attention as well. When used in conjunction with other aspects of policy analysis, benefit–cost analysis contributes productively to sound climate-policy decision making.

NOTES

*   I am grateful to Kenneth Arrow, James Griffin, Peter Hammond and Ronald Wendner for helpful suggestions.
1.   In climate-change discussions, environmental impacts are usually considered within the benefit category, while non-environmental (narrowly economic) impacts are considered within the cost column. This categorization method is inherently arbitrary. Note that negative values are possible for both 'benefits' and 'costs'. For example, in Russia climate change could yield a more temperate climate and boost agricultural productivity. Thus, climate policy would have a negative 'benefit' insofar as it prevented this moderation of climate. Similarly, if a policy causes producers to discover cheaper methods of producing than they had previously recognized, it can produce a positive non-environmental impact; that is, the 'cost' will be negative.
2.   See, for example, Manne and Richels (1997), Nordhaus (1999), Edmonds and Wise (1998), and Bernstein et al. (1999).
3.   For a review of results from various cost-effectiveness studies, see Gaskins and Weyant (1996) and Chapter 7 by Edmunds and Sands in this volume.
4.   While these two different definitions of benefit often yield similar values, they can sometimes differ significantly. For a discussion, see Hanemann (1991).
5.   If measured as required compensation, the benefit can be expressed as ΔY such $U(Y + \Delta Y, Q_L) = U(Y, Q_H)$. That is, it is the increase in income that would make a person just as well off in the world with lower environmental quality as he or she would be if there had been no reduction in such quality.
6.   Even if reductions in environmental quality imply a finite damage, we might still believe that the complete loss of all environmental assets and all of the goods and services they generate is worth everything we have (or more). Fortunately, societies seldom are faced with a situation where all natural capital and every environmental good or service that flows from such capital is jeopardized.
7.   For a clear and relatively non-technical presentation of valuation methods, see Goodstein (2002). A more technical presentation is in Freeman (1993).
8.   Several of the issues discussed here are examined in more detail in the collection of essays in Portney and Weyant (1999).
9.   According to economic theory, the productiveness of capital is reflected in the market interest rate, which is jointly determined by the supply of investible funds by individuals and institutions and the demand for such funds by businesses. The supply of investible funds is considered to be a function of time preference (the tendency to attach more psychic value to having or consuming a given commodity today than to having or consuming it in the future), while the demand for such funds is regarded as a function of the perceived profitability of investment opportunities.
10. In addition, there is uncertainty about the likely benefits and costs that future generations will experience from a policy introduced today. We discuss this issue below.
11. In fact, using a lower discount rate does not necessarily raise benefits relative to costs. If most of a project's benefits are in the near term, and its costs are in the more distant future, a lower discount rate will *lower* the present value of net benefits. A strip-mining project involving significant costs at the end (aimed at restoring the stripped land) could fall into this category.
12. The same sort of problem arises when a benefit–cost assessment to deal with income distributional concerns is modified by giving different weights on the benefits of rich and poor persons.
13. This chapter has emphasized the supply-side approach to discounting, an approach that links the discount rate to the productivity of capital and the market interest rate. Under this approach, efficiency and equity considerations are kept separate. However, some economists take a different, 'demand-side' approach, in which equity considerations influence the choice of discount rate. This latter approach endorses a discount rate that is based on the 'social rate of time preference' plus a term that reflects how future genera-

tions' valuations of consumption might differ from those of the current generation. Under this approach, intergenerational equity considerations are embodied in the social rate of discount. For a discussion of this approach, see Arrow et al. (1996).

14. For an insightful analysis of how analysts can deal with the uncertainties associated with the impacts of climate-change policies, see Moss and Schneider (2000).
15. For an interesting debate on this issue, see the series of *Nature* commentaries by Grabler and Nakićenović (2001) and Schneider (2001). The present chapter supports Schneider's point of view.
16. Strictly speaking, specifying a concentration target does not necessarily imply a given environmental impact. The environmental consequences and benefits depend on the time profile of emissions that leads to the target. See Chapters 2 and 3 by William Schlesinger and Gerald North in this volume.
17. Note that, to a large extent, the 'losers' from climate policy are the present generation, who bear the costs, not the future generations, who enjoy the benefits (avoided damages). Thus, much of the missing compensation is from future generations to current generations.
18. For a discussion, see Heal (1998).
19. See Dasgupta and Heal (1979). These authors define an exhaustible resource as 'essential' if the elasticity of substitution is less than one. If the resource is essential and there is no technological progress, then there is no growth path that permanently sustains consumption.
20. See, for example, Mendelsohn (1999).
21. One potential response to this problem is to perform a benefit–cost assessment which imputes to poorer nations the willingness to pay that they would exhibit *if* they had higher incomes. This would increase the estimated benefits. But such an approach is artificial. The more appropriate response, I think, is to put the efficiency calculation in perspective rather than to 'correct' it.
22. For a useful general discussion of the notion of a social welfare function, see Stokey and Zeckhauser (1978).
23. For an insightful discussion of these issues, see Ackerman (1996).
24. The issue is a thorny one. It is one thing to make the ethical case that the jawboning policy would improve well-being relative to the status quo. It is another to show that this policy is superior to the tax policy.

REFERENCES

Ackerman, Frank (1996), *Why Do We Recycle? Markets, Values, and Public Policy*, New York: Island Press.

Arrow, K.J., W.R. Cline, K.-G. Mäler, M. Munasinghe, R. Squitieri and J.E. Stiglitz (1996), 'Intertemporal equity, discounting, and economic efficiency', in J.P. Bruce, H. Lee and E.F. Haites (eds), *Climate Change 1995: Economic and Social Dimensions of Climate Change, Contribution of Working Group III to the Second Assessment Report of the Intergovernmental Panel on Climate Change*, Cambridge, UK: Cambridge University Press, pp. 125–44.

Bernstein, P.M., W.D. Montgomery, T. Rutherford, and G.-F. Yang (1999), 'Effects of restrictions on international permit trading: the MS–MRT Model', in J. Pan, N. van Leeuwen, H. Timmer and R. Swart (eds), *Economic Impact of Mitigation Measures*, The Hague, The Netherlands: Central Planning Bureau, pp. 27–56.

Dasgupta, Partha and Geoffrey Heal (1979), *Economic Theory and Exhaustible Resources*, Cambridge, UK: Cambridge University Press.

Edmonds, J. and M. Wise (1998), 'The economics of climate change: building backstop technologies and policies to implement the Framework Convention on Climate Change', *Energy and Environment* **9** (4): 383–97.

Freeman, A. Myrick III (1993), *The Measurement of Environmental and Resource Values*, Washington, DC: Resources for the Future.

Gaskins, Darius and John Weyant (eds) (1996), *Reducing Global Carbon Dioxide Emissions: Costs and Policy Options*, Stanford, CA: Stanford University Energy Modeling Forum.

Goodstein, Eban (2002), *Economics and the Environment*, 3rd edn, Upper Saddle River, NJ: Simon & Schuster.

Grabler, Arnulf and Nebojsa Nakićenović (2001), 'Identifying Dangers in an Uncertain Climate', *Nature*, **412** (5 July): 15.

Hanemann, W. Michael (1991), 'Willingness to pay and willingness to accept: how much can they differ?', *American Economic Review* **81** (3): 635–47.

Heal, Geoffrey (1998), *Valuing the Future: Economic Theory and Sustainability*, New York: Columbia University Press.

Lind, Robert C. (1999), 'Analysis for intergenerational decisionmaking', in Portney and Weyant (eds), pp. 173–80.

Manne, Alan and Richard Richels (1997), 'On stabilizing CO_2 concentrations – cost-effective emission reduction strategies', *Environmental Modeling & Assessment* **2** (4): 251–66.

Mendelsohn, Robert (1999), *The Greening of Global Warming*, Washington, DC: American Enterprise Institute.

Moss, Richard H. and Stephen H. Schneider (2000), 'Uncertainties in the IPCC TAR: recommendations to lead authors for more consistent assessment and reporting', in Pachauri, R., T. Taniguchi and K. Tanaka (eds), *Guidance Papers on the Cross Cutting Issues of the Third Assessment Report of the IPCC*, Geneva: World Meteorological Organization, pp. 33–51.

Nordhaus, William D. (1994), *Managing the Global Commons*, Cambridge, MA: MIT Press.

Nordhaus, William D. (1999), 'Requiem for Kyoto: An Assessment of the Economics of the Kyoto Protocol', *The Energy Journal*, Special Issue.

Portney, Paul and John Weyant (eds) (1999), *Discounting and Intergenerational Equity*, Washington, DC: Resources for the Future.

Schneider, Stephen (2001), 'What is "Dangerous" Climate Change?', *Nature*, **411** (3 May): 17–19.

Solow, Robert (1992), 'An almost practical step toward sustainability', Resources for the Future 40th Anniversary Lecture, Resources for the Future, Washington, DC.

Stokey, Edith and Richard Zeckhauser (1978), *A Primer for Policy Analysis*, New York: W.W. Norton.

5. Assessing the market damages from climate change

Robert Mendelsohn

1 INTRODUCTION

In order to determine the optimal amount of greenhouse gases that should be controlled over time, society must weigh the benefits from control against the cost. This weighing is especially complicated with greenhouse gases because of the long lags between emissions and impacts and the long duration of impacts once they occur (Houghton et al., 1996). The weighing is also challenging because of the global nature of climate changes and the likelihood that effects will not be uniform or even unidirectional. The weighing is also made obscure by the pervasive uncertainties inherent in evaluating effects never before experienced and effects that are far into the future. Although uncertainty persists in measuring the costs of controlling greenhouse gases (see Edmonds and Sands, Chapter 7), the uncertainty surrounding the measurement of greenhouse gas damages may be as much as an order of magnitude larger.

We begin our detailed review of market damages from climate change with a careful discussion of the uncertainty surrounding impact estimates. For this discussion, we include the links between emissions and all final effects. We then move to a discussion of market impacts in the United States where a great deal of analysis has occurred. Finally, we move to the world and discuss what is currently understood about impacts on the global economy and each region. Our discussion of market impacts will assume that climate is in fact going to change. For a more detailed discussion linking greenhouse gas emissions to climate change, see North (Chapter 3).

2 UNCERTAINTY OF IMPACTS

Uncertainty pervades damage estimates across all pollution control problems. However, the global nature, the uniqueness of climate change as a phenomenon, and the fact that climate change occurs so far into the future combine to cloud any estimate that we make concerning the damages from accumulating greenhouse gases.

There are several sources of uncertainty. The link between emissions, climate change, and ecosystem change, the link between these changes and the quality of life, and the link between these changes and impacts on the economy are all sources of uncertainty. As discussed in Chapter 2, the fact that human emissions of carbon dioxide is causing increases in the observed concentrations of carbon dioxide is one of the more certain facts about greenhouse gases. However, even this link is uncertain in the future. We cannot be sure that the carbon cycle will continue to behave as it now does. Sinks might get overloaded and sources might suddenly appear from the biosystem as the climate changes. The link between concentrations of greenhouse gases and radiative forcing also seems well understood although the complexity of how gases behave at different altitudes and how clouds might change, make this link uncertain as well. The link between increased radiative forcing and changes in our climate has always been poorly understood. It is very difficult to know how a complex system such as climate will be affected by a change that may never have happened before. It is clear that more heat will be trapped on the Earth's surface and that this will speed the hydrological cycle. However, the magnitude of temperature and precipitation changes remains uncertain. Even less well understood is how the distribution of climate change will unfold across the Earth's geography. Ecosystems are undoubtedly going to be affected by changing climates. Precisely how they will react over time is not known. Productivities will certainly change and biomes are likely to shift. How quickly this will occur and what will happen during the transition is not known at this moment. In short, the science underlying damage estimates is uncertain as to the magnitude and distribution of effects.

Even if the natural science were completely understood, precise estimates of the damages from climate change would continue to elude us. We do not know what our economic system or lifestyle will be like even without climate change in a few decades much less by the end of the century. We do not know how sensitive our future economic sectors or quality of life will be to changes in climate. We do not know how important society judges these changes to be – what values to associate with each change.

The impacts of specific climate scenarios on the American economy have been studied at depth. Despite this effort, uncertainty pervades even here. The size of impacts will depend upon how quickly the economy grows in general and specifically how quickly climate-sensitive sectors grow. The impacts will also depend upon the climate sensitivity of these future sectors. We can study how sensitive the current economy appears to be, but this may provide only an indication of future sensitivity. Future impacts will undoubtedly be dependent on how large each sector becomes in each region and what new technologies are adopted. Our ability to perform accurate long-run forecasts of all these phenomena are limited.

Estimating the impacts to the world economy is far more problematic. Our ability to estimate world economic development is even more primitive than forecasting American growth. Conditions across the world are far more heterogeneous and dependent on social, political, and cultural phenomena that are beyond our current understanding. Further, American climate responses suggest a hill-shaped relationship between economic welfare and temperature. These results imply that countries currently in warmer climates will be more vulnerable to warming. Unfortunately, these same vulnerable countries (low-latitude nations) are also the least developed, which likely compounds their sensitivity. Further, there is no clear economic theory why so many low-latitude countries are less developed. Our inability to explain the current growth rates of these countries clearly is not a good indication for our ability to make long-run projections. In summary, we are especially concerned about predicting what will happen in low-latitude countries. Current economic conditions are more uncertain, forecasts of growth are more uncertain, and measurements of climate sensitivity are more uncertain for tropical and subtropical countries.

Measuring the impacts of climate change to the quality of life could well be the most challenging of all the links between emissions and damages. Changes in ecosystems, life expectancy, and weather are all likely to be important to people. However, even today, we do not know how important these aspects of quality of life are to Americans. Compound this problem by extending the analysis to the entire world, across myriad cultures and beliefs and forward an entire century and you quickly realize that the uncertainty of damage estimates in this domain cannot be understated. This is one area where we could argue that the uncertainty so dwarfs our understanding that it calls into question whether we understand anything useful about these impacts at all.

3   MARKET IMPACTS IN THE UNITED STATES

Even though the United States is sometimes accused of doing very little about climate change, it cannot be accused of doing very little research about climate change. Vast resources have been spent over the last two decades trying to understand what will happen to the United States and the world as greenhouse gases increase. Initial research by climate scientists and geographers focused more on the actual change in climate. This research indicated that climates were in fact going to warm (although this was not initially understood) because of greenhouse gases. The presumption by these initial researchers was that proving that climate would change was enough evidence to begin controlling greenhouse gases. Perhaps if greenhouse gases could have been controlled relatively inexpensively, the scientists would have been correct. Unfortunately, because greenhouse gases require substantial resources to control, society wanted more evidence than just the change in climate in order to make the commitment to this new effort. Society wanted to learn what would happen if climate changed and whether these effects would justify large abatement programs.

The impact literature relies on two critical sources of data in order to estimate climate impacts. First, researchers examine the results of scientific experiments done in controlled settings (Adams et al., 1989; Sohngen and Mendelsohn, 1998; Mendelsohn and Neumann, 1999). Holding all other environmental and management factors constant, the experiments explore the net effect of changing temperature, precipitation, and carbon dioxide. The results are then fed into simulation models that try to extrapolate from the experiments to the world. Second, scientists examine cross-sectional evidence (Mendelsohn et al., 1994; Mendelsohn and Neumann, 1999). By looking at how farms and homes do in one climate versus another, they hope to learn how systems will adjust to climate change. For example, Mendelsohn (2001) found that farmers expand the percent of land in cropland in better climates and contract cropland in more marginal conditions. Cross-sectional and simulation results also suggest that farmers choose different crops in each climate zone and adjust their planting dates with temperature.

There are strengths and weaknesses to each approach. Because each experimental site is expensive, the studies are often limited to just a few sites. The experimental approach has to work hard to make the results representative. The cross-sectional approach, in contrast, is generally performed across the relevant sector and so is automatically representative. The experimental approach includes other factors only to the extent that the modeler remembers to include them. Thus the experimental approach has been criticized for not including human adaptation and possibly ecosystem adaptations (such as insects and disease) as well. The cross-sectional approach includes these factors because they are built in to what is happening at each place today.

However, the cross-sectional approach has its own weaknesses. It is difficult to control for all the things that vary across space. It is easy for unwanted factors to influence the results, raising questions of cause and effect. The experimental approach with its carefully controlled settings does not have this problem. The cross-sectional approach also cannot predict the effect of factors that have not yet appeared. For example, the cross-sectional approach cannot predict the consequences of higher CO_2 levels because every site in the cross-section has the same CO_2 level. The experimental approach can create these new conditions. Because the strengths and weaknesses of the two approaches are so very different, we strongly recommend that both approaches be applied whenever practical. The two methods check each other so that if results differ, both must be aware that there is a problem. However, if the results are the same, scientists can have confidence that they have obtained reliable results since the two methods rely on such different assumptions.

The initial research into climate impacts was in search of large damages. That is, the researchers were asked to find out whether there were sufficiently harmful effects that would justify a substantial greenhouse control program. The first systematic analysis of climate effects based on climate scenarios from climate models was conducted by the US Environmental Protection Agency (USEPA) at the request of Congress (Smith and Tirpak, 1989). This study examined agriculture, timber, energy, water, coastal resources, ecosystem change, health, migration, and pollution. We discuss in this chapter the part of the report that found impacts on the American economy (see Chapter 6 for a discussion of the quality of life impacts). The study examined the effects of doubling greenhouse gases on the US economy as it looked in 1990. The study found that impacts on all five economic sectors could well be large, depending on the climate scenario and the role of carbon fertilization. Agriculture could have large damages of up to $10 billion in a hot and dry climate scenario if there were no fertilization effects (Adams et al., 1989). Ecosystems were predicted to collapse by gap models as many key species would not regenerate in the warmer climate. Many ecosystem modelers also predicted that existing trees would die as biomes shifted from one type to another. This dieback effect would reduce key stocks of timber. Warming was expected to increase electricity demand as homes and businesses increased air-conditioning in the summer. Large damages in water resources were expected from reductions in runoff in arid regions of the country and increases in floods in wetter regions. Coastal resources were expected to be inundated by rising seas of 1 meter by 2100. Developed land would have to be protected by expensive sea walls and undeveloped land would be lost to the sea. All of these individual market impacts were large, although aggregate estimates of damages were not reported in the study.

The first aggregate estimates of damages from climate change did not come forth until the cost-benefit paradigm for greenhouse gases was first developed (Nordhaus, 1991). In this seminal paper, Nordhaus not only laid down a framework to make decisions about greenhouse gas policy, but he also compiled the results of the USEPA study into an estimate of aggregate damages. The predicted damages for the United States from this initial study are presented in Table 5.1. Again, the measurement is the predicted impacts of doubling CO_2 on the 1990 economy. Nordhaus did not estimate damages in all sensitive market sectors but he provided estimates for agriculture,

Table 5.1   Initial market damage estimates (billions 1998 US$/year)

Sector	Nordhaus	Cline	Fankhauser	Tol
Agriculture	−11 to +10	−20.7	−9.9	−11.8
Timber	−	−3.9	−0.8	−
Water	−	−8.3	−18.4	−
Energy	−0.6	−11.7	−9.3	−
Coastal	−14.4	−8.3	−10.6	−10.0
Total market	−26 to −5.0	−52.8	−49.1	−21.8
GDP (%)	−0.5 to −0.1	−0.9	−0.8	−0.4

Note: Table does not present the authors' estimates of quality of life impacts.

Sources: Nordhaus (1991); Cline (1992); Fankhauser (1995); Tol (1995).

energy, and coastal structures. He estimated the net impact from doubling greenhouse gases on market sectors to be between $5 and $26 billion of damages a year or between 0.1 and 0.5 percent of 1990 GDP. Including impacts to non-market sectors, the aggregate impact was estimated to be around 1 percent of GDP.

Following Nordhaus, a series of authors re-examined the data from Smith and Tirpak (1989) and included further analyses done elsewhere (Cline, 1992; Fankhauser, 1995; Tol, 1995). Although they rely largely on the same set of evidence, these authors generated wildly different estimates of the impacts on the US economy. The additional estimates are presented in Table 5.1 as well. Note that the authors rarely agreed about the size of the impact in each sector although they did agree that all impacts were harmful. After adding all the market impacts together, we can see that the authors did not agree about the magnitude of aggregate market impacts either, with estimates ranging from damages of $5 to $53 billion per year. One explanation for this range is that some of the authors discounted the role of carbon fertilization on crops and forests. The authors also varied the price inelasticity of the demand for agriculture and the importance of heating benefits.

Mendelsohn and Neumann (1999) conducted the second systematic analysis of market impacts on the United States with the help of many of the same experts involved in the first USEPA study. This second study made several improvements over the earlier literature, although it by no means eliminated the enormous uncertainty surrounding the estimates. One improvement that Mendelsohn and Neumann made was to estimate impacts on a future economy that will likely be in place by the time that greenhouse gases double. Forecasting the economy into the future increases the uncertainty of the estimate

because it compounds the climate sensitivity analysis with an uncertain economic forecast. It is a less precise measure but it measures a more relevant
phenomenon. That is, estimating what will likely happen when climate finally changes is much more important than guessing how a future climate
change might affect our current economy. The Mendelsohn and Neumann set
of studies consequently estimate damages in each sector in 2060 not in 1990.

Another important change in Mendelsohn and Neumann is that every
author went to great lengths to include adaptation. There is a lot of controversy about the extent to which victims and governments can adapt to climate
change. The analysis did not assert that adaptation will eliminate all damages, but merely that adaptation is likely to occur and should be taken into
account. The inclusion of private adaptation in agriculture, energy, and timber proved to have significant effects. In some ways, however, the study may
have been too optimistic about adaptation. The study assumed that sectors
would adapt even when the adaptation decision had to be made by many
people jointly. Although it is reasonable to expect that governments will
provide these public adaptations, it is not at all clear whether governments
will be efficient (Mendelsohn, 2000). In some circumstances, it is easy to
imagine that governments will be too eager to act and will protect too much
too early. For example, governments may well build sea walls too soon, to
protect powerful interests with expensive coastal property. On the other hand,
governments may be slow to react, for example, by failing to reallocate
scarce water to the highest valued use. We are confident that private adaptation will be efficient. Private adaptation involves cases where people and
firms change to make only themselves better off. However, it is not at all
clear that public adaptation will be efficient.

A third innovation in the Mendelsohn and Neumann study was to include
dynamic studies for sectors with sizeable capital stocks. Many impact analysts are concerned with the speed not just the magnitude of climate change.
The speed of climate change is particularly important for capital-intensive
sectors because these sectors are slow and expensive to change. The
Mendelsohn and Neumann study consequently includes a dynamic analysis
of the timber industry and coastal structures. In both these sectors, the path of
change is just as important as the final equilibrium outcomes. The timber
study consequently projects a path of ecosystem changes over time and
examines decisions by foresters both after the fact and in anticipation of these
changes. The model harvests forests that are expected to decline and die back
and it plants new forests that are expected to be able to thrive in the future
climate. Harvesting and planting, however, occurs on only a small fraction of
the land each year so that this process takes many decades to transform the
landscape. A similar forward-looking approach was taken with respect to
coastal protection. Structures that were about to be inundated were allowed to

depreciate. This reduces final damages slightly. However, the most important innovation of the study was to build sea walls only as needed. That is, the decision to build and raise sea walls and to count inundation damages was re-examined each decade. The model consequently built protection only as needed. This dynamic approach reduces the present value of the costs of building coastal protection and the damages of inundation by an order of magnitude.

The Mendelsohn and Neumann study includes the beneficial impact of carbon fertilization. The USEPA study both included and excluded fertilization, allegedly to demonstrate how important fertilization was. However, many subsequent analysts misinterpreted this choice as suggesting that carbon fertilization might not occur (see Nordhaus, 1991 and Cline, 1992). Scientific experiments, however, leave little doubt about carbon fertilization and especially its effects on crops. Studies made on many crops in many locations almost universally revealed that increased carbon dioxide levels increase crop productivity (Reilly et al., 1996). Studies made on trees suggest a similar effect for forests, although these results are less reliable because they were conducted largely on young trees in plantation type settings. Including carbon fertilization is empirically important. In the USEPA study, the agricultural analysis found that aggregate impacts go from $11 billion in damages to $10 billion in benefits by including carbon fertilization (Adams et al., 1989). Reilly et al. (1996) estimate that carbon fertilization increases crop productivity by an average of 30 percent, which is comparable with the magnitude of damages in the most severe climate scenarios. The inclusion of carbon fertilization thus turns initial concerns of large damages in agriculture and timber into likely benefits or small net impacts.

One final improvement in Mendelsohn and Neumann is that the studies went to great length to be representative of entire sectors. Whereas the earlier studies had a tendency to focus on the part of each sector that was most vulnerable to climate change, the Mendelsohn and Neumann study examined everything in the sector. This led to the discovery of a number of benefits from climate change that had been overlooked before. For example, the agriculture sector had previously overlooked fruits and vegetables yet these crops tend to prosper in warmer conditions. The energy sector had previously focused just on electricity and had overlooked oil and natural gas, which are used more frequently just for heating. The timber models had focused on species migrating away but not on species arriving. Many of the benefits from climate change were simply not counted in the early studies.

The net effect of all these changes in Mendelsohn and Neumann shifts the expected value of market impacts in the United States (see Table 5.2). Whereas the earlier studies all predicted damages from doubling greenhouse gases, this new study predicted benefits as long as climate outcomes did not exceed

Global climate change

Table 5.2   New estimates of national US market impacts in 2060 (billions 1998 US$/year)

Sector	0% P	7% P	15% P
Climate: Scenario: 1.5°C			
Agriculture	30.0	30.9	31.4
Forestry	0.9	3.8	6.7
Energy	−1.7	−3.1	−4.5
Water	−2.6	−0.4	2.7
Coastal	−0.1	−0.1	−0.1
Total	26.5	31.0	36.1
Climate: Scenario: 2.5°C			
Agriculture	25.3	25.8	26.1
Forestry	1.5	4.2	6.9
Energy	−5.3	−6.9	−8.3
Water	−4.8	−3.1	0.6
Coastal	−0.2	−0.2	−0.2
Total	16.5	19.8	25.1
Climate: Scenario: 5.0°C			
Agriculture	14.1	16.1	17.0
Forestry	1.5	9.1	7.8
Energy	−21.3	−25.7	−26.9
Water	−11.3	−9.0	−5.4
Coastal	−19.9	−9.9	−7.8
Total	−19.9	−9.9	−7.8

Note: Sea level is assumed to rise 33, 66, 100 cm by 2100 in 1.5°C, 2.5°C, and 5.0°C scenarios. Climate change is assumed to be uniform across country and season. P is precipitation. 7% P implies 7% increase in precipitation.

Source: Mendelsohn (2001).

2.5°C. When warming reached 5°C, the Mendelsohn and Neumann study also predicts damages. The biggest change in estimates was for agriculture, where impacts become beneficial and large. It is the large benefits in the agricultural sector that make the 1.5°C and 2.5°C scenarios deliver net benefits. Benefits are now also predicted for the timber sector, partially because of dynamic adaptation but primarily because the new ecological predictions are more optimistic. Damages continue to be estimated in the energy and water sectors as earlier predicted. In fact, the damages to the energy sector are estimated to be larger because cooling is expected to be more universally adopted in future firms and homes. The earlier studies missed this effect because they focused on existing structures. Although damages are also predicted for the coastal sector, the present values of these damages are much smaller than previously considered. The net effect of this second wave of studies is to shrink our estimates of the market damages from climate change and to even imagine them being beneficial to the United States. These new results are gradually making their way into the literature and into recent assessments. Although these studies have made some significant improvements, it should be reiterated that they have not eliminated uncertainty. Impact estimates remain highly uncertain.

In the last few years, a third set of impact studies have been conducted in the United States. The US Global Change Research Program conducted a National Assessment Report that examines the effect of climate change on each region of the country (National Assessment Synethesis Team, 2001). The authors of the original Mendelsohn and Neumann study have also conducted a regional assessment using the methods in their national study (Mendelsohn 2001). The two sets of studies use many of the same authors to examine regional effects. However, the studies use very different climate scenarios. The National Assessment Report relies on the climate predictions of two General Circulation Models: the Canadian Climate Center and the Hadley models. These two models have many attractive characteristics that led to their being chosen from the myriad of possible climate models. Unfortunately, the two models generate similar and unusual scenarios that differ from the rest of the predicted scenarios by other climate models. This does not necessarily make the scenarios wrong but it does suggest that the National Assessment Report is not representative of the full range of outcomes predicted by climate models. The Mendelsohn study is also limited by the climate scenarios chosen because it relies primarily on uniform change scenarios. Although the Mendelsohn study makes an attempt to examine regional climate variation, most of the results are based on scenarios that assume uniform changes in climate across regions and across seasons. The advantage of the uniform scenarios is that one can examine a full suite of climate outcomes including low and high temperature increases and low and high precipitation changes. However, the uniform scenarios do not capture the variation in climate change across space and time that the climate models do. Thus, both studies could be criticized for their choice of climate scenarios.

Both the National Assessment Report and Mendelsohn (2001) find that regional impacts vary. That is, the impacts from climate change are not uniform across the country. The National Assessment Report finds this result partially because they utilize climate scenarios which themselves vary from region to region. However, the Report also generally finds that northern regions are much less vulnerable to warming than southern regions. The Report also finds that the regional distribution of impacts will vary across sectors. Regions that have important agricultural sectors will consequently be heavily affected by that sector. Regions with large vulnerable coasts and forests, such as the southeast, will be relatively more vulnerable to impacts in those sectors.

The Mendelsohn (2001) study is able to discern how regional impacts will change depending upon the severity of the forecasted climate change. Because the study relies solely on uniform climate scenarios, the differences across regions are due just to differences in climate sensitivity and initial climates. Despite the fact that all the scenarios assume uniform change across regions, as can be seen in Table 5.3, the impact in each region depends upon the climate-change scenario. With a relatively mild scenario such as 1.5°C, with a 15 percent increase in precipitation (P), the effects are more uniform across the entire country. In this scenario, there is very little change in temperature so that the harmful effects of climate change are small. This allows the beneficial impact of carbon fertilization to be the dominant factor in the scenario and carbon fertilization helps every region. Every region benefits in this scenario and every sector benefits, except the energy and coastal sectors. With a 2.5°C increase, the effect of temperature begins to be felt. The warming offsets the carbon fertilization benefits in the southern regions. Benefits shrink and damages increase, leaving these regions with almost a zero net effect. The warmer temperatures are not particularly harmful in the cooler north. Benefits from warming continue to occur in the north although they are slightly smaller than in the 1.5°C scenario. The Pacific Northwest acts more like a southern than a northern region because of its mild current climate. With a 5°C increase, temperatures begin to dominate the impacts. Damages in the southern regions become severe and all the southern regions are hurt. This can be seen most clearly in the energy sector where the costs of cooling far outstrip the reduced heating bills. In the north, the temperature increase is now large enough to be harmful. Compared to the 2.5°C case, benefits fall and damages start to appear. This scenario places the northern regions back to where they were without climate change. The study consequently suggests that the damages from warming are not likely to be uniformly felt across regions unless the climate scenarios turn out to be mild. With warming of 2.5°C or more, the southern regions will be the first to be damaged and these damages will accelerate as warming continues.

The Mendelsohn (2001) study made another useful insight. For market sectors such as agriculture and timber, the impact falls as much on demanders as suppliers. Prices for both agricultural goods and timber products are expected to change as a result of climate change. The distribution of who wins and loses in consumption does not depend upon where the goods are pro-

Table 5.3   *US regional estimates of market impacts in 2060 (billions 1998 US$/year)*

Region	Agriculture	Forest	Energy	Water	Coast	Total
Climate: Scenario: 1.5°C, 15%P						
Northeast	3.1	1.5	–0.7	0.0	–0.0	3.9
Midwest	7.5	1.3	–0.5	0.1	–0.0	8.4
N. Plains	5.3	1.1	–0.2	0.2	–0.0	6.5
Northwest	2.2	0.1	1.5	1.0	–0.0	4.8
Southeast	6.7	1.1	–2.0	0.2	–0.1	5.8
S. Plains	3.3	0.4	–1.7	0.2	–0.0	2.2
Southwest	2.7	1.1	–0.9	1.1	–0.0	4.0
Climate: Scenario: 2.5°C, 7%P						
Northeast	3.2	2.2	–0.4	0.0	–0.1	4.9
Midwest	6.5	1.3	–0.2	–0.1	0.0	7.5
N. Plains	3.9	0.8	–0.1	–0.3	0.0	4.4
Northwest	2.0	–0.3	1.6	–1.8	–0.0	1.5
Southeast	5.7	–1.0	–3.5	–0.5	–0.1	0.6
S. Plains	2.0	0.3	–2.9	–0.2	–0.0	–0.8
Southwest	2.1	1.0	–1.4	–0.2	–0.0	1.4
Climate: Scenario: 5.0°C, 0%P						
Northeast	1.8	2.6	–2.6	–0.1	–0.2	1.6
Midwest	3.6	1.0	–1.6	–0.5	0.0	2.4
N. Plains	2.7	0.5	–1.2	–1.2	0.0	0.8
Northwest	1.7	–0.6	1.6	–5.7	–0.0	–3.1
Southeast	3.6	–2.8	–9.5	–0.5	–0.2	–9.4
S. Plains	0.5	0.1	–6.7	–0.9	–0.0	–7.0
Southwest	0.5	0.6	–1.5	–2.5	–0.0	–2.7

Note: Sea level is assumed to rise 33, 66, 100 cm by 2100 in 1.5°C, 2.5°C, and 5.0°C scenarios. Climate change is assumed to be uniform across country and season.

Source: Mendelsohn (2001).

duced. With mild scenarios, the supply of food is expected to increase, causing prices to decline. Across all the scenarios, timber supplies are expected to increase, especially in the long run. As prices fall, consumers of food and wood benefit everywhere. The consumer impacts of warming are shared across regions depending on population, not farmland or forestland.

Places that are very hot or that have little farming will still receive these consumer benefits because overall market conditions are better, even if that is not evident locally.

4 GLOBAL MARKET IMPACTS

Estimating global impacts is far more difficult than estimating impacts for the United States, the most heavily studied country in the world. First, one needs to know how climate will change across the globe. Each climate model makes a different prediction of the geographic pattern of change, especially with respect to precipitation. However, there are some consistent patterns across models. In general, precipitation is expected to increase worldwide. Temperatures are also expected to increase everywhere although they are expected to increase more in the higher latitudes.

Given the climate change, the next task is to determine the size of the sensitive sectors that will be exposed in each country. We have reasonable information about the size of economic sectors in every country today. However, the exact location of these sectors can be important in large heterogeneous countries. For example, there are several low-latitude countries that have low-altitude regions that are very hot and high-altitude regions that are temperate. The agriculture in these countries is concentrated in the temperate regions. Unfortunately, subnational economic data is difficult to obtain for the entire world and our current impact models miss this important geographic detail. Long-term forecasts of economic growth are also difficult to make. One can be optimistic and expect that the poorest countries of the world will grow most rapidly, equilibrating long-run global per capita incomes. In contrast, it is possible that low-income countries suffer from long-lasting constraints (natural, social, political, or cultural) that prevent them from developing rapidly. In this scenario, income differences across countries could grow wider over time. These alternative assumptions about economic development have important implications for impacts because the poorest countries of the world are clustered in the low latitudes whereas the richest countries are located primarily in the mid to high latitudes. Low-latitude countries are more likely to be damaged by warming and high-latitude countries are more likely to benefit from warming. Thus changes in the relative growth rates of the two regions of the world could determine the extent to which net global effects are beneficial or harmful.

Perhaps the hardest third task in impact assessment is to determine the climate sensitivity of each country. Impact analysts first thought that every country would be damaged by warming. For example, Fankhauser (1995) assumes that every region is hurt by warming although he assumes that the

Organization for Economic Cooperation and Development (OECD) (developed) countries would suffer damages of only 1.3 percent whereas the poorer developing countries would have damages closer to 1.6 percent. Tol (1995) allows the former Soviet empire to benefit from warming but assumes that all other regions will be hurt. Tol assumes that the OECD countries would suffer damages of 1.6 percent and the poorer developing countries would have damages closer to 2.8 percent of GDP. Pearce et al (1996) predict damages between 1 and 2 percent for all developed countries and between 2 and 9 percent for developing countries. Nordhaus and Boyer (2000) assume that aggregate climate damages would vary between 0.5 and 3 percent of GDP for a 2.5°C warming, Russia would gain 0.7 percent, and the poorer low-latitude countries would suffer damages between 2 and 4 percent. All of the above estimates include both market and non-market impacts.

Although the above estimates seem to imply that impact studies have been done worldwide, economic analyses of sectoral climate sensitivity are rare outside the United States. Many of the impact estimates for other countries come from the climate-sensitivity functions estimated for the United States and have simply been fit to conditions in each country (Fankhauser, 1995; Tol, 1995; Mendelsohn et al., 2000). Empirical climate-sensitivity studies are quite limited for the rest of the world. There has been one study of world agriculture (Rosenzweig and Parry, 1994). There have also been a host of agricultural studies in each country (El-Shauer et al., 1997; Iglesias and Minguez, 1997; Reilly et al., 1996). Most of these studies are agronomic analyses that might have examined some adaptations but did not examine whether the adaptations were efficient or not. An exception to this is the cross-sectional and experimental study of agriculture impacts in India (Dinar et al., 1998). This study used both traditional crop models and a Ricardian (cross-sectional) analysis to determine how sensitive India would be to climate change. The crop-model analysis confirmed earlier results by Rosenzweig and Parry (1994) that the yields of at least some crops could fall by 30–40 percent with warming. The cross-sectional analysis suggested that warming would be strictly harmful to India but that the economic effects would be much smaller, with damages of between 9 and 21 percent depending on the climate scenario.

Sohngen et al. (2001) completed a global timber study. This study relies on a global model of ecological change (Haxeltine and Prentice, 1996) and a complex global dynamic general equilibrium model of forestry (Sohngen et al., 1999). However, the dynamic ecological model is a crude construction and the estimates of forest responses across the world are highly uncertain. In short, we have only crude guesses of world impacts at the moment.

The studies in the United States strongly suggest that the level of climate is very important. The impacts depend upon the absolute temperature and precipitation of a region and this relationship appears to be hill-shaped. Warming will consequently have different impacts depending upon the current climate of a country. For example, significant warming is harmful to the southern but not the northern regions of the United States because the south is already warm (Mendelsohn, 2001). The Pacific Northwest gets included as a southern region in this analysis despite its northern location because of its warm climate. The southern regions start to be harmed as soon as warming reaches 2.5°C. The northern regions of the United States, in contrast, benefit from this initial warming. These benefits shrink to zero as warming reaches 5°C, but by 5°C, the southern regions are suffering large damages.

All the American studies also suggest that temperature has a quadratic effect on economic impacts in every market sector (except coastal structures which have a quadratic relationship with sea-level rise). That is, at low temperatures, warming is beneficial. However, each sector has a point where further warming becomes harmful. The point where impacts turn from benefits to damages varies across sectors. The maximum benefit temperatures for the water and energy sectors tend to be relatively low, close to the northern temperatures found in the United States. Agriculture seems to maximize near the current US mean temperature. Outdoor recreation seems to maximize near the temperatures currently found in the southern US and forestry has the highest maximum temperatures, apparently close to subtropical climates.

These results imply that countries further north than the United States will tend to benefit from warming as they will enjoy benefits in virtually every sector from warming. Countries with similar climates to the United States will probably enjoy similar effects as the US. Countries in lower latitudes, however, are expected to be damaged by warming. These countries are already too warm and any further warming will push them further down the hill in each sector.

Another interesting insight from the US regional study is that impacts in agriculture and forestry will affect consumers (Mendelsohn, 2001). That means that the impact in each country will depend upon how much food and forest products they consume, regardless of whether they have farms or forests. As prices fall or rise, these effects will be felt worldwide. These consumer effects are universal and will not depend on location or national production.

Comparing results found in the United States, Brazil, and India suggest that development also has a role to play. Cross-sectional studies have been completed on agriculture in these three countries and the results suggest that the more developed a country, the less climate sensitive it will be (Mendelsohn et al., 2001). For example, as India moved through the green revolution, production increased but it also become less temperature sensitive. Comparing the temperature sensitivity of India and the United States suggests that the Indian response function is far steeper to temperature. Relying on these three studies, new impact estimates were computed for every country in the world.

Two sets of results for the world are presented in Tables 5.4 and 5.5 for 2060. We assume that CO_2 levels in the atmosphere have doubled to 550 ppmv in this scenario. Because the global economy is predicted to grow over the century, world GDP is expected to be equal to $75 trillion by 2060. In Table 5.4, we rely on estimates that have been generated by experimental-simulation models. In Table 5.5, we use climate-sensitivity results from cross-sectional studies. Both sets of studies rely on the University of Illinois Urbana Campaign (UIUC) climate model to predict how temperature changes in each country and how precipitation changes. The UIUC model tends to

Table 5.4   Global market impacts by region for 2060 (experimental-simulation) (billions 1998 US$/year)

Region	Agriculture	Forest	Energy	Water	Coast	Total
Climate: Scenario: 2.5°C						
Africa	−30.8	0.2	−2.4	−8.9	−0.0	−41.8
Asia	5.1	4.6	−9.9	34.4	−0.3	34.1
Lat. America	−3.8	0.7	−6.2	−1.4	−0.0	−10.8
Oceania	−17.1	0.1	−0.8	−0.5	−0.0	−18.4
USSR+EE	134.6	1.5	4.0	−27.6	−0.0	112.6
W. Europe	12.1	1.8	−3.5	−5.4	−0.2	4.8
N. America	54.6	2.6	−2.9	−8.8	−0.1	45.4
World	154.9	11.5	−21.8	−18.1	−0.6	125.8
Climate: Scenario: 5.0°C						
Africa	−60.8	0.2	−5.3	−15.9	−0.0	−81.8
Asia	−69.2	8.1	−23.6	75.7	−1.1	−10.0
Lat. America	−20.6	1.0	−13.6	0.8	−0.1	−34.0
Oceania	−17.4	0.8	−1.8	−0.8	−0.0	−19.9
USSR+EE	172.8	2.4	5.8	−51.3	−0.0	129.6
W. Europe	−14.3	2.8	−11.9	−9.9	−0.7	−33.9
N. America	33.6	4.0	−9.4	−15.6	−0.5	12.1
World	24.2	18.7	−59.7	−18.5	−2.6	−37.9

Note: Sea level assumed to rise 0.5 m with 2.5°C and 1.0 m with 5.0°C scenarios. CO_2 is assumed to be 550 ppmv and world GDP is $75 trillion. EE is Eastern Europe.

Source: Forecasts with GIM2.2 and UIUC climate model.

⚡ *Table 5.5*   *Global market impacts by region for 2060 (cross-sectional)*
                (billions 1998 US$/year)

Region	Agriculture	Forest	Energy	Water	Coast	Total
Climate: Scenario: 2.5°C						
Africa	3.9	−0.4	−2.4	−8.9	−0.0	−7.8
Asia	8.3	1.8	−1.7	34.4	−0.3	42.6
Lat. America	8.2	−0.2	−1.2	−1.4	−0.0	5.4
Oceania	4.7	0.0	−0.5	−0.5	−0.0	3.6
USSR+EE	11.9	4.2	5.2	−27.6	−0.0	−6.3
W. Europe	11.5	2.2	10.6	−5.4	−0.2	18.7
N. America	30.0	2.1	−1.0	−8.8	−0.1	22.2
World	78.4	9.8	9.0	−18.1	−0.6	78.4
Climate: Scenario: 5.0°C						
Africa	−2.4	−1.1	−6.7	−15.9	−0.0	−26.1
Asia	−40.5	2.0	−11.1	75.7	−1.1	25.0
Lat. America	1.8	−0.8	−4.1	−0.8	−0.1	−4.0
Oceania	3.7	0.1	−1.2	−0.8	−0.0	1.6
USSR+EE	−3.2	7.1	5.5	−51.3	−0.0	−41.9
W. Europe	12.8	3.1	12.6	−9.9	−0.7	17.9
N. America	34.7	2.6	−9.7	−15.6	−0.5	11.4
World	6.9	12.9	−14.8	−18.5	−2.6	−16.0

Note: Sea level assumed to rise 0.5 m with 2.5°C and 1.0 m with 5.0°C scenarios. CO_2 is assumed to be 550 ppmv and world GDP is $75 trillion. EE is Eastern Europe.

Source: Forecasts with GIM2.2 and UIUC climate model.

predict more uniform temperature changes across the globe than other climate models. The predicted changes in temperature are therefore relatively larger for low latitudes and smaller for high latitudes than results from other models. The UIUC model also predicts relatively large increases in precipitation over Asia and reductions in precipitation over the former Soviet Union.

The results in Tables 5.4 and 5.5 imply that a mid-range temperature increase of 2.5°C would create small net benefits for the world of between 0.1 to 0.2 percent of world GDP. In Table 5.4, the net benefits are about $126 billion/year for the world, a 0.17 percent increase in GDP. The low-latitude countries of Africa, Asia, Latin America and Oceania suffer damages of $37 billion whereas the mid- and high-latitude countries of Europe, North America, and the former Soviet Union enjoy benefits of $163. With the cross-sectional results, the global net effect from this climate scenario is $78 billion/year of benefits or 0.1 percent of GDP. However the cross-sectional model predicts less regional difference. The low-latitude countries enjoy benefits of $44 billion and the mid- to high-latitude countries gain $35 billion of benefits per year. With a more severe 5°C warming, net effects become harmful in both scenarios. According to the experimental results, net global effects are $38 billion/year in damages (0.05 percent of GDP). A $108 billion benefit in mid- and high-latitude countries mitigates a $146 billion loss in low-latitude countries. According to the cross-sectional model, harmful effects are more widespread but milder. Global impacts amount to $16 billion in damages (0.02 percent of GDP) with low-latitude countries suffering net damages of $4 billion and mid- to high-latitude countries losing $12 billion annually. These simulations suggest that net global impacts on economies are likely to be small, especially compared to the expected size of the world economy by 2060 of $75 trillion.

Note that agriculture plays a large role in the estimates in Tables 5.4 and 5.5. Net market impacts are heavily influenced by the size of agricultural impacts. Agriculture is the single most important sector. Energy and water also play a big role in more severe scenarios. Timber and coastal impacts, in contrast, are much smaller. Although previous studies support the direction of many of these sectoral findings, the shrinking role of coastal impacts is in contrast with the early literature that thought coastal impacts would be the single largest impact. This study predicts sea-level rise will have a much smaller impact because the model spreads sea-level protection costs across a century as needed. This dramatically reduces the present value of the costs. The estimates are also lower because scientists have reduced their projected estimate of the size of sea-level change.

One could also contrast the results across countries by income. For example, if a per capita income of $10,000 was used as a boundary, then almost three-quarters of the world population would be low income in 2060. These low-income countries would share 21 percent of world GDP. In the 2.5°C scenarios, the low-income countries would share net benefits of between $18 and $45 billion from warming. In these same scenarios, the wealthy countries would enjoy net benefits of $60 and $80 billion, respectively. In the 5.0°C scenarios, the low-income countries would now suffer damages equal to between $42 and $48 billion annually. In contrast, the wealthy countries would enjoy small net benefits of between $26 and $10 billion, respectively. The impacts of global warming will not be felt equally across countries by income.

5   CONCLUSION

The IPCC has recommended that action be taken to prevent climate from changing enough to present a danger to humankind and the world. This policy initiative implies that there may be some clear threshold that society does not want to cross. Such a threshold for climate change has eluded researchers to date, despite an avid search. It is clear that the more severe the temperature change, the higher the damage, above at least 2.5°C. However, the evidence suggests a steadily increasing risk, not a threshold phenomenon. The impact research alone cannot generate an acceptable atmospheric concentration or an acceptable temperature change. The damages from the impacts must be weighed against the costs of abatement. When the temperature change is low, the results imply that only inexpensive abatement efforts are justified. As the temperature change rises, the research implies that abatement expenditures should increase to reflect the increasing harm.

These results have important implications for abatement. The results provide little evidence that near-term emissions are harmful. The emissions in the next few decades are expected to have only a small impact on temperature. Small changes in temperature do not appear to cause net harm in market sectors. In order to justify reducing near-term emissions, evidence of harm must be found in non-market impacts (see Chapter 6 by Smith, Lazo, and Hurd). Long-term emissions over the century, in contrast, may cause temperature to rise enough to be harmful. Even here, however, policy must be cautious because the magnitude of market damages appears to be a lot smaller than originally thought. Again, ambitious abatement programs would have to be justified on the basis of non-market impacts, which is not yet the case.

On a more technical level, the more recent impact results have not yet been taken into account in integrated assessment models (see Manne in Chapter 8). These models continue to rely on the older impact estimates reflected in the Second Assessment Report of the IPCC (Pearce et al., 1996). The integrated assessment models need to update their estimates and reflect the much smaller size of aggregate net market impacts. They need to capture the fact that small increments of temperature could well have beneficial impacts that will slowly become damages as temperatures rise. The integrated assessment models also need to capture the likely distributional outcomes with mid-high-latitude countries enjoying benefits and low-latitude countries suffering damages.

Policymakers must also cope with these new insights into distributional impacts. The impacts from global warming are not going to be shared equally as originally thought. Cooler countries are likely to benefit, temperate countries are likely to be unaffected at first, and warm countries will be hurt. Island countries will probably also be disproportionately affected. With winners and losers from warming, rather than just losers, it will be more difficult to achieve an international consensus on climate policy. As more and more countries become aware of these impacts, they will demand that global warming policy deal with these distributional consequences.

The results call for compensation of some kind to be paid to the most severely impacted nations. Compensation could take many forms: emergency relief from weather catastrophes as they occur, payments today for future potential effects, or subsidies for abatement. Somehow, carbon emitters should help the most vulnerable nations cope with the damages from global warming. Compensation is an immediately attractive policy action. Since the net impacts of today's carbon emissions are ambiguous, there is very little justification for spending vast amounts of resources on abatement in the near term. Paying compensation, in contrast, equal to the present value of future damages is not that expensive since damages paid today are small compared to most mitigation programs. Helping poor nations develop today lowers their climate sensitivity in the long run. Helping other countries develop may lead to future markets and trade that benefit everyone. Last but not least, compensating poor nations for the consequences of actions taken by rich nations addresses an important equity problem associated with greenhouse gases (see Victor, Chapter 9).

Although impact research does suggest important policy actions, uncertainty continues to dominate impact results. The uncertainty surrounding impact estimates is a great weight that both scientists and policymakers concerned with climate change must carry. It depresses the bright enthusiasm of researchers to unfold the mysteries of climate and climate's relationship with the human race. It burdens anyone bold enough to recommend a climate policy to the world's population. Unfortunately, it is a weight that is unlikely to be lifted in the near term. Decisions about what to study and what to do about climate change will have to cope with this uncertainty for decades. Perhaps as we go through the experience of changes in the Earth's climate, we shall learn a great deal about both what will happen and what will happen to us. However, it is unlikely that the next few decades will provide the strength of signal over noise for us to learn a great deal. It may well be true that we will have to be far into the experience of climate change before much of the inherent uncertainty will be lifted.

REFERENCES

Adams, R., D. Glyer and B. McCarl (1989), 'The economic effects of climate change in US agriculture: a preliminary assessment', in D. Tirpak and J. Smith (eds), *The Potential Effects of Global Climate Change on the United States: Report to Congress*, Washington, DC: US Environmental Protection Agency, EPA-230-05-89-050.

Cline, W. (1992), *The Economics of Global Warming*, Washington, DC: Institute of International Economics.

Dinar, A., R. Mendelsohn, R. Evenson, J. Parikh, A. Sanghi, K. Kumar, J. McKinsey and S. Lonergan (eds) (1998), *Measuring the Impact of Climate Change on Indian Agriculture*, World Bank Technical Paper No. 402, Washington, DC.

El-Shaer, H.M., C. Rosenzweig, A. Iglesias, M.H. Eid and D. Hillel (1997), 'Impact of climate change on possible scenarios for Egyptian agriculture in the future', *Mitigation and Adaptation Strategies for Global Change* **1**: 233–50.

Fankhauser, S. (1995), *Valuing Climate Change: The Economics of the Greenhouse*, London: Earthscan.

Haxeltine, A., and C. Prentice (1996), 'BIOME3: an equilibrium terrestrial biosphere model based on ecophysiological constraints, resource availability, and competition among plant functional types', *Global Biogeochemical Cycles* **10** (4): 693–709.

Houghton, J., L. Meira Filho, B. Callander, N. Harris, A. Kattenberg and K. Maskell (eds) (1996), *Climate Change 1995: The State of the Science*, Intergovernmental Panel on Climate Change (IPCC), Cambridge University Press: Cambridge.

Iglesias, A. and M.I. Minguez (1997), 'Modelling crop–climate interactions in Spain: vulnerability and adaptation of different agricultural systems to climate change', *Mitigation and Adaptation Strategies for Global Change* **1**: 273–88.

Mendelsohn, R. (2000), 'Efficient adaptation to climate change', *Climatic Change* **45**: 583–600.

Mendelsohn, R. (ed.) (2001), *Global Warming and the American Economy: A Regional Assessment of Climate Change*, Cheltenham, UK and Northampton, MA, USA: Edward Elgar.

Mendelsohn, R., A. Dinar, and A. Sanghi (2001), 'The effects of development on the climate sensitivity of agriculture', *Environment and Development Economics* **6**: 85–101.

Mendelsohn, R., W. Morrison, M. Schlesinger and N. Adronova (2000), 'Country-specific market impacts from climate change', *Climatic Change* **45**: 553–69.

Mendelsohn, R. and J. Neumann (eds) (1999), *The Economic Impact of Climate Change on the Economy of the United States*, Cambridge, UK: Cambridge University Press.

Mendelsohn, R., W. Nordhaus and D. Shaw (1994), 'The impact of global warming on agriculture: a Ricardian analysis', *American Economic Review* **84**: 753–71.

National Assessment Synthesis Team (2001), *Climate Change Impacts on the United States: The Potential Consequences of Climate Variability and Change*, Cambridge: Cambridge University Press.

Nordhaus, W. (1991), 'To slow or not to slow: the economics of the greenhouse effect', *Economic Journal* **101**: 920–37.

Nordhaus, W. and J. Boyer (2000), *Warming the World*, Cambridge, MA: MIT Press.

Pearce, D., W. Cline, A. Achanta, S. Fankhauser, R. Pachauri, R. Tol and P. Vellinga (1996), 'The social cost of climate change: greenhouse damage and the benefits of control', in J. Bruce, H. Lee and E. Haites (eds), *Climate Change 1995: Economic and Social Dimensions of Climate Change*, Cambridge: Cambridge University Press.

Reilly, J. et al. (1996), 'Agriculture in a changing climate: impacts and adaptations', in IPCC (Intergovernmental Panel on Climate Change), R. Watson, M. Zinyowera, R. Moss and D. Dokken (eds). *Climate Change 1995: Impacts, Adaptations, and Mitigation of Climate Change: Scientific-Technical Analyses*, Cambridge University Press: Cambridge.

Rosenzweig, C. and M. Parry (1994), 'Potential impact of climate change on world food supply', *Nature* **367**: 133–8.

Smith, J. and D. Tirpak (1989), *The Potential Effects of Global Climate Change on the United States: Report to Congress*, Washington, DC: Environmental Protection Agency.

Sohngen, B. and R. Mendelsohn (1998), 'Valuing the market impact of large-scale ecological change: the effect of climate change on US timber', *American Economic Review* **88**: 686–710.

Sohngen, B., R. Mendelsohn and R. Sedjo (1999), 'Forest conservation, management, and global timber markets', *American Journal of Agricultural Economics* **81**: 1–13.

Sohngen, B., R. Mendelsohn and R. Sedjo (2001), *The Impact of Climate Change on Global Timber Markets*, New Haven, CT: Yale School of Forestry and Environmental Studies.

Tol, R. (1995), 'The damage costs of climate change: toward more-comprehensive calculations', *Environmental and Resource Economics* **5**: 353–74.

6. The difficulties of estimating global non-market damages from climate change

Joel B. Smith, Jeffrey K. Lazo and Brian Hurd*

1 INTRODUCTION

The potential non-market damages[1] from climate change are a strong motivation for control of greenhouse gas emissions. The term 'non-market' damages applies to impacts to sectors that do not have goods and services traded in the marketplace. The potential for disruption of ecosystems, loss of endangered species, harm to human health, and other non-market effects have been cited by many as sufficient reason to limit the extent of climate change. As noted in Edmonds and Sands (Chapter 7), the costs of limiting greenhouse gas emissions to substantially reduce global warming are not trivial. The tradeoffs between investing in reductions of greenhouse gas emissions versus absorbing market and non-market damages will be substantial.

An additional consideration is that should climate change be less than about 2 to 3°C, the net global market impacts may be less than a few percent of world product (Smith et al., Chapter 6; Mendelsohn, Chapter 5).[2] Given the limited total market damages, it is critical to determine the extent and value of non-market damages. A fundamental question is whether non-market damages so extensive as to justify controlling greenhouse gas emissions is enough to limit warming to a few degrees or less?

This raises some interesting questions about the extent and value of non-market damages from climate change:

- How well have we understood and quantified non-market climate-change impacts?
- Can the value of non-market impacts be credibly determined?
- Are non-market impacts similar across the globe or do they differ by latitude (for example, do higher latitudes have non-market benefits while lower latitudes have non-market damages)?

- Is it appropriate to monetize global non-market impacts of climate change?

These questions will be addressed in this chapter. We briefly review the literature on non-market impacts, particularly, impacts on ecosystems and human health. We then review methods for valuing non-market impacts. Most of this chapter is devoted to reviewing studies in the literature estimating the monetary value of non-market impacts from climate change. We address different approaches for estimating the value of non-market impacts including expert judgment, willingness-to-pay surveys, and site-specific analyses. We also review studies that estimate the monetary damages from impacts to human health, recreation, tourism, amenity values, and catastrophic impacts.[3]

2   A BRIEF REVIEW OF NON-MARKET IMPACTS

Space does not permit an adequate summary of the extensive literature on how climate change could affect non-market sectors. Readers are encouraged to consult IPCC (2001) for the Intergovernmental Panel on Climate Change's summary of impacts. Here, we briefly review what may happen to ecosystems and human health.

Ecological Impacts Could be Very Significant

Climate change is very likely to have substantial impacts on global ecosystems. We expect a general movement of ecosystems and species towards the poles (that is, to the north in the Northern Hemisphere) and to higher elevations because of higher global temperatures. This could result in the reduction or loss of some ecosystems and the expansion of others. The rate of climate change, for example, how quickly temperatures warm, is a very important factor affecting ecosystems. A more gradual transition may allow many more species to survive and the transitions may be less catastrophic. A more rapid change is likely to be more destructive.

The combination of climate change and human development is likely to result in significant loss of biodiversity and these losses are likely to be experienced across the world (for example, NAST 2000). Many ecosystems and species are already under stress from development and pollution. These stresses, unless relieved, will be exacerbated by climate change. The combination of other stresses and climate change will result in reduction of populations or loss of many individual species as well as substantial reduction or loss of some ecosystems (for example, mountain tundra, Cape Floral

Kingdom in South Africa; IPCC, 2001). It is not clear what the marginal effect of climate change is, but it is expected to be a contributing factor to adverse ecological impacts.

Human Health Impacts Are Generally Complex and Uncertain

The effects of climate change on humans appears to be more uncertain because of uncertainties about future societies' capacity to cope with climate change. In addition, there is the complexity of having not only adverse effects in some regions, but positive effects in others.

The risk of vector-borne diseases, such as malaria, will probably increase because of warmer (and wetter) conditions (for example, McMichael and Githeko, 2001). That is, more areas will become suitable for the spread of vector-borne diseases. Whether or not the number of cases increases and by how much is difficult to predict and depends on many factors (for example, Balbus and Wilson, 2000). A strong public health system should be sufficient to minimize the risk and contain any outbreaks. Indeed, increased levels of development could reduce the risk of climate change increasing the spread of vector-borne disease, although it would probably not eliminate it (Tol and Dowlatabadi, in press.) Thus, the risk of increased vector-borne disease is greatest for developing countries.

Mortality from heat stress could increase, particularly among the elderly and in inner cities. Estimates are for several hundred additional deaths per year in the United States (for example, Kalkstein and Greene, 1997). The number of cases of heat stress in developing countries would probably be much greater than the number of cases in developed countries. However, increased penetration of air-conditioning and other preventive measures could reduce heat-stress mortality (Chestnut et al., 1998).

Mortality related to low temperatures could drop, particularly in mid- and high-latitude countries. In some countries the reduction in winter mortality could be greater than the increase in summer mortality (for example, Martens, 1998). There is much uncertainty about changes in winter mortality, particu- larly because behavior is an important factor affecting it.

Today, most of the world's population lives in the tropics, where they are more likely to face increased risk of death from vector-borne disease and heat-stress mortality. Furthermore, the percentage of global population in the tropics will increase (United Nations, 1999). The percentage of the world's population living in high-latitude areas that may have reduced mortality will become smaller over time. If we also factor in the lower quality of health care in most low-latitude countries, it appears more likely than not that climate change will increase global mortality.

Quantifying Non-market Impacts of Climate Change

The discussion above presents many qualitative statements about impacts. In general, the literature indicates that climate change will have adverse effects on ecosystems and human health. There are few credible quantitative estimates of impacts, but there are exceptions. For example, Martens et al. (1999) estimate that under climate change, 100 to 300 million more people will be at risk of contracting malaria by 2100. Such estimates are scenario dependent and can be substantially changed by different assumptions about development and adaptation (for example, see Tol and Dowlatabadi, in press). There appear to be no credible estimates of how many endangered or threatened species would become extinct or how many ecosystems would be disrupted (although some studies have tried to identify ecosystems at substantial risk from climate change, for example, Malcolm and Markham, 2000). Thus, based on a review of the literature, it does not appear possible to reliably quantify nonmarket impacts of climate change.

3   VALUING NON-MARKET IMPACTS

The following is a brief discussion of the complex topic of valuing non-market impacts of climate change.

The prices of commodities can be used as an indication of the relative value of those commodities to society. This is true for market goods because prices reflect the aggregation of individual preferences that are implicit in the concepts of demand and supply. Behind the concepts of demand and supply and the price they yield are the economic notions of willingness to pay (demand) and willingness to accept (supply), both of which are commonly measured in monetary terms. Both willingness to pay and willingness to accept reflect the assignment of value by individuals. As Brown (1984) insightfully describes, assigning value is the end result of a process in which the individual applies a preference relationship to his or her set of 'held values'.

A taxonomy of held values includes personal values (for example, happiness, wisdom), professional values (for example, dedication, hard work), national values (for example, loyalty, patriotism), or issues such as the environment (for example, beauty, uniqueness). Such held values are not directly observable or measurable, but are key, along with the individual's experience and social context, in determining relative preferences and assigned value. Assigned values for market goods are routinely observed because they emerge as market prices. It is much more difficult to observe assigned values for non-market goods and thus, prices. Even notions of willingness to pay and willingness to accept can be inadequate proxies for describing and relating the underlying held values of a society or culture.

What Are Non-market Values?

Environmental commodities generate services, which often are not valued (that is, bought and sold and priced) in regular economic markets. A significant concern of environmental economists has been to understand and explain these values. Figure 6.1 from Reiner and Sussman (1994) presents one of many possible taxonomies used to characterize such values. Defining non-market values can be controversial. A commonly accepted approach of defining different types of value is to refer to active-use and passive-use values. These are roughly equivalent to the use and non-use values illustrated by Reiner and Sussman.

Any attempt to define and measure different types of values must recognize that different individuals have different 'ethical structures' underlying their preferences toward environmental commodities. Does the ethical system underlying these values matter? Economists work within the paradigm of 'utility' (that is, satisfaction or well-being) and 'individual welfare'. The extent that an individual's utility is based on different ethical systems is not relevant. Whether a commodity or a service generates utility is all that matters. This becomes inherently difficult, though, when an ethical system does not 'permit' tradeoffs to occur, because tradeoffs are the basis for economists' approach to understanding and measuring values.

Valuation Methods

Several authors discuss the theory and methods of non-market valuation (Mitchell and Carson, 1989; Freeman, 1993; Garrod and Willis, 1999), and we do not attempt to provide a thorough review of this topic. Two general types of non-market valuation approaches are used by economists: revealed preference and stated preference. The primary issue is that different methods capture different values presented in Figure 6.1. Revealed preference methods rely on actual (observed or revealed) choices individuals make in order to infer the value of environmental commodities. Revealed preference methods are thus useful to measure some types of use values presented in the figure.

Revealed preference methods include travel cost, hedonic wage and hedonic property values, and averting behavior approaches. Briefly, the hedonic price approach assumes that the value of a market commodity implicitly reflects the value of all of the services that constitute that commodity, including non-market characteristics. The price of a house thus reflects, in part, the value of environmental amenities, such as the view and where that house is located.

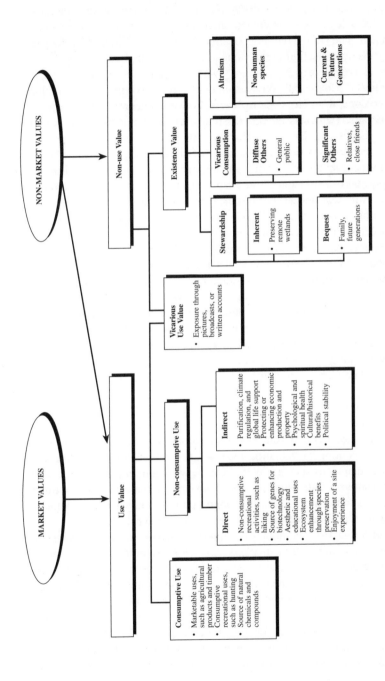

Source: Reiner, D.M. and F.G. Sussman (1994), Perceptions of Ecosystem Damages and Economic Prescriptions, ICF Incorporated, paper presented at the Western Economic Association meeting, 29 June–3 July.

Figure 6.1 A taxonomy of economic values for ecological systems

119

Similarly, the hedonic wage approach assumes that comparing two identical jobs, one with a low risk of death and one with a high risk of death, the extra wage that has to be paid to the 'high death risk' employee (divided by the risk differential) is an indication of the value of death or injury on the job.

The travel cost approach is based on the economic assumption that if prices are lower, people will consume more of a good. For travel to a site that provides ecological services, if trip costs are lower, people will take more trips to that site. Trip costs include the time and travel expenses that people expend to visit a site. By calculating the number of trips to the site as a function of these trip costs, a demand curve can be derived. Averting behavior is based on the assumption that the amount of money someone is willing to spend to prevent or avoid a negative environmental impact is an indication of the damage from that impact. For instance the amount someone spends on in-house microbial water filters is an indication of how much it is worth to them to avoid illnesses from water-borne microbes.

Alternatively, stated preference methods (for example, contingent valuation method, conjoint choice) can be used to capture both use and non-use values, and are the only approach for capturing non-use values.[4] Stated preference methods generally survey individuals, asking them to express their preference over potential changes in non-market goods described to them in the survey. The term 'stated preference' encompasses all survey-based research in which people are asked questions about their preferences with the intent of estimating values for goods or services by analyzing what people say (that is, state). This is in contrast to studies that analyze what people do (that is, reveal).

Stated preference methods are often split into (i) direct valuation questions and (ii) stated choice questions. Direct valuation questions include questions such as 'How much would you be willing to pay for ...?'. These are often referred to as contingent valuation method questions. Choice questions include yes–no questions such as 'Would you be willing to pay $X for ...?' and questions where an individual chooses between alternatives with multiple attributes. The latter are sometimes called conjoint analyses, a term taken from the market research literature where this approach originated.

The total value of a commodity comprises active-use and passive-use values. For some use values, markets exist, for example, private hunting reserves, whereas for other use values, no markets exist, for example, the value of a scenic drive. For non-use values, by their nature, markets cannot and do not exist, for individuals cannot be charged a price for something from which they cannot be excluded, for example, simply knowing that blue whales exist. Market valuation methods (for example, market prices) thus can capture only some use values and no non-use values. Therefore, stated preference methods, both direct valuation and stated choice approaches, are important in that they are the only methods available to measure non-use values. By definition, non-use values do not leave a behavioral trail and thus revealed preference methods cannot be used to derive non-use values. Of additional importance is that stated preference methods can present scenarios of change that are beyond those currently experienced by individuals. Stated preference methods thus may be useful for considering the impacts of climate change that are beyond individuals' current experiences. However, non-use values identified through stated preference methods cannot be verified through observation of behavior.

A further problem with valuing non-market impacts of climate change has to do with when the impacts will be realized. Whatever method is used to value environmental and health changes, it can only measure the values of current generations. Revealed preference methods in general measure current generations' values for current conditions. However, the non-market impacts of climate change may well be greatest for generations yet to be born or too young to state or reveal a preference. Applying revealed preference values for climate-change impacts requires assuming that utility functions do not change over time. Stated preference methods can be used to value current generations' values for future conditions by presenting the valuation scenario as future conditions. Stated preference methods can thus be used to elicit current generations' values to prevent future changes. Alternatively, stated preference methods can be used to elicit current generations' values for changes in current conditions and then assume that these can be applied to future generations' values for future changes. In any event, stated preference methods cannot determine future generations' values for future changes without making the same assumption that revealed preference requires: that preferences do not change over time.

Benefits Transfer

Most approaches that attempt to derive aggregate values involve some sort of benefits transfer – that is, the application of values measured in one setting for one group to another setting for another group. Any valuation of future impacts on future individuals also involves a benefits transfer. A key assumption underlying such a transfer is that the utility function of future individuals in one place is reasonably equivalent to the utility function of similar individuals who may be in another place. To be sure, values between generations can change substantially. For example, past generations talked about 'swamps' as having low values, while we now talk about the importance of 'wetlands'. However, lacking any information on how future values may change, benefits transfer appears to be the best approach available. Another key aspect of such a transfer is that the choices of current individuals are based on the currently available choice set. The choice sets that future individuals will face will most likely be significantly different. These differences will occur because of the choices we make now, because of the impacts of climate change between now and the future, and because of new choices made available to future generations by both technological progress and the depletion of current resources.

Estimating the Value of Natural Ecosystems

One rather controversial topic that some economists have dared to tackle is the value of all ecosystems. We briefly review this literature not to derive such a number, because we think it lacks credibility and usefulness (we do not foresee a situation in which we shall consider losing or saving all of the world's ecosystems), but to demonstrate the difficulty of arriving at such a number. Natural resource economics tends to focus on deriving the value of ecosystems on the margin. For example, there are many studies estimating the value of few acres of wetland. It is not unreasonable to try to trade off the value of a marginal acre of wetlands versus a market good, such as housing. This is far different from trying to derive the value of *all* wetlands. Indeed, climate change poses the risk of losing or substantially damaging entire ecosystems.

While we are uncertain about climate-change impacts on natural ecosystems and how to value them, we have knowledge of the services that ecosystems provide. Several authors have developed or reviewed taxonomies of ecosystem services, including Christensen and Franklin (1997), Costanza et al. (1997), and Daily (1997). Some authors develop taxonomies for specific ecosystem types; for example, Whigham (1997) identified a wide range of services provided by wetlands other than commercial or recreational fishing. In Daily (1997), several contributing authors discussed functions and services of ecosystems that should be considered when evaluating the importance of ecosystems to society.[5] While not all of these services are discussed in terms of economic value, all are offered as important functions that society depends on in some manner. A partial compilation of these services as discussed in Daily (1997) includes:

- sequestration of materials and gases (including methane, carbon, and nitrogen or nitrous oxides);
- genetic material and maintenance of a genetic library;
- amelioration of weather and climate regulation;
- pest control;
- insect pollination;
- fisheries;

- soil retention, formation and maintenance of fertility;
- flood control and regulation of hydrologic cycles;
- cycling of matter;
- cultural values;
- building materials;
- food and fiber;
- fuel (biomass);
- waste assimilation and detoxification;
- recreation – including hunting and fishing;
- surface albedo;
- medicines and pharmaceuticals; and
- industrial use of bioproducts such as oils and pigments.

Drawing on Brown's concepts of valuing resources, Alexander et al. (1998) investigated several approaches to valuing global ecosystem services. The authors view the ecosystem as a productive economic input that supports the global economy. Their research seeks to identify the 'maximum amount that could feasibly be paid for these [ecosystem] services'. The scenario they pose is that of a discriminating monopolist who owns all ecological services in the global economy, and they ask, 'How much could this monopolist charge humans for using these services?'. At the upper extreme is the value of the world's output less the amount required for subsistence; in 1987, the authors estimated this value to be \$16.2 trillion (88 per cent of world GDP, in 1987 US dollars).[6]

Alexander's approach, as with other attempts to value the globe's ecosystems, such as Costanza et al. (1997), seems rather narrow and reductionist. In the case of Alexander et al. (1998), their recognition that society's *willingness to pay* is fundamentally constrained by its *ability to pay* is compelling, but it rests on assumptions that ecosystems and their services are valuable *only* in as much as they contribute to societies' capacity to generate economic activity. Certainly without clear air and clean water our capacity to do work is diminished. However, the value of clean air and water is not simply that it better enables the labor force to produce, but that utility is enhanced directly – not only because income is greater but also because clean air and water enhance the value of all of our activities and enjoyments. Having good health, knowing that wildlife and ecosystems are not damaged, and enjoying the experience of not breathing and drinking fouled air and water provide, arguably, as much or more value than income from our labor. The estimates of Alexander et al. ignore the possibility that ecosystems are part of an endowment, and that perhaps implicit in that there is a right to the enjoyment of the resource that is independent of a capacity to pay for it.[7]

4 ESTIMATED DAMAGES FROM CLIMATE CHANGE

This section of the chapter reviews estimated non-market damages to natural ecosystems, human health, tourism and recreation, and amenity values. This is not a comprehensive assessment of the literature; instead, some interesting studies from the recent literature that are typical of the kind of research being conducted are reviewed and used to evaluate the state of the literature in estimating climate-change damages.

Estimates of Value of Natural Ecosystem Impacts

The estimates of the value of natural ecosystems impacts based on a few published studies are reviewed. Readers should bear in mind Tol's (1998, p. 7) warning about valuing such impacts: 'Climate economists therefore face a double problem, i.e., how to derive a total value of something which is unknown in quantity and price'. Examples of three approaches that have been used are given: using expert judgment to estimate damages, determining willingness to pay to avoid damages, and estimating site-specific damages using benefits transfer.

Expert judgment on global damages

Nordhaus and Boyer (2000) used the RICE-98 model to estimate global values of market and non-market impacts of climate change. Their basic approach, for both market and non-market sectors, was to measure *willingness to pay* (WTP) to prevent future change. This approach is akin to estimating the 'insurance premium' that different societies are willing to pay to prevent climate change and its associated impacts. That is, for each sector and region, they developed an estimate of WTP to avoid a 2.5°C increase in global mean temperature as a share of each region's GDP at a given point in time (usually a current time period), and then project future values by scaling with an adjustment factor based on future and current per capita GDP and income elasticity.

Nordhaus and Boyer assumed that the capital value of human settlements and ecosystems, which varies by region, ranges from 5 to 25 per cent of GDP (for example, for the United States this is estimated at 10 percent of GDP or about $500 billion in 1990 GDP levels[8]). They further assumed that each region has an 'annual WTP of 1 percent of the value of the vulnerable system (which is one-fifth of the annualized value at a discount rate on goods of 6 percent per year) to prevent climate disruption associated with a 2.5°C rise in mean temperature' (p. 86). On a global basis, Nordhaus and Boyer estimated that settlement and ecosystem damage represents about 9.5 percent of all damages (including extreme events). For the United States, they estimated the damages of 2.5°C warming on ecosystems at 0.10 percent of GDP.

Table 6.1   Estimated natural ecosystem damages for 1 °C increase in global mean temperature

Region	Monetary damages (US$ billion)
US & Canada	15
Western Europe	19
Pacific OECD	8
Eastern Europe/Former USSR	12
Middle East	2
Latin America	4
South/SE Asia	5
China	2
Africa	2
Total	69

Source: Based on Tol (1998, Table 3).

Another example of expert judgment is Tol (1998), who calculated a combined WTP to avoid damages to natural ecosystems. He stated that his estimated damages capture use, option, and existence values. He assumed a WTP of $50 per person per habitat and that one habitat per year is lost. He adjusted the WTP for GDP/capita and assumed a positive income elasticity for WTP. The results are displayed in Table 6.1. Tol's estimate of global WTP to avoid ecosystem damages is about 0.2 percent of current global GDP.

One interesting outcome of such studies is whether total non-market damages exceed total market damages. Nordhaus and Boyer (2000) estimate that the non-market damages related to health, ecosystems, and settlements (0.27 percent of global product) nearly cancel the non-market amenity benefits related to improved recreation and leisure (0.29 percent of global product) at 2.5°C of global mean temperature increase. So, their estimate of net non-market damages is close to zero. On the other hand, Nordhaus and Boyer estimate that the absolute value of non-market impacts is 0.56 percent of global product, while the absolue value of market impact is 0.50 percent of global product. So, their estimate of the absolute value of the non-market impacts is quite close to their estimate of the absolute value of market impacts.[9]

Studies such as Nordhaus and Boyer (2000) and Tol (1998) have the advantage of providing specific monetary estimates of climate-change damages, but their limitation is that they are largely based on expert judgment. There are substantial uncertainties with these estimates and little indication of confidence limits. Thus, there is low confidence even in estimates of relative non-market versus market damages.

Willingness-to-pay surveys

In contrast to the global approach and expert judgment of Nordhaus and Boyer is Layton and Brown (undated; and 1998), who used a stated preference survey to elicit individuals' WTP to prevent ecosystem change due to climate change over 60- and 150-year intervals. The ecosystem change valued is a shift of forests to higher elevations along the Front Range of Colorado, with prairie ecosystems replacing the forests. Layton and Brown conclude that WTP to prevent a change occurring over 60 years is not statistically different from the same changes over 150 years: $20 a month for altitudinal shifts of 600 feet to $80 a month for 2500 feet. Layton and Brown's results are reasonably robust to various model specifications and modeling approaches and show that individuals are willing to pay significant amounts to prevent potential future changes in ecosystems in response to global climate change. As Layton and Brown state, 'Little research has attempted to value ecosystems in their entirety, and none to our knowledge along with global climate change' (p. 8). They also state that 'we are aware of no markets that reveal the preferences of those alive today to help others 150 years in the future' (p. 22).

Studies such as Layton and Brown (1998) have the advantage of being replicable. It would be interesting to conduct similar studies of WTP and see if results are consistent. The results of these studies are difficult to interpret because it is not clear if respondents are embedding larger concerns about climate change in their answers (Kahneman and Knetsch, 1992). As Layton and Brown state 'perhaps the greatest challenge is in disentangling the willingness to pay (WTP) to prevent forest loss, from WTP to prevent all the other expected impacts of global climate change' (p. 9). Respondents could be giving a WTP to avoid *all* impacts of climate change, not just the one they are asked to respond to. Thus, even if we knew the quantitative ecological impacts from climate change, it is not clear whether results such as this can be scaled up by different impacts and population to arrive at a credible national or global damage estimate.

Kinnell et al. (forthcoming) use a contingent valuation survey to elicit values from Pennsylvania duck hunters for reducing impacts on the Prairie Pothole Region from climate change and agricultural activities. The Prairie Pothole Region is a major breeding ground in central US and Canada for ducks that migrate through Pennsylvania. Mean annual WTP to prevent agricultural or climate-change impacts on the pothole region is about $11. The stated values for preserving Prairie Potholes were higher when the source of the impact was indicated as climate change as opposed to agricultural causes and was larger for larger potential impacts on the Prairie Pothole Region. An interesting aspect is that individuals indicate a WTP to prevent climate-change impacts on an ecosystem that is spatially distinct from themselves.

Kinnell et al. also note that the values stated by respondents could incorporate embedding for prevention of a broader array of ecosystem impacts rather than those just to the Prairie Pothole Region.

Site-specific analyses
A third approach is to examine site-specific ecosystem impacts and use benefits transfer to estimate damages. For example, the World Bank (2000) and Stratus Consulting (2000) found that climate change could significantly affect low-lying island nations, which are particularly vulnerable to changes in sea level. The coral reefs that surround many of these islands may be highly sensitive to warmer temperatures and increased CO_2 concentrations, both of which inhibit coral growth (for example, Kleypas et al., 1999).

Coral reefs support nearshore commercial, recreational, and subsistence fisheries, and other economically valuable marine species. They serve important functions as atoll island foundations, natural protective structures along the coast by dampening of waves, sources of beach sand, sources of aggregate for construction, and tourist attractions. Bleaching events, which kill reefs, are expected to be more frequent, leading to declines in reef fisheries and long-term coastal protection.

For Fiji, the damages from climate change are estimated to average between $5 and $14 million annually by 2050 (in 1998 US dollars). These values were derived by estimating impacts to key services such as fisheries, tourism, and coastal protection, and estimating their current values and sensitivity to climate changes. For example, to estimate the value of mangroves (that is, WTP) for providing valuable habitat to support both commercial and subsistence fishing, recreation, supply medicinal plants, habitat support for wildlife, and coastal protection, per hectare values were developed from a variety of economic studies and applied to the current stock of Fijian mangroves (about 23,500 ha). The values include the value of goods or services delivered through a market (for example, local fish bought and sold in the local market) and non-market context (for example, fish caught by subsistence anglers).

The authors of these studies note that their economic analyses are based on a series of assumptions, models, and professional judgment. The methods used are intended to produce conservative (that is, lower-bound) estimates. In particular, there are many omissions, biases, and uncertainties acknowledged by the authors, and most of these are believed to result in underestimates of the losses. Examples of values that may not be covered in these damage estimates include non-use values (for example, existence, bequest, option values), trade in aquarium species, infrastructure maintenance and repair costs, and biodiversity.

Studies such as those described here have the advantage of being very specific. A disadvantage in addressing global damages from climate change is the difficulty of replicating such studies in enough cases to have sufficient examples upon which to develop a credible global estimate. In addition, there are problems with benefits transfer. It is not clear that other cultures share what are essentially Western values. They may put less or more value on ecological systems such as coral reefs. Studies such as this are interesting, particularly for identifying relative damages, but it appears to be premature to use them to develop estimates of global damages.

Human Health

While there are relatively more reliable quantitative estimates of the loss of human life of natural systems impacts, and there are more established techniques for valuing human life than valuing ecosystem impacts, the topic of the value of human life has been particularly controversial.

The controversy over valuing human life exploded during review of the IPCC's Second Assessment Report, which included estimates of global willingness to pay to avoid risk to human life (Pearce et al., 1996). The controversy arose because some studies adjusted the value of a statistical life (VSL) based on per capita GDP. This can lead to the conclusion that there is a higher WTP to avoid risk to people in wealthier countries than in poor countries.[10]

There is no right approach for valuing global health impacts. The prescriptive view, the 'moral imperative', treats all lives as equal and values them using the OECD (Organization for Economic Cooperation and Development) value of life for all lives under the polluter pays principle. However, this has a weak economic theoretic basis.

Assigning a single value to all lives based on the value estimates derived mainly from studies in developed countries results in a misallocation of resources in developing countries. VSL estimates are based in theory on individuals' attitudes toward risk and their willingness to pay to avoid risk – and this WTP is thus based on their actual income. Using an inflated value estimate for reductions in mortality will likely shift resources from other programs, which are valued in 'local' value terms. The VSL in a developing country is based on attitudes toward risk that cannot necessarily be transferred from developed countries, even if income levels can be scaled on per capita GDP measures.

In contrast, the descriptive view examines how much people are willing to pay to reduce risk to human life.[11] The human capital approach treats people as economic machines and values life according to the net value of produced output. The human capital approach is not the correct measure for policy analysis because it does not measure individuals' values as defined in welfare economics. Human capital does not capture individuals' attitudes toward risk and does not measure consumer surplus losses which are relevant in welfare analysis. Similarly, cost-of-illness approaches, which encompass more than just human capital, do not capture WTP measures and furthermore may be distorted because of social insurance programs.

The theoretical economic approach involves willingness to pay for reduced risk to human health or willingness to accept compensation for increased risk to human health. This requires a clear understanding of the hypothesized risk from climate change. Another problem is that it depends on other factors like the distribution of wealth; that is, the value of poor people's lives is constrained by their net income.

In the climate-change literature, different approaches have been used, from using a single average value (for example, Cline, 1992; Titus, 1992; and Fankhauser, 1995) to a varying approach that depends on regional per capita GDP (for example, Nordhaus and Boyer, 2000 and Tol, 1998).

For example, Nordhaus and Boyer (2000) relied on data from Murray and Lopez (1996) on the current prevalence of climate-related diseases (for example, malaria, dengue fever). These data are given for both the years of life lost (YLLs) and disability adjusted lives lost (DALYs). They use three approaches to estimate the effects of climate change: (i) assume that one-half (one quarter in sub-Saharan Africa) of the gains in health estimated by Murray and Lopez for 1990 to 2020 will be lost as a result of 2.5°C warming, (ii) adjust health impacts for each region to approximate changes in climate analogue regions, and (iii) apply a regression approach estimating the relationship between illness and mean regional climate. In all cases, life-years are valued as two years of per capita income. For the United States, Nordhaus estimates the health-related damages are approximately 2.7 percent of total damages (0.02 percent of GDP), or roughly $1.4 billion.

Our view is that if it is necessary to apply a VSL, it should be in a manner consistent with the level at which decisions are being made. If a decision is being made just for India, for example, on protection of human life versus other investments, then it is reasonable to use a VSL appropriate for the Indian economy and Indian values. Using a VSL from an OECD country might result in overinvestment for protection of human life compared to other investments such as education. For climate change, we can think of a single global decision maker. In this case a single value of human life across the globe is appropriate (so we do not inadvertently value lives in one country more than another). This single value could be based on global average GDP per capita.

Recreation

A few studies have attempted to derive monetary estimates of climate-change impacts on recreation.

Loomis and Crespi (1999) estimated across a range of activities that a warming of 2.5°C and a 7 percent increase in precipitation across the United States could generate net gains in recreation benefits of $2.5 billion (1992 dollars), because activities such as golf and fishing and other freshwater stream and lake uses increase much more than cold-weather recreation, such as skiing, declines.

Mendelsohn and Markowski (1999) similarly estimated that modest warming leads to a net increase in outdoor recreation benefits, as hunting, fishing, and boating gains in consumer surplus outweigh losses in camping, skiing, and wildlife viewing. The authors estimate the value of this impact to the United States to be between $1.7 and $6.3 billion (in 1991 dollars) for a 2.5°C increase in temperature and a 7 percent rise in precipitation.

Robinson and Godbey (1997) surveyed time use by Americans and report that less than 5 percent of non-market time is climate sensitive (about 2.2 hours out of 39.4 hours per week). A slight positive impact is estimated for amenity impacts such as gains in camping and golf at the expense of skiing and hockey. A 2.5°C warming leads to an amenity increase of 0.3 percent of US GDP (the value reaches a maximum at about 20°C mean temperature, after which it declines). They applied this relationship to other regions (extrapolating from the United States) and find positive impacts for temperate and cold high-latitude regions and negative for warm regions (that is, those with monthly mean temperatures above 20°C).

Nordhaus and Boyer (2000) estimated slight increases in global welfare associated with changes in climate-sensitive recreation (about 0.28 percent of US annual GDP, $19 billion in 1995 baseline).

Tourism

A few studies have attempted to estimate economic impacts of changes in tourism. For example, Maddison (forthcoming) developed a pooled travel cost model to look at the impact of climate variables (temperature and precipitation) on choice of vacation site for British tourists using aggregated country data to estimate change in the number of trips to a site (87 countries) as a non-linear function of temperature. Using this model, Maddison identified an optimal destination temperature and derived welfare estimates based on changes in temperature and precipitation under different scenarios. Using data from the United Kingdom Meteorological Office's (UKMO) general circulation model, which indicated a uniform increase of around 2°C for Southern Europe by 2030, Maddison valued impacts on tourism for Greece, Spain, and the Seychelles. As an example, Maddison shows that there would be a small increase in consumer surplus of just over £11.6 million ($16 million), and the flow of British tourists increases by 2.9 percent for Greece.

If the whole of the Seychelles were inundated, the total consumer surplus loss would be £2.2 million pounds per year (1995 values; $3 million).

Maddison's model deals only with use values (Maddison is very explicit on this point). Thus values for some low-lying island countries are found to be smaller even if they are totally inundated because they tend to be far away for British tourists and have lower visitation rates. It is noted, though, that there may be large passive use values (Maddison calls these 'existence' values) for these countries. The paper further recognizes that it does not deal with substitution among sites or changes in the total number of visits across all sites.

Others have examined the impact of climate change on tourism, but there has been little work on estimating the economic impacts of such changes (Smith, 1993; Schackleford and Olsson, 1995; Wall, 1998).

Amenity Values

A number of studies have attempted to estimate changes in amenity values. Amenity value is human centered and is largely related to time and leisure activities. On a global basis, Nordhaus and Boyer (2000) estimate amenity benefits from a 2.5°C warming of $19.4 billion. This result derives from surveys and analyses by the authors showing a rise in time allocated to outdoor recreation and leisure activities as temperatures rise. For example, Nordhaus and Boyer observe that the positive gains from activities such as hiking and camping outweigh the losses to activities such as skiing.

Case and Leary (1995) used a hedonic price model to test the hypothesis that climate amenity values are capitalized in housing rents and wages, and to estimate the implicit price of such amenity values. They find that mild climates are preferred (that is, cooler rather than hotter summers and warmer rather than colder winters). Their estimates for decreased prices of single family homes as a result of higher summer temperatures range from –$30 to –$160 (1990 dollars) per degree Fahrenheit increase. On the winter side, the authors find an average increase of $5 per degree in winter temperatures. They also find less cloud cover preferable to more cloud cover. Graves (1980, as cited by Leary, 1994) demonstrated that outmigration and inmigration patterns are influenced by temperatures and temperature variations. This result is not robust, since other studies suggest that the effect of climate is insignificant compared to the driving force of economic opportunity.

One of the more detailed amenity value studies was recently conducted by Maddison and Bigano (undated). Using housing, wage, climatic, and regional data, they developed a hedonic model of the impact of climate variables on net household income differentials as an indication of the amenity values of climate in Italy. The analysis controlled for the influence of coastal and alpine areas, the presence of metropolitan areas, population density, and latitude and longitude in addition to climate variables (temperature, precipitation, and percent of clear sky). Their analysis found significant disamenity values for both high July temperatures and January precipitation. Climate-change models predict increases in July temperatures and January precipitation, and the analysis suggests that there would be significant amenity welfare losses in Italy due to climate change. Maddison and Bigano calculated implicit prices for climate variables for five metropolitan areas but did not calculate projected welfare losses under climate change. Maddison and Bigano report implicit prices by city for amenity values of climate variable in thousands of Italian lira per household per year (undated, Table 4). These implicit prices indicate the welfare effects of marginal changes in the level of climate amenities. Converting to US dollars,[12] for a household in Milan, a 1°C increase in July temperature would lower welfare by $286 per year. Similarly, for a household in Milan, a 1 mm increase in precipitation in January would lower welfare by $19 a year, a 1 percent increase in clear skies in January would increase welfare by $140, and a 1 percent increase in clear skies in July would lead to a $274 per year increase in welfare. They note that such calculations would be upper bounds since the model does not allow for relocation due to changes in climate amenities.

It seems reasonable to conclude that lower latitudes, where temperatures are already relatively high, would most likely face a loss of amenity values whereas higher latitudes, where temperatures are relatively low, would most likely experience an increase in amenity values.

Catastrophic Impacts

There is very little published literature addressing the WTP to avoid catastrophic impacts of climate change such as break-up of the West Antarctic Ice Sheet or slowdown of the North Atlantic Thermohaline Circulation. However, Nordhaus and Boyer (2000) examined the issue of catastrophic loss and developed some stylized estimates using results from a 'survey' of experts, in which they were asked to assign probabilities to several climate and high-consequence events. The results led them to estimate WTP to avoid catastrophic losses in the United States associated with a 2.5°C warming to be 0.45 percent of GDP and 2.53 percent of GDP with a 6°C warming, where catastrophic loss is given as a 30 percent drop in income. Note that this estimate of willingness to pay to avoid catastrophe dwarfs estimates of willingness to pay to avoid damages in other impact categories. The literature contains virtually no information on the economic consequences of catastrophic impacts of climate change (that is, whether such impacts will lead to a 30 percent loss of GDP).

A Possible Approach

It appears to be almost fruitless to try to develop estimates of global WTP to avoid non-market damages from climate change – at least using the methods reviewed here. Another approach, however, is possible. This involves first monetizing what can credibly be quantified about benefits and costs of greenhouse gas emissions control. This would mainly involve effects of climate change on markets, where values of goods and services are much better established. The market benefits of controlling greenhouse gas emissions should be subtracted from the costs of emissions control.[13]

The net costs of control can be compared with qualitative or quantitative descriptions of non-market impacts of climate change. The non-market impacts can be expressed in terms that may be more meaningful to people than monetary value. The net number of people who may die can be quantified and ecosystem impacts can be quantified (for example, species loss) or described. People could then indicate their preference as to whether it is better to (i) invest in greenhouse gas emissions control or (ii) allow the impacts of climate change to happen. This could be done for different control levels, indicating the cost of reducing emissions to different levels and the consequences of the emissions in terms of non-market impacts.

This approach is similar to a referendum question used in stated preference valuation approaches. A key aspect of this approach would be clearly explaining the potential negative and positive impacts with and without a climate-change policy and the associated costs the individual would face. The individual would also have to understand the market impacts he or she would face and then state a preference over the potential non-market impacts and control costs.

The major limitation in applying such an approach is that we currently lack good information on non-market impacts. This is particularly true for ecosystem impacts. This suggests that more research to better understand and quantify ecosystem and other non-market impacts of climate change is needed.

5 FINAL THOUGHTS

Assessing economic damages from climate change to non-market systems, that is, ascribing monetary value, is, to say the least, a very difficult and challenging exercise. This chapter reviews a number of approaches, none of which appears to provide results that give us much confidence. The expert judgment approaches give comprehensive numbers but there is no information about the confidence limits of the results. The 'bottom-up' approaches, such as surveys or estimates of willingness to pay for specific impacts, cover such a small portion of the potential impact that they leave us wanting with regard to how these narrow results can be aggregated to a credible and meaningful global number.

Some interesting insight can be gained from the available literature on non-market damages. While the magnitude of these damage estimates may have little credibility, the sign of the impact is of interest and may hold up over time. The literature generally reports that there will be damages associated with ecosystem impacts. Even though some species could gain and there could be temporary increases in productivity (for example, Cramer et al., 2001), the literature on climate-change impacts consistently concludes that species and ecosystem diversity would be reduced by climate change. Thus, there appears to be little doubt that there will be net damages associated with ecosystem impacts.

The literature predominantly shows damages to human health, primarily based on estimated increases in mortality. However, as the IPCC Third Assessment (IPCC, 2001) points out, there may be mixed human health impacts in many countries. Given the large populations in tropical countries and their relatively poor health-care systems, it appears more probable that there will be increased rather than decreased global deaths from climate change.

In contrast, the studies on recreation impacts show a net positive effect. This is because the value of increased 'warm' weather activities appears to outweigh the value of decreased 'cold' weather activities. These studies have only limited geographical application (the United States) and need to be extended to more areas before global conclusions can be drawn.

Studies on amenity values and tourism appear to be more equivocal. Maddison and Bigano's study estimates reduction in amenity values, but only for one country. One would expect that higher-latitude countries may have increased amenity values, while lower-latitude countries may have decreased values. Studies on tourism indicate that tourist activities may shift location. This seems reasonable since people will continue to travel for vacation but may choose different destinations based on change in climate. There may be little net change, but there will certainly be winners and losers.

On the whole, it appears as if we are far away from being able to derive a credible and useful estimate of global non-monetary damages from climate change. However, readers should not assume that all attempts to estimate monetary value of non-market damages are fruitless. Indeed, while it is extremely difficult to credibly monetize *total global* non-market damages, quantifying non-market impacts of climate change and identifying services that can be lost, both of which are necessary in order to estimate non-market damages, will provide very useful information to policymakers on the consequences of climate change. In addition, we believe that credible regional or local estimates of the monetary value of many non-market impacts can be established. Such estimates can be very useful in understanding the relative values of non-market climate change impacts and how those values may change as climate change becomes more severe.

NOTES

*   The authors would like to thank Jim Griffin, Ann Fisher, and Richard Tol, for their careful review and extensive comments. The staff at Stratus Consulting Inc. helped us enormously with this chapter. Shiela DeMars coordinated the production, Christina Thomas did the editing, while Sara Garland and Erin Miles provided word-processing support. Megan Harrod helped us with research. Any mistakes are the responsibility of the authors.

1. The term 'damages' is typically used to describe economic impacts from pollution. In the case of global warming, not all impacts are negative. Should there be net benefits, the sign of damages would be negative. However, as noted below, we expect that net impacts of climate change on natural ecosystems and human health will be negative.

2. As Mendelsohn notes, at such a level of warming, impacts to markets in developed countries in mid- and high latitudes may be positive, while the impacts to markets in developing countries in low latitudes may be negative. As Goulder (Chapter 4) notes, when equity is considered, the net market may be negative even at a few degrees of warming.

3. It should be noted that many of the studies we survey were not designed to arrive at global estimates of non-market damages. Many are more appropriate for estimating regional or local non-market damages from climate change.

4. Although there have been several critiques of the contingent valuation method (for example, Kahneman and Knetsch, 1992; Desvousges et al., 1993), others agree with EPA's statement that 'We believe that contingent valuation (CV) is a useful methodology, particularly for determining passive use damages that cannot be measured in any other way. The practical choice is between using CV or implicitly assigning a zero value to passive use damages. We believe that CV, when carefully done, can provide reliable results for determining damages at a reasonable cost' (USEPA, 1994, p. iii).

5. Some of the service flows mentioned by Daily and others are compiled from other authors and not discussed in depth here.

6. In 1997 dollars, Alexander et al.'s estimate would be \$18.4 trillion, based on the chain-type price indexes for gross domestic product (CEA, 2000). As a percentage of current global product, the estimate would be about \$35 trillion.

7. The difference between capacity to pay for ecosystems and willingness to pay to reduce risks to ecosystems is similar to the difference between cost-of-illness (COI) and value of statistical life (VSL) approaches to valuing morbidity risks. It is generally recognized that the COI approach is not necessarily the correct measure for policy analysis and that it may not directly measure welfare changes. VSL measures are also known to be related to, but not constrained by, income levels since they are based on willingness to pay to avoid the risk of death, not willingness to pay to avoid death. In a similar manner the appropriate measure of the value to prevent climate-change impacts to ecosystems is a risk-based measure and thus may not be constrained by income.

8. It would be about \$100 billion based on current US GDP.

9. In addition, Nordhaus and Boyer assume that at 2.5°C of mean global temperature increase, there is a willingness to pay of 1 percent of global product to avoid catastrophes such as very high sea-level rise or the runaway greenhouse effect (see below). Such catastrophes would cause both market and non-market damages and the authors do not identify the relative share of such damages.

10. This conclusion can be verified through observation of such behavior as the difference in safety investments in wealthy and poor countries.

11. It is important to note that there is very little discussion of the potential morbidity impacts from climate change. There is also generally much less information on individuals' values for morbidity compared to estimates of mortality estimates. Another issue in using VSL estimates is that these are often based on wage risk studies for middle-aged working individuals. How to adjust VSL estimates for the young, elderly, or specific susceptible populations is unclear.
12. www.oanda.com/convert/classic June 20, 2001: 1,000 Italian lira = 0.44125 US dollars.
13. We recognize that there still remain substantial uncertainties and disagreement about the cost of greenhouse gas emissions control and the market impacts of climate change.

REFERENCES

Alexander, A.M., J.A. List, M. Margolis and R.C. d'Arge (1998), 'A method for valuing global ecosystem services', *Ecological Economics* **27**: 161–70.

Balbus, J.M. and M.L. Wilson (2000), *Human Health and Global Climate Change: A Review of Potential Impacts in the United States*, The Pew Center on Global Climate Change, Arlington, VA.

Brown, T.C. (1984), 'The concept of value in resource allocation', *Land Economics* **60** (3): 231–46.

Case, B. and N. Leary (1995), *Human Amenity Values of Climate: Evidence from U.S. Housing Markets*, US Environmental Protection Agency, Washington, DC.

(CEA) Council of Economic Advisors (2000), *Economic Report of the President*, US Government Printing Office, Washington, DC.

Chestnut, L.G, W.S. Breffle, J.B. Smith and L.S. Kalkstein (1998), 'Analysis of differences in hot-weather-related mortality across 44 U.S. metropolitan areas', *Environment Science & Policy* **1**: 59–70.

Christensen, N.L., Jr. and J.F. Franklin (1997), 'Ecosystem function and ecosystem management', in R.D. Simpson and N.L. Christensen, Jr. (eds), *Ecosystem Function and Human Activities: Reconciling Economics and Ecology*, Chapman & Hall, New York, pp. 1–25.

Cline, W.R. (1992), *The Economics of Global Warming*, Institute for International Economics, Washington, DC.

Costanza, R., R.C. d'Arge, R. de Groot, S. Farber, M. Grasso, B. Hannon, K. Limburg, S. Naeem, R. O'Neil, J. Paruelo, R. Raskin, P. Sutton and M. van den Belt (1997), 'The value of the world's ecosystem services and natural capital', *Nature* **387**: 253–60.

Cramer, W. and 16 co-authors (2001), 'Global response of terrestrial ecosystem structure and function to CO_2 and climate change: results from six dynamic global vegetation models', *Global Change Biology* **7**: 357–73.

Daily, G.C. (1997), 'Introduction: what are ecosystem services?', in G.C. Daily (ed.), *Nature's Services; Societal Dependence on Natural Ecosystems*, Island Press, Washington, DC, pp. 1–10.

Desvousges, W.H., F.R. Johnson, R.W. Dunford, K.J. Boyle, S.P. Hudson and K.N. Wilson (1993), 'Measuring natural resource damages with contingent valuation: tests of validity and reliability', in J.A. Hausman (ed.), *Contingent Valuation: A Critical Assessment*, North-Holland, Amsterdam, pp. 91–164.

Fankhauser, S. (1995), *Valuing Climate Change: The Economics of the Greenhouse*, Earthscan, London.

Freeman, A.M. (1993), *The Measurement of Environmental and Resource Values: Theory and Methods*, Resources for the Future, Washington, DC.

Garrod, G. and K.G. Willis (1999), *Economic Valuation of the Environment*, Edward Elgar, Cheltenham, UK and Northampton, MA, USA.

Graves, P. (1980), 'Migration and climate', *Journal of Regional Science* **20**: 227–37.

(IPCC) Intergovernmental Panel on Climate Change (2001), *Climate Change 2001: Impacts, Adaptation, and Vulnerability*, J. McCarthy, O. Canziani, N. Leary, D. Dokken and K. White (eds), Cambridge University Press, Cambridge, UK.

Kahneman, D. and J.L. Knetsch (1992), 'Valuing public goods: the purchase of moral satisfaction', *Journal of Environmental Economics and Management* **22**: 57–70.

Kalkstein, L.S. and J.S. Greene (1997), 'An evaluation of climate/mortality relationships in large U.S. cities and the possible impacts of a climate change', *Environmental Health Perspectives* **105** (1): 2–11.

Kinnell, J., J.K. Lazo, D.J. Epp, A. Fisher and J. Shortle (forthcoming), 'Perceptions and values for preventing ecosystem change: Pennsylvania duck hunters and the prairie pothole region', *Land Economics*.

Kleypas, J.A., R.W. Buddemeier, D. Archer, J.-P. Gattuso, C. Langdon and B.N. Opdyke (1999), 'Geochemical consequences of increased atmospheric carbon dioxide on coral reefs', *Science* **284**: 118–20.

Layton, D.F. and G. Brown (undated), 'Heterogeneous preferences regarding global climate change', Working Paper, Department of Environmental Science and Policy, University of California, Davis.

Layton, D.F. and G. Brown (1998), 'Application of stated preference methods to a public good: issues for discussion', Paper prepared for the NOAA Workshop on the Application of Stated Preference Methods to Resource Compensation, Washington, DC, June 1–2.

Leary, N. (1994), 'The amenity value of climate: a review of empirical evidence from migration, wages, and rents', Discussion Paper, US Environmental Protection Agency, July.

Loomis, J. and J. Crespi (1999), 'Estimated effects of climate change on selected outdoor recreation activities in the United States', in R. Mendelsohn and J.E. Neumann (eds), *The Impact of Climate Change on the United States Economy*, Cambridge University Press, Cambridge, UK, pp. 289–314.

Maddison, D. (forthcoming), 'In search of warmer climates? The impact of climate change on flows of British tourists', *Climatic Change*.

Maddison, D. and A. Bigano (undated), 'The amenity value of the Italian climate', Centre for Social and Economic Research on the Global Environment (CSERGE), University College London / University of East Anglia and the Centre for Economic Studies (CES).

Malcolm, J.R. and A. Markham (2000), *Global Warming and Terrestrial Biosphere Decline*, World Wildlife Fund, Gland, Switzerland.

Martens, W.J.M. (1998), 'Climate change, thermal stress and mortality changes', *Social Science Medicine* **46**: 331–44.

Martens, P., R.S. Kovats, S. Nijhof, P. de Vries, M.T.J. Livermore, D.J. Bradley, J. Cox and A.J. McMichael (1999), 'Climate change and future populations at risk of malaria', *Global Environmental Change* **9**: S89–S107.

McMichael, A.J. and A. Githeko (2001), 'Human health', in J. McCarthy, O. Canziana, N. Leary, D. Dokken, and K. White (eds), *Climate Change 2001: Impacts, Adaptation, and Vulnerability*, New York, Cambridge University Press.

Mendelsohn, R. and M. Markowski (1999), 'The impact of climate change on outdoor recreation', in R. Mendelsohn and J.E. Neumann (eds), *The Impact of Climate Change on the United States Economy*, Cambridge University Press, Cambridge, UK, pp. 267–88.

Mitchell, R.C. and R.T. Carson (1989), *Using Surveys to Value Public Goods: The Contingent Valuation Method*, Resources for the Future, Washington, DC.

Murray, C.J. and A.D. Lopez (eds) (1996), *The Global Burden of Disease*, Harvard University Press, Cambridge, MA.

NAST (National Assessment Synthesis Team) (2000), *Climate Change Impacts on the United States: The Potential Consequences of Climate Variability and Change*, US Global Change Research Program, Washington, DC.

Nordhaus, W. and J. Boyer (2000), *Roll the DICE Again: Economic Modeling of Climate Change*, MIT Press, Cambridge, MA.

Pearce, D.W., W.R. Cline, A.N. Achanta, S. Fankhauser, R.K. Pachauri, R.S.J. Tol and P. Vellinga (1996), 'The social costs of climate change: greenhouse damage and the benefits of control', in J.P. Bruce, H. Lee, and E. F. Haites (eds), *Climate Change 1995: Economic and Social Dimensions of Climate Change*, Cambridge University Press, Cambridge, UK.

Reiner, D.M. and F.G. Sussman (1994), 'Perceptions of ecosystem damages and economic prescriptions. ICF Incorporated', Paper presented at the Western Economic Association Meeting, June 29–July 3.

Robinson, J.W. and G. Godbey (1997), *Time for Life: The Surprising Ways Americans Use Their Time*, Pennsylvania University Press, University Park, PA.

Schackleford, P. and L.E. Olsson (1995), 'Tourism, climate and weather', *World Meteorological Organization Bulletin* **44** (3): 239.

Smith, J.B., H.J. Schellnhuber and M.Q. Mirza (2001), 'Lines of evidence for vulnerabilty to climate change: a synthesis', in J. McCarthy, O. Canziana, N. Leary, D. Dokken and K. White (eds) *Climate Change 2001: Impacts, Adaptation, and Vulnerability*, New York, Cambridge University Press, pp. 913–67.

Smith, K. (1993), 'The influence of weather and climate on recreation and tourism', *Weather* **48** (12): 398.

Stratus Consulting Inc. (2000), *Economic Implications of Climate Change in Two Pacific Island Country Locations: Case Illustrations of Tarawa, Kiribati, and Viti Levu, Fiji*, Stratus Consulting Inc., Boulder, CO.

Titus, J.G. (1992), 'The costs of climate change to the United States', in S.K. Majumdar, L.S. Kalkstein, B. Yarnal, E.W. Miller, and L.M. Rosenfeld (eds), *Global Climate Change: Implications, Challenges, and Mitigation Measures*, Pennsylvania Academy of Science, Philadelphia, PA, pp. 384–409.

Tol, R.S.J. (1998), 'New estimates of the damage costs of climate change', D-98/06, Working Paper, Free University, Amsterdam, April.

Tol, R.S.J. and H. Dowlatabadi (in press), 'Vector-borne diseases, development, and climate change', *Integrated Environmental Assessment*.

United Nations (1999), Population Division of the Department of Economic and Social Affairs of the United Nations Secretariat, *Long-Range World Population Projections: Based on the 1998 Revision*, ESA/P/WP.153, http://www.undp.org/popin/wdtrends/longrange/tab2.htm. Accessed March 20, 2001.

(USEPA) US Environmental Protection Agency (1994), 'Comments on Proposed NOAA/DOI Regulations on Natural Resource Damage Assessment', US Environmental Protection Agency, Washington, DC 20460, October.

Wall, G. (1998), 'Implications of global climate change for tourism and recreation in wetland areas', *Climatic Change* **40** (2): 371.

Whigham, D.F. (1997), 'Ecosystem functions and ecosystem values', in R.D. Simpson, J. Norman and L. Christensen (eds), *Ecosystem Function and Human Activities*, Chapman & Hall, New York, pp. 225–239.

World Bank (2000) (Draft), *Cities, Seas and Storms: Managing Change in Pacific Island Economics. Volume IV: Adapting to Climate Change*, World Bank, Washington, DC.

7. What are the costs of limiting CO_2 concentrations?*

James A. Edmonds and Ronald D. Sands

1 INTRODUCTION

In 1992 the United Nations Framework Convention on Climate Change (UNFCCC) emerged from the environmental meetings held in Rio de Janeiro, Brazil. The convention has subsequently entered into force with the United States and more than 160 other parties joining.

> The ultimate objective of this [The Framework] Convention ... is ... the ... stabilization of greenhouse gas concentrations in the atmosphere at a level that would prevent dangerous anthropogenic interference with the climate system. Such a level should be achieved within a time frame sufficient to allow ecosystems to adapt naturally to climate change, to ensure that food production is not threatened and to enable economic development to proceed in a sustainable manner. (Article 2, UNFCCC, 1992)

While the framers of the UNFCCC never seriously considered the question, cost has been a central feature of subsequent discussions about attaining the ultimate objective of the framework convention. This chapter is about that issue.

We begin with a consideration of the core features of the global climate-change problem, which shape and determine the cost of limiting carbon dioxide (CO_2) concentrations. We shall next turn to consider the scale of the problem, and the technological and resource options available to address the question. Finally, we consider some of the implications of alternative policy frameworks for the cost and performance of options to limit the CO_2 concentration.

2 THE NATURE OF THE CLIMATE ISSUE

The most prominent feature of the global climate-change problem is that it is inherently global. There are many greenhouse gases (GHGs) in the atmosphere including water vapor (H_2O), ozone (O_3), carbon dioxide, methane (CH_4), nitrous oxide (N_2O), and a suite of human manufactured hydrocarbon compounds. In addition, there are a variety of aerosols and particulates that affect climate. Gases such as CO_2, CH_4, N_2O, the hydrocarbon compounds, and the aerosols and particulates are emitted in sufficient quantity by human activities that they can affect global biogeochemical cycles.

The presence of GHGs in the atmosphere affects the Earth's climate. As a consequence, the climate-change problem is inherently a public goods problem. That is, the climate that everyone enjoys is the product of everyone's behavior. No single individual or nation can determine the composition of the world's atmosphere. Any individuals' or nations' actions to address the climate-change issue, even the largest emitting nation acting alone, can have only a small effect. As a consequence, individuals and nations acting independently will provide, together, fewer resources than all individuals and nations would if they acted in concert. This characteristic provides an important motivation for collective, global-scale action.

At the same time it must be recognized that not all nations emit equally. The four largest emitters of CO_2 from fossil-fuel use in 1995 – the United States, China, the Russian Federation, and Japan – accounted for half of the world's emissions. The next nine nations account cumulatively for another 20 percent of the total.[1] The other 177 nations in the Oak Ridge National Laboratory database[2] each contribute one percent or less to the final 30 percent.

Several greenhouse-related gases are long-lived. The lifetime for methane is a decade or more. Nitrous oxide has a lifetime of multiple decades. And, a significant fraction of CO_2 emissions (at present 20 percent) remains in the atmosphere for a thousand years. The emissions of one generation become the heritage of the next. Intergenerational transfers are thus inevitable. The present generation has inherited its atmosphere and associated climate from its ancestors. While individuals and governments make many decisions that affect future generations, most of these decisions are undertaken inadvertently.

It is impossible to avoid the intergenerational wealth-transfer issue when addressing the climate problem. The fact that most of the affected parties are not present to participate in the decision-making process raises complicated ethical questions. The implications of their absence are not immediately obvious. Future generations have a stake both in the environmental resources, such as climate, that they inherit, and in other wealth that is passed down to them. Decisions that are taken by the present generation for the good of its descendants will shape the composition of wealth (for example, environmental versus material) that is transferred from the present to the future, as well as the magnitude of the transfer.

Since climate change depends on cumulative emissions each generation has limited ability to determine its own climate. Thus, those who live in the future will reap most of the benefits that accrue to near-term actions to limit greenhouse gas emissions.

Climate change is related to the concentration of greenhouse gases and not to any individual year's emissions. CO_2 concentrations are closely related to the net accumulation of emissions over long periods of time.[3] That is, it is the sum of emissions over time that determines the atmospheric concentration. Any individual year's emissions are only marginally important. While non-CO_2 GHGs with relatively short lifetimes, such as methane and even nitrous oxide, have an atmospheric concentration that is stable with a stable rate of annual emissions, CO_2 does not. In other words, any positive and stable rate of CO_2 emissions from fossil sources eventually implies a continuously increasing concentration of CO_2 in the atmosphere. Strategies to control net emissions must account for long periods of time in a meaningful way.

The natural carbon cycle governs the relationship between emissions and concentrations of CO_2. Anthropogenic emissions originating from net changes in land use and fossil-fuel oxidation initially enter the atmosphere, but are eventually partitioned between the atmosphere and the ocean. While the oceans ultimately take up much of the net release, a fraction of any net emission remains in the atmosphere for more than a millennium. As a consequence, the pre-industrial level of 275 parts per million volume (ppmv) concentration of CO_2 is no longer accessible in the present millennium without reversing the net flow from fossil-fuel oxidation and land-use change. Society's ability to remove carbon from the atmosphere is presently limited, although in principle the technology exists to accomplish this end. Beyond that, it is conceivable that technologies, which have not yet been imagined, could be brought into being for that purpose. But, to date no effort has ever been undertaken to systematically lower atmospheric CO_2 concentrations through direct human intervention.

Stabilizing the concentration of CO_2 in the atmosphere therefore implies that no positive net emission of CO_2 is possible indefinitely. Emissions must eventually become arbitrarily small. While present (1999) levels are in excess of 6 petagrams[4] of carbon per year (PgC/yr), net emissions will almost surely rise before falling. Since cumulative emissions determine the long-term steady-state concentration of CO_2, an infinite number of alternative time-paths of emissions exist for any long-term CO_2 concentration. It also means that to satisfy the cost-effectiveness objective of the UNFCCC, emissions could rise before finally declining.

Most emissions scenarios anticipate that carbon emissions will rise steadily over the course of the next century unless climate change leads to policies and measures that alter that trajectory. This is almost universally the case for emissions scenarios that focus on the first half of the twenty-first century

(Nakićenović et al., 2000). Under such circumstances most of the emissions mitigation (defined as the difference between a future emissions path without climate policy and a path with climate policy) required to stabilize the concentration of carbon must occur in the long term. The difference between reference emissions and the control case becomes increasingly great as the scenario progresses into the future. Control of GHG concentrations implies eventual limitations on global, energy-related emissions.

Energy is the single largest source of GHG emissions. It is responsible for approximately 80 percent of net carbon emissions to the atmosphere. While net emissions of carbon are associated with fossil-fuel combustion, the carbon-to-energy ratio varies between high-carbon fuels, such as coal, and low-carbon fuels, such as natural gas (methane or CH_4), by a factor of approximately two. Technologies such as hydroelectric power, nuclear fission, wind power, and solar power are generally treated as if they have little or no direct carbon emissions.[5]

Technologies exist that can capture and sequester carbon. Thus, in principle, controlling energy-related carbon emissions is possible without forgoing fossil-fuel use. Technologies that capture and sequester carbon are generally divided into two categories. The first category includes those technologies that use terrestrial ecosystems to do the job. For example, changing cropping practices can store carbon in soils. Or, forest planting can be used to accomplish the same end. The second category directly removes carbon in the energy transformation process, for example during electricity generation, and transports the carbon to a geologically isolated site.[6]

Finally, as noted above, carbon capture and storage technologies open the technical possibility of negative emissions. This can be accomplished at present by growing biomass, whose carbon was absorbed from the atmosphere, and depositing that carbon to a storage site removed from the ocean-atmosphere. Technologies also exist that can in principle remove carbon directly from the air. These issues will be discussed later in the chapter.

Finally, there is as yet no scientific basis for preferring one CO_2 concentration to another. Pre-industrial concentrations of carbon dioxide, for example, were in the neighborhood of 275 ppmv. They had risen to 368 ppmv by 1999. Under a variety of scenarios this concentration rises to anywhere from 500 ppmv to more than 700 ppmv over the course of the twenty-first century.[7]

3 EMISSIONS UNDER INNOVATION-AS-USUAL SCENARIOS WITHOUT CLIMATE LIMITS

There is no physical constraint that will prevent cumulative emissions from rising substantially. While the resource base of *conventional* oil and gas is limited, the amount of carbon stored in fossil fuels is not. Table 7.1 describes the distribution of carbon in fossil-fuel resources.

Table 7.1   Carbon content of fossil-fuel energy resources potentially available after 1990

Energy form	Resource base (PgC)	Range of resource base estimates (PgC)	Additional occurrences (PgC)	Resources plus additional occurrences (PgC)
Conventional oil[a]	170	156–230	200	156–430
Conventional gas[a]	140	115–240	150	115–390
Unconventional gas[a]	410	–	340	750
Coal[1,a,c]	3,240	–	3,350	3,240–6,590
Tar sands & heavy oils[2,b]	720	600–800	–	600–800
Oil shale[2,c]	40,000	–	–	40,000
Gas hydrates[a]	–	–	12,240	12,240

Notes:
1. Assumes 50 percent unrecoverable coal in the resource base.
2. Range estimates not available due to abundance of resource.

Sources:
a. IPCC (1996), p. 87.
b. Rogner (1997).
c. Edmonds and Reilly (1985).

The extent of carbon stored in the form of conventional oil and gas is only about half the mass of carbon existing in the atmosphere. The extent of carbon stored in the form of coal resources could exceed the amount of carbon in the atmosphere by as much as an order of magnitude. Further, the extent of carbon stored in the form of unconventional liquids and gases exceeds the carbon stored in the form of coal. There is no serious prospect for 'running out' of fossil fuels during the course of the twenty-first century. And therefore, the idea that society will soon, and as a matter of a transition dictated by nature, develop non-carbon energy forms because there is no fossil-fuel alternative, is unlikely. This is different from saying that society may choose to leave fossil-fuel resources unexploited.

Future emissions can potentially range widely. Nakićenović et al. (2000) examined the literature and confirmed the essential findings of Alcamo et al. (1995). That is, emissions remain potentially uncertain due to a wide array of factors and that by the end of the twenty-first century, emissions can potentially vary by an order of magnitude.

This range is due to a variety of factors which can be loosely grouped into four somewhat overlapping aggregations:

1. *scale factors* factors that determine the scale of human activities such as population and gross domestic product (GDP);
2. *cost factors* factors that determine the absolute cost of energy and the relative cost of alternative energy forms including for example, technology, subsidies and taxes, energy resources, agricultural resources, market structure, and institutions;
3. *policy* the direct intervention on the part of society to change private decision making, including for example, environmental or development policy; and
4. *global context* factors that determine the context in which the other three factors operate, including for example, international relations or trade policies that move the world either toward an increasingly interdependent or increasingly independent mode of interaction.

The range of scenarios found by the IPCC Special Report on Emissions Scenarios (SRES; Nakićenović et al., 2000) writing team is shown in Figure 7.1.

What is interesting to note is that while the median scenario examined anticipates that emissions will more than double between 2000 and 2100, there are numerous scenarios that are both higher and lower. In fact, there is a suite of scenarios, some of which assume no explicit control of carbon emissions, that are characterized by paths that are consistent with the stabilization of the concentration of carbon in the atmosphere. That is, they exhibit the critical emissions peak and subsequent monotonic decline in emissions.

The SRES considered six scenario groups that span a range of uncertainties underlying projections of future carbon emissions. Primary driving forces are population, economic development, and technological change. Assumptions about population in the year 2100 range from 7 to 15 billion people across scenarios. Even though most of the scenarios assume no policy intervention to limit carbon emissions, a tremendous amount of technical innovation is assumed to occur, especially with future energy systems. This results in

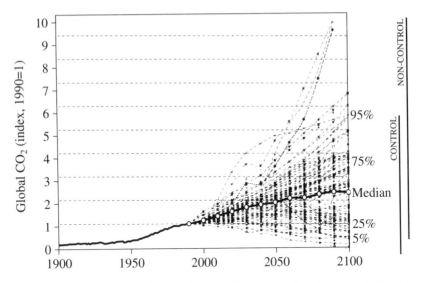

Note: The emissions paths indicate a wide range of future emissions. The range is also large in the base year 1990. In order to separate the variation due to base-year specification from different future paths, emissions are indexed for the year 1990, when actual global energy-related CO_2 emissions were about 6 GtC. Altogether, 232 different scenarios from the database were included in the figure. Two vertical bars on the right-hand side indicate the ranges for scenarios with emissions control measures (labeled 'control') and for those without controls ('non-control').

Sources: Data: Nakićenović et al. (1998); Morita and Lee (1998). Figure: Nakićenović (1999).

Figure 7.1   *Global carbon emissions and historical development in different scenarios*

steadily declining energy consumption per unit of GDP in all of the scenario groups.

Each scenario group contains an illustrative 'marker' scenario, with annual global carbon emissions shown in Figure 7.2. Emissions increase in the early years for all scenarios. The A1 family of scenarios represents a world of rapid economic growth and rapid introduction of new technologies. Three A1 groups are distinguished by dominant energy source: fossil intensive (A1FI), non-fossil energy sources (A1T), or a balance across all sources (A1B). Other SRES scenario groups (A2, B1, B2) are differentiated by assumptions on population growth, economic development, pace and diversity of technological change, and coordination between countries. Even though carbon emissions are falling after 2050 in several of the illustrative SRES scenarios, concentrations of carbon dioxide continue to rise. Figure 7.3 shows concentrations of CO_2 corresponding to the carbon emissions paths from Figure 7.2. Note that

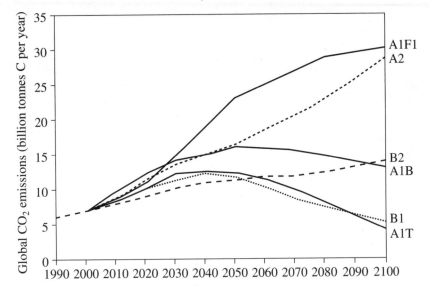

Data source: IPCC (2000).

*Figure 7.2   Annual global carbon emissions from fossil fuels for six
illustrative SRES scenarios*

CO_2 concentrations increase over time for all of the scenarios, with concentrations ranging from 540 to 970 ppmv in year 2100, well above the present CO_2 concentration of approximately 370 ppmv.

4   EMISSIONS PATHS THAT STABILIZE CO_2 CONCENTRATIONS

We have argued that there is no unique emissions path that leads to a given concentration of CO_2 in the atmosphere. Rather there are an infinite number. For some combinations of reference emissions paths and concentrations, there is no need for policy intervention to limit cumulative emissions. The choice of path therefore has implications for cost. The question of cost and path has been the source of a great deal of debate. Emissions trajectories consistent with five alternative concentrations limits are shown in Figure 7.4. These paths were derived by Wigley, Richels and Edmonds (WRE) and are labeled as WRE carbon emissions paths, with one emissions path for each concentration ceiling (Wigley et al., 1996). Of the infinite number of carbon emissions paths consistent with any given CO_2 concentration ceiling, the

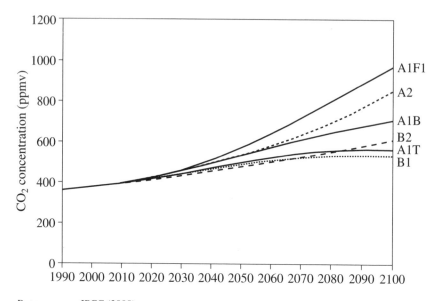

Data source: IPCC (2000).

Figure 7.3 CO_2 concentrations implied by six illustrative SRES scenarios

WRE path represents a gradual transition in early years away from a baseline, avoiding early retirement of energy-consuming capital stock. Figure 7.4 includes carbon emissions from both the energy system and deforestation, although this is dominated by carbon emissions due to energy combustion.

Key characteristics associated with the WRE emissions paths, consistent with alternative CO_2 concentrations limits, are shown in Table 7.2. Taking the WRE 550 curve as an example, carbon emissions first diverge from the IS92a baseline in 2013, reaching a global maximum in 2033, and return back to 1990 levels around 2100. Figure 7.5 provides CO_2 concentrations implied by the WRE emissions paths. The time-scale in Figure 7.5 is extended to 2300 to show that a steady-state CO_2 concentration is reached after 2100 for the greater concentration ceilings.

5   TIMING OF EMISSIONS MITIGATION

The cost of stabilizing the concentration of carbon in the atmosphere depends on the emissions path chosen (for a discussion of the variety of definitions of cost used in this chapter, see Appendix 7A). The problem of finding a cost-minimizing path for a finite available resource is not new. Hotelling first

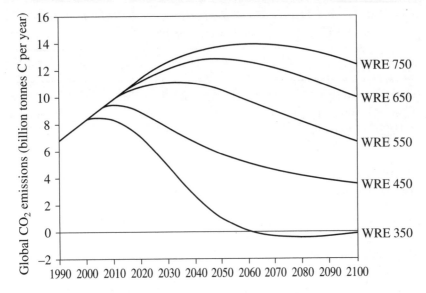

Source: Wigley et al. (1996).

Figure 7.4   Fossil-fuel carbon emissions consistent with alternative CO₂ concentration ceilings

solved it in 1931. Hotelling (1931) showed that the cost-minimizing path was obtained by setting discounted marginal cost equal across time and space. Thus, all parties should face the same value for a tonne of carbon emissions mitigation regardless of where they reside and in which human activity they are engaged, and regardless of when they are alive. Since the cost in one period of time differs from that in another by the interest rate, the value of a tonne of carbon should rise at the rate of interest to eliminate the possibility of lowering present discounted cost by shifting emissions mitigation from one period to the next.

One implication of the Hotelling approach is the gradual transition. Initial deviations of control cases from reference cases begin modestly, but eventually depart substantially. Economic models tend to exhibit a gradual departure from their reference path. This behavior reflects the influence of several factors. First, energy-using and energy-producing capital stock (for example, power plants, buildings and transport) are typically long-lived. The current system was put into place based upon a particular set of expectations about the future. Large emission reductions in the near term will require accelerated replacement. This is apt to be costly. There will be more opportunity for reducing emissions cheaply at the point of capital stock turnover.

*Table 7.2   Characteristics of potential emissions trajectories that limit
            cumulative atmospheric CO_2 emissions*

Ceiling (ppmv)	350	450	550	650	750
Date when emissions are lower in the control case than in the reference case, IPPC IS92a	Today	2007	2013	2018	2023
Maximum global emissions from energy combustion (PgC per year)	6.0	8.0	9.7	11.4	12.5
Year of maximum global emissions	2005	2011	2033	2049	2062
Rate of long-term emissions decline	–	1.10%	0.80%	0.60%	0.50%
Cumulative emissions 1990 to 2100 (PgC)	363	714	1,043	1,239	1,348

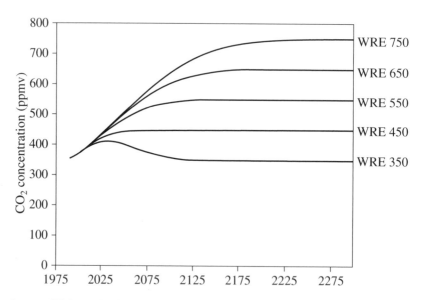

Source: Wigley et al. (1996).

*Figure 7.5 CO_2 concentrations corresponding to carbon emissions paths
            from Figure 7.4*

Second, low-cost opportunities to control emissions are limited on both the supply and demand sides of the energy sector. Deep near-term cuts in carbon emissions therefore come at a substantial cost. With the anticipated improvements in the efficiency of energy supply, transformation and end-use technologies, such reductions should be less expensive in the future.

Third, because of positive returns on capital, future reductions can be made with a smaller commitment of today's resources. For example, assume a net real rate of return on capital of 5 percent per year. Further, suppose that it costs $50 to remove a tonne of carbon – regardless of the year in which the reduction occurs. If we were to remove the tonne today, it would cost $50. Alternatively, we could invest only $19 today to have the resources to remove a tonne of carbon in 2020.

The fact that the least-cost mitigation pathway tends to follow the baseline in the early years is not an argument for inaction. Wigley et al. (1996) note that this is far from the case:

First, all stabilization targets still require future capital stock to be less carbon-intensive than under a business-as-usual scenario. As most energy production and end-use technologies are long-lived, this has implications for current investment decisions. Second, new supply options typically take many years to enter the marketplace. To ensure sufficient quantities of low-cost, low-carbon substitutes in the future requires a sustained commitment to research, development and demonstration today. Third, any 'no regrets' measures for reducing emissions should be adopted immediately. Last, it is clear that one cannot go on deferring emission reductions indefinitely, and that the need for substantial reductions in emissions is sooner the lower the concentration target.

6 TIMING AND ENDOGENOUS TECHNOLOGICAL CHANGE

To the extent that the cost of reducing emissions is lower in the future than at present, the overall cost of stabilizing the CO$_2$ concentration is reduced if emissions mitigation is shifted toward the future. This shift occurs in all models, because all models face the common problem of allocating a fixed cumulative emission over time. For a common reference case this means they also face fixed cumulative emissions mitigation over all time as well. The extent of that shift that minimizes the cost of limiting the concentration of atmospheric CO$_2$ depends, at least in part, on the treatment of technological change. Without technological change, the problem is simple and the results of Hotelling (1931) apply. With endogenous technological change, the problem becomes more complex.

As pointed out by Grubb (1997), there are several key assumptions imbedded in the energy-economy models that influence the shape of the least-cost mitigation pathway. These relate to the determinants of technical change; capital stock turnover and the inertia in the energy system; discounting; and, the carbon cycle.

At present no adequate theory of endogenous technological change exists, which is a major handicap in modifying the basic Hotelling results. The present state of understanding is such that our knowledge is partial and not necessarily fully consistent. No complete theory of technological change exists; however, two elements have been identified and explored in the literature: induced technological change and learning by doing.

Goulder and Mathai (1998) have shown that when endogenous technological change takes the form of induced technological change, it is preferable to concentrate more abatement efforts in the future. The reason is that when society can invest in research and development (R&D) it has the power to order up improved technologies when needed. This effect lowers the costs of future abatement relative to current abatement, making it more cost-effective to place more emphasis on future abatement. Goulder and Schneider (1999), Weyant and Olavson (1999), and Goulder and Mathai (2000) obtain similar results.

This line of research implies that R&D can be an important investment in a strategy to minimize the cost of limiting the concentration of GHGs. When private agents cannot capture the full value of R&D, an R&D market failure exists. This market failure tends to compound the environmental market failure that fails to internalize the costs of climate change. In the presence of an R&D market failure, subsidies for R&D are justified (Goulder and Schneider, 1999; Schneider and Goulder, 1997).

When the channel for technological change is learning by doing, the presence of induced technological change has an ambiguous impact on the optimal timing of abatement. Learning by doing is a happy consequence of those investments, in which learning essentially comes 'free' as a result of cumulative experience with new technologies. Learning by doing typically refers to reductions in production cost, in which learning takes place on the shop floor through day-to-day operations, not in the R&D lab.[8]

Including learning by doing in a model has two, countervailing effects.[9] On the one hand, induced technological change makes future abatement less costly, which suggests emphasizing future abatement efforts. On the other hand, there is an added value to current abatement because such abatement contributes to experience or learning and helps reduce the costs of future abatement.

Work by Ha-Duong et al. (1997), Grubb et al. (1995), Grubb (1997), and Grübler and Messner (1998) has examined the implication of learning by doing and inertia within the context of uncertainty and an imperative to preserve the option of concentration ceilings such as 450 ppmv. They conclude that emissions mitigation can be shifted from the future toward the present under special circumstances. But such circumstances are not necessarily common.

Finally, it should be noted that different emission pathways for achieving a given concentration target not only imply different mitigation costs but also different benefits in terms of environmental impacts averted including the environmental co-benefits of reducing GHG emissions. These benefits are difficult to quantify adequately. Shifting emissions mitigation from the present toward the future means incurring higher near-term rates of climate change, despite the fact that long-term concentrations are identical. Wigley et al. (1996) show that these are at best second-order effects.[10] Whether or not they are important is at present impossible to determine unambiguously.

7   EMPIRICAL RESULTS

Figure 7.6 shows the results of a recent Stanford Energy Modeling Forum project to measure the empirical difference between a gradual transition away from the reference emissions trajectory and an accelerated departure from the near-term, reference emissions path. The Stanford Energy Modeling Forum asked six modeling groups to compute the cost of stabilizing the concentration at 550 ppmv under four alternative conditions – following the WG1 emissions trajectory without trade, following the WG1 emissions trajectory with trade, following the WRE emissions trajectory without trade, and following the WRE emissions trajectory with trade. The WG1 emissions trajectory has more stringent emissions limitations in the near term than does the WRE trajectory.

All modeling groups found that the more modest early emissions limitations of the WRE was associated with lower economic costs than the WG1 trajectory whether the scenario allowed trade in emissions rights or not. Similarly, allowing trade always resulted in lower cost than either emissions trajectory without trade. For each modeling group the lowest cost combination was the WRE trajectory with trade in emissions rights. For each modeling group the most expensive cost combination was the WG1 emissions trajectory without trade in emissions rights. Of course, different modeling groups found quantitatively different costs.

8   THE COST OF EFFICIENT PATHS

One of the most important results to emerge over the last decade is the observation that the minimum cost of stabilizing the concentration of carbon

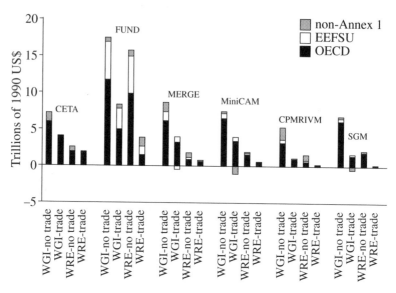

Note: Six global models were used to make the requested calculations. In each instance, two emission pathways to stabilization were examined. The Working Group I or S pathway and the WRE pathway. The former requires a more rapid departure from the baseline than the latter. Costs were calculated assuming no international trade in carbon emission rights and full global trade. Costs are reported for the (i) OECD, (ii) Eastern Europe and the former Soviet Union (EEFSU) and (iii) non-Annex I countries.

Data source: Energy Modeling Forum Study, EMF-14.
Figure source: IPCC (2001, p. 545).

*Figure 7.6   Costs (discounted present value) of stabilizing concentrations
              at 550 ppmv*

in the atmosphere varies inversely with the concentration. Furthermore, costs drop dramatically as the stabilization concentration rises, for example, from 450 ppmv to 550 ppmv. At higher concentrations, reductions in total cost become smaller. Three principal effects are at work:

1. *Cumulative emissions*   Allowable cumulative emissions during the course of the twenty-first century rise sharply as the concentration ceiling rises from 450 ppmv to 550 ppmv. The increase is more modest for increases between higher concentrations.
2. *Technology*   Higher concentrations have a greater share of emissions in the future where technologies have evolved and the marginal cost of emissions mitigation is lower. For example, in the second half of the century, the cost of substituting solar power for coal-generated electricity is lower

because the technology for producing electricity from solar radiation is assumed to have been reduced relative to coal by technology advance.

3. *Discounting*   There is a time value to money and the more stringent cumulative emissions limit for low concentrations means that a greater share of costs occur near the present rather than in the future.

Figure 7.7 shows the results derived from the Energy Modeling Forum. The rapid decline is in part related to the sharp increase in cumulative emissions over the twenty-first century that occurs as the concentration rises from 450 ppmv to 550 ppmv as shown in Table 7.2. These results hold for efficient concentration control regimes. There is no limit to the mischief that can occur under inefficient regimes. Not only will costs be higher, but also the relationship of present discounted cost to concentration need not mirror the pattern of efficient regimes. Manne and Richels (1997) and Edmonds and Wise (1997)

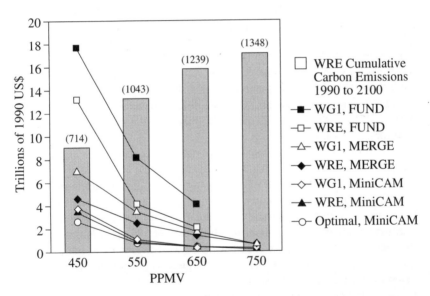

Note: Costs are calculated using three global models. In each instance, costs were calculated based on two emission pathways for achieving the prescribed target: WGI or S and WRE. (WGI = Working Group I, IPCC, 1995; WRI = Wigley–Richels–Edmonds, 1996.) The MiniCam model was also used to identify the least-cost emissions pathway. The bar chart shows cumulative carbon emissions between 1990 and 2100 for WRE scenarios.

Data source: Energy Modeling Forum Study, EMF-14.

Figure 7.7   Costs (discounted present value) of stabilizing CO$_2$ concentrations at 450–750 ppmv

showed that in a regime with early emissions mitigation and without international trade in emissions permits, global costs could remain high until the
concentration rose to 650 ppmv.

There is, of course, no reason to believe that the world will choose to
employ an efficient path for stabilizing the concentration of GHGs. Human
institutions are notoriously imperfect. Prospects are good that costs will be
higher than along an efficient path. Inefficient paths can be considerably
more expensive. For example Richels et al. (1996) showed that if done badly,
costs could be an order of magnitude greater than the minimum.

9   BURDEN SHARING AND THE DISTRIBUTIONAL CONSEQUENCES OF VARIOUS POLICY INSTRUMENTS

Stabilizing the concentration of carbon in the atmosphere requires limiting
cumulative emissions. This implies the need to identify either directly or
indirectly the roles for different parties over time. Because the benefits of
cumulative emissions limitations are distributed independently of the efforts
undertaken by any individual party, the control of cumulative emissions is
subject to the 'global commons problem'. It is in every party's interest to
have all the other parties incur the greatest share of the costs of control and to
bear as little of the burden as possible. After all, the benefits are the same
regardless of individual effort.

The formulation of an international policy response takes place under
particularly difficult circumstances. There are a wide variety of policy interventions that can affect such a limit on cumulative global carbon emissions.
The choice of policy instrument carries with it cost implications and potentially large wealth redistribution consequences that change over time.

Efficient instruments are those that fully exploit all opportunities to reduce
the total cost of achieving a specified limit. This means that at any point in
time all emitters must face the same marginal value for the next tonne of
carbon emissions mitigation. This observation has led to a clear preference
among policymakers for fiscal instruments – that is either taxes or tradeable
emissions permits. The Kyoto Protocol (United Nations, 1997) is at heart a
tradeable emissions permit structure.

Even efficient emissions control systems have non-emission implications
for income and wealth transfers. These implications occur both within and
between nations. Two economic theorems have important implications for
international policy.

The Coase theorem argues that efficiency and equity are in principle sepa-
rable. That is, everyone should value carbon equally and undertake emissions

mitigation up to the same marginal cost. Side-payments can, in principle, be made to address problems that the equal-marginal-cost principle creates in the realms of justice and equity. While humanity may be only one set of side-payments away from a 'fair and just' distribution of the burdens of emissions mitigation, economics cannot prescribe what is in fact 'fair and just'.

The Hotelling principle argues that efficient paths should value carbon at a rate that rises over time at the rate of interest. This principle describes behavior over time. Taken together, the Coase and Hotelling theorems provide strong guidance in shaping the overall architecture of international agreements. But, they leave important elements of the architecture undetermined. Fairness and equity is one problem.

The determination of fairness would be much easier if the ratio of environmental cost to wealth allocation were larger. For example, in an international regime in which all nations participate, following a WRE550 global emissions path, the cost of emissions mitigation in the year 2020 is calculated by Edmonds et al. (1997) to be approximately $11 billion per year, yet the value of emissions to be allocated through international trade in emissions permits is approximately $170 billion per year. It is no wonder then that for many countries, emissions limitation negotiations are primarily viewed as fairness and equity negotiations. The principal issue to be negotiated is the fair and equitable distribution of wealth associated with emissions limitations.

Edmonds et al. (1993) and Rose et al. (1998), among others, have explored the financial implications of alternative emissions allocations. Among the most popular allocation rules examined are: 'grandfathered' emissions, equal per capita emissions, equal emissions per unit GDP, and historical responsibility.

By far the most popular emissions allocation regime in practice is the grandfathered emissions allocation. This emission allocation creates an allocation that is proportional to some historical emission. The value of emissions is given to those who are currently emitting. As a consequence it minimizes the wealth transfer burden to current emitters. In a world in which all parties have access to the same technology options and in which emissions growth is expected to be roughly similar for all parties to the agreement, the emissions mitigation cost distribution is roughly proportional to emissions. Under such a regime there is actually relatively little trade in emissions permits. There is no need as all parties, by assumption, have access to the same technology and therefore share similar marginal abatement cost curves. Trade in emissions permits is used merely to balance accounts, but is not a significant feature of the system. All of this comes undone when time and circumstance cause anticipated emissions across parties to grow in proportions different from the initial allocations. Under such circumstances trade in emissions permits can be very substantial. Regions with small initial allocations, but rapidly growing economies find themselves buying permits from regions with slower-growing economies, but historically high emissions. In climate-change regimes that have been studied, grandfathered emissions allocations eventually imply large eventual transfers of wealth from developing nations to developed nations.

The allocation of emissions permits on another basis, such as population, has very different effects. Equal per capita emissions allocations lead to transfers of wealth from low-population, high-emission economies to high-population, low-emission countries. Edmonds et al. (1993) showed that it is possible for developing countries that have high populations, rapidly growing economies and declining population growth rates, to find themselves shifting from sellers of permits to buyers over a few decades. This creates the potential for a 'dropout' problem in which countries participate for as long as they receive income transfers, but leave the system when these income transfers no longer cover the cost of emissions mitigation.

Similar distributional implications accompany other allocation rules. In addition to the simple rules outlined above, hybrids are also possible. For example, emissions rights could initially be allocated on the basis of historic emissions, but adjusted for economic growth. But the fundamental problem, that valuing carbon implies the creation of a new asset to be allocated, stalks any emissions mitigation negotiation.

10   TRADE

Most global analysis assumes a world in which trade in emissions rights is free and open. This assumption is non-trivial. The cost of meeting an obligation is strongly affected by an open and smoothly operating trading system that leads to the equilibration of marginal costs across all parties. The absence of such mechanisms causes costs to be higher. Virtually all economic analysis supports this finding. Results from the Stanford Energy Modeling Forum exercise, EMF-16 shown in Figure 7.8, are a prime example of the universality of this finding.

This result is echoed in Edmonds et al. 2000; see Table 7.3.[11] Because the underlying assumptions and model structures differ, so do the marginal abatement costs, net costs (GDP costs plus purchases of permits), and effects on GDP. However, all of the models show substantial savings from trade. Marginal abatement costs are generally about 18 to 50 percent lower than without trade, net costs 15 to 75 percent lower, and GDP losses 0 to 2.2 percent lower.

Emissions mitigation activities will almost certainly involve something less than universal participation. That is, some countries may abstain from participation. Remaining outside the agreement, however, does not mean that

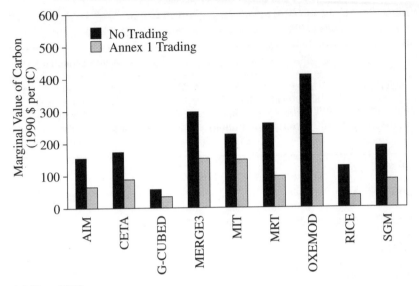

(a) Year 2010

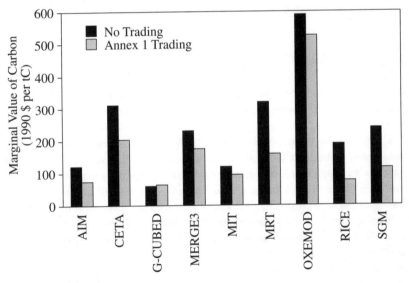

(b) Year 2020

Figure 7.8 Marginal value of carbon

Table 7.3   *Costs in US of achieving carbon emissions 7 percent below 1990 levels (1992 $)*

Model	Year	No trade			Annex I trading		
		Marginal abatement cost ($/ton)	Net abatement cost ($ billion)	GDP %	Marginal abatement cost ($/ ton)	Net mitigation obligation cost ($ billion)	GDP %
EPPA	2010	243	na	−1.5	160	na	−1.5
	2020	134	na	−1.5	109	na	−1.5
MERGE	2010	256	67	−1.0	104	16	−0.5
	2020	229	74	−1.0	172	67	−1.0
IIAM	2010	269	75	−2.1	100	42	−1.3
	2020	288	101	−2.4	160	75	−1.7
NEMS	2010	317	86	−4.2	149	57	−2.0
	2020	278	94	−0.8	129	60	−0.6
SGM	2010	201	59	−0.4	91	50	−0.2
	2020	261	100	−0.4	129	93	−0.2

Note: Net abatement cost, net mitigation cost, and GDP are changes relative to a no-control case. Net mitigation cost is the loss of GDP, plus the cost of permits purchased, minus the value of permits sold.

there are no consequences to the existence of the agreement. The actions of the mitigating nations can have significant consequences for those nations that choose not to participate.[12] For some these consequences will be beneficial, for others, the actions of mitigating nations may impose unforeseen costs.

Studies of the effects of emissions mitigation on non-mitigating nations show some consistent patterns. First, the oil price always falls in the near term. As a consequence, oil exporters receive less for their exports. For some countries this can have profound adverse effects on GDP and welfare. For oil-importing nations, the decline in prices comes as a benefit. If this were the only effect, oil-importing nations would all benefit. However, as Bernstein et al. (1999) point out, the costs borne by nations reducing their emissions imply that they have lower GDPs and therefore their demands for imports decline. For non-oil-exporting, non-emissions-mitigating parties, the effect of emissions mitigation by other nations is ambiguous.

The policy instruments that are employed to effect emissions mitigation within the trading regions can have a significant influence on both regional and the overall costs. This raises the important question of the interface between domestic and international policy instruments. Hahn and Stavins

(1999) and Stavins (1997) have argued that unless domestic and international policy regimes are compatible, inefficiencies will inevitably develop in implementing an international emissions limitation regime. For example, if the international protocol adopts a cap-and-trade instrument, domestic policies that employ regulatory or tax instruments are unlikely to result in sales and purchases that equate marginal costs across nations and activities. Real-world emissions limitations will almost inevitably be 'second best'. The existence of these potential impediments limits the extent to which gains to emissions permit trading can be captured in fact.

11 DOMESTIC IMPLEMENTATION OF MEASURES TO LIMIT EMISSIONS

Even within the context of a domestic emissions limitation regime there are a wide variety of measures that can be undertaken to limit emissions. These measures include taxes, domestic emissions trading, technical standards, voluntary agreements, and subsidies for the production and consumption of energy.

Taxes are one of the most commonly analyzed policy instruments. Most of the researchers using economic models reduce emissions through the introduction of a tax. The cost of the tax is measured in terms of lost welfare or some proxy for welfare such as GDP. This welfare loss is the consequence of the fact that marginal costs faced by producers and consumers are no longer the same as the prices faced by producers and consumers. In an economy where there are already taxes creating distortions, the potential exists for a reconfiguration of the tax system to result not in reductions in welfare, but increases in welfare.

There has been considerable interest in the question of whether or not existing distortions in real-world economies are of sufficient magnitude to afford an opportunity for revenue-neutral carbon taxes to be employed to improve overall economic efficiency. Of particular interest have been pre-existing taxes on income, payroll, and sales. The 'double dividend' therefore, refers to a tax swap – carbon tax for income, payroll or sales – that could both (i) improve the environment and (ii) reduce market distortions and simultaneously improve economic performance. (The same potential opportunity exists if nationally auctioned permits are used.) Goulder (1995a) defines two different degrees of the double dividend, 'weak' and 'strong'. A strong double dividend occurs when the reduction in economic distortions accompanying the revenue-neutral tax swap are so great as to eclipse the entire cost of the carbon tax. The former occurs when the offset is only partial.

Several numerical studies, including Goulder (1995b) and Jorgenson and Wilcoxen (1993), confirm that the gross costs of meeting given abatement targets can be significantly reduced by using the revenue of carbon taxes to finance cuts in the existing payroll taxes, as compared with the situation where the revenues are returned to the economy in a lump-sum fashion. Other studies undertaken within the context of the Energy Modeling Forum EMF-16 failed to report a double dividend. Studies of European economies tend to find double dividends more frequently than studies of the US economy. The IPCC explains 'differences between results concerning the US and European Economies by the fact that labour taxes represent one of the most important sources of distortion in the European countries given the type of regulation of the labour market prevailing in these countries' (IPCC, 2001, Third Assessment Report, Chapter 8).

Obtaining the benefits of even a 'strong' double dividend may be easier in theory than practice. The execution of the double dividend assumes the existence of strong political will and commitment to improve economic performance and the political fortitude to forgo the opportunity to increase government revenues. In fact, there is no guarantee that the same process that created a system sufficiently inefficient that a double dividend was possible, would not create a revised tax system even less efficient than the one it replaced. Second, even if the double dividend was paid in the first period, there is no way to guarantee that the process will not change in the future and devolve toward its former inefficient state.

12   'NO REGRETS'

There are always opportunities to reduce emissions and improve economic welfare and these opportunities are enormous. These opportunities exist because technology, knowledge, information, and institutions do not stand still. Improvements in technology imply that as new investments occur or capital stocks are replaced, the system can be improved.

Reference cases typically include a great deal of energy technology improvement. Edmonds (1999) calculated the effect on global carbon emissions of fixed technology for a commonly cited reference case, IS92a (Leggett et al., 1992) and an emissions path consistent with stabilizing the concentration of CO_2 in the atmosphere at 550 ppmv (Wigley et al., 1996). The gap between fixed technology emissions and the emissions path needed to stabilize concentrations widens rapidly with time because the underlying population and economic growth implies expanding demands for energy services, as shown in Figure 7.9.

The difference between the IS92a (1990 technology) emissions trajectory and the IS92a emissions trajectory is due entirely to differences in assumed technology opportunities.[13] These technology opportunities occur in the model

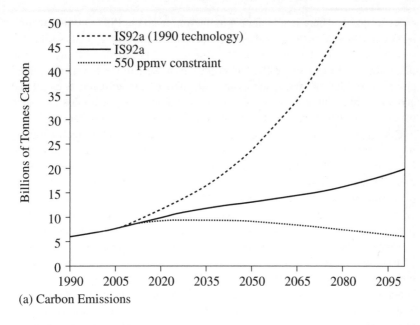

(a) Carbon Emissions

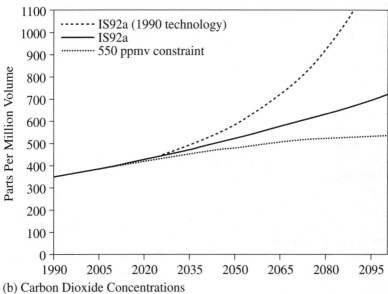

(b) Carbon Dioxide Concentrations

Source: Battelle (2000).

Figure 7.9   The future with and without technological change

by assumption. There is no net cost in moving from the IS92a (1990 technol-ogy) emissions trajectory to the IS92a emissions trajectory. And, while it is possible to debate the ability of the system, in the absence of any climate imperative to in fact make the technology transformations that are assumed possible in IS92a,[14] those technological changes are affected because the economy takes advantage of advancing technology opportunities. As such these improvements can be thought of as no-cost or 'no regrets' actions.

One question that arises in the literature is, 'Can even more technological improvement be obtained without cost?'. This question has been explored by a literature that is commonly referred to as the 'bottom-up' literature. In contrast to the economic-based approach to analysis that anchors itself in economic behavior as well as theory, the bottom-up literature is anchored in engineering and technology. The approach taken in the bottom-up literature is to meet energy service demands at least cost using all available technology. In general, the bottom-up literature shows that opportunities exist to reduce emissions relative to a fixed technology reference case that are in excess of those exhibited in economic models. The results from this literature for economically attractive opportunities are summarized in Figure 7.10. There is a sharp divide between the results from the bottom-up literature and the standard economic literature, the former showing emissions mitigation op-portunities available at lower cost than the latter.

Recent efforts have gone into trying to understand how this is possible. EMF-13 brought together members of the bottom-up community to under-take analysis under standard conditions. In general differences between the cost-effective emissions mitigation opportunities shown in bottom-up studies and those shown in economic models have their roots in a small number of critical analytical differences.

The first, and perhaps most important difference is the internal rate of return required for an investment to be undertaken. Bottom-up models typi-cally employ a 'social' or risk-free discount rate. Economic models employ internal rates of return consistent with *ex post* behavior of firms, and these are much higher. The lower internal rate of return employed in the bottom-up analyses leads to higher rates of deployment of energy-efficient technologies. A second difference between the top-down and bottom-up approaches is the treatment of non-climate externalities. Bottom-up studies frequently include the social benefits of reduced emissions of non-greenhouse gases. These additional benefits expand deployment of energy-efficient technologies still further. Differences in results between bottom-up and top-down economic models reflect the existence of market failures. In fact, the existence of market failures is well known in the economic literature. What are less clear are the policy implications that flow from the existence of such market failures.

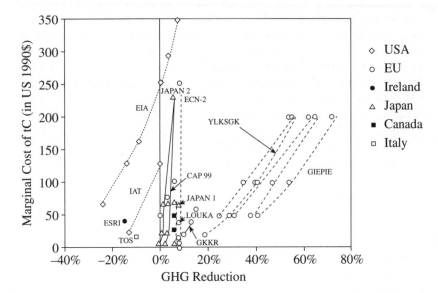

Note: Negative GHG reduction implies an increase of emissions from 1990 level. This increase implies a positive marginal cost when it corresponds to a lower increase than would have occurred in the absence of climate policy.

Source: IPCC (2001, p. 508).

Figure 7.10   *Analyses of carbon emissions mitigation opportunities from bottom-up studies*

Furthermore, correction of the market failures could result in substantially less emissions mitigation than bottom-up analysis calculates. The reason is that undercapitalization is a pervasive market failure. That is, it occurs for all investment opportunities, not just energy-technology investment opportunities. If all investments that were attractive using the social discount rate were taken up, then the demand for loanable funds at every interest rate would increase dramatically. Since savings behavior is unchanged, the total investment in the economy can rise only if the interest rate is bid up and entices savers to provide more resources to the economy. This higher interest rate will in turn choke off some of the investments that are assumed in the bottom-up analyses.

Even if we assume that this market failure can be corrected, we are still left with the problem that this is a one-time opportunity. Once the economy shifts to a more efficient allocation of resources, there are no more static efficiency gains to be had. The rate of improvement in overall emissions intensity of the economy reverts to the rate of overall technological change.

Finally, it is worth pointing out that while the qualitative differences between top-down and bottom-up approaches are substantial, quantitative differences are not always as great as might be expected. The United States Department of Energy (1997) shows that US emissions could be returned to 1990 levels in the year 2010 at a marginal cost of approximately $100 per tonne carbon (though $50 per tonne carbon would be recovered in ancillary benefits). The Inter-laboratory Working Group (2000) obtained similar results.

How large, important, and amenable to correction the bottom-up technology gap turns out to be remains a matter for future research to illuminate.

13   TECHNOLOGY AND EFFICIENT PATHS

While bottom-up analysis has illuminated the potentially positive role of accelerated technology deployment, that opportunity harvests the fruits of previous investments in technology development. As Figure 7.9 shows, the continued development and deployment of new and better technologies is assumed to provide for substantial reductions in CO_2 emission relative to a fixed-technology alternative.

Energy technologies with low and no GHG emissions are favored relative to others in any regime that stabilizes the concentration of GHGs in the atmosphere. Energy-economy models generally include explicit representations of such technologies as hydro, wind, solar, nuclear, natural gas, and energy conservation. Other technologies, such as fuel cells, hydrogen, commercial biomass, carbon sequestration in terrestrial ecosystems, and carbon capture and disposal in geologic repositories present challenges to modelers. The latter set of technologies is not part of the historical experience and therefore introduces a degree of uncertainty into the analysis that is unavoidable. On the other hand, these technologies hold the potential for massive deployment under appropriate circumstances. As a group they provide a mechanism by which fossil fuels can continue to be employed in the delivery of energy services to the economy.

Land-use Emissions, Soils and Commercial Biomass

GHGs are emitted in the use of land as well as in the use of fossil fuels. Land-use change is associated with the release of carbon through net reductions in the stock of terrestrial biomass. Whereas approximately 6.0 billion tonnes of carbon per year were released in the use of fossil fuels in 1990, about 1.3 billion tonnes of carbon per year were estimated to have been released through land-use changes, primarily deforestation, but also through agricultural practices that release soil carbon. In comparison with the thousands of billions of tonnes of carbon estimated to be contained in various fossil-fuel resource bases, terrestrial systems contain significantly less. All above-ground biomass is estimated to contain approximately 550 PgC, while soils are estimated to contain about 1200 PgC.

In the long term, most models anticipate that the forces driving deforestation, such as population growth and rising demands for food, that cannot be offset by increases in agricultural productivity, will subside. Most forecasts of net land-use emissions tend toward zero by the end of the twenty-first century, and in some instances emissions become negative as reforestation dominates (IPCC, 1995; IPCC, 2000).

Several technologies exist that can be employed to remove carbon from the air, in effect creating a negative emission. Carbon can be sequestered in forests or in agricultural soils. Over the course of the past two centuries IPCC (1996) estimates that between 40 and 80 PgC were released into the atmosphere from soil tillage practices. The return of previously lost carbon to vegetation and soils in agricultural lands may have value as part of a least-cost strategy for stabilizing atmospheric concentrations of GHGs. But, as Cole et al. (1996, p. 765) point out in the Second Assessment of the IPCC (1996), 'the world's farmers, ranchers and pastoralists will not volunteer to implement practices proposed to mitigate greenhouse-forced climate change. This will happen only if the producer is convinced that profitability will improve if these practices are implemented.'

Two levels of economic analysis are relevant. On a local scale, we must understand the economic incentives facing land managers, and how management behavior might change if a value is placed on the amount of carbon stored. On a global scale, sequestering carbon in plants and soils will be compared to other options for reducing net GHG emissions on the basis of cost. The economic potential to store carbon in plants and soils depends on the availability of other options and their relative costs. It is important to note that carbon sequestration in terrestrial ecosystems is not necessarily permanent. For direct emissions reduction we can imagine a market in carbon emissions rights priced in dollars per tonne. But the valuation of carbon stored in the biosphere would likely have a time element, for example dollars per tonne of carbon sequestered and held for some period of time. Even temporary storage of carbon in the terrestrial ecosystem can have value as a way to buy time for the development of energy technologies and to limit early retirement of capital during the initial years of a carbon policy.

Many Annex I nations are in the process of reforesting, and therefore have net accumulation of carbon that reduces net anthropogenic emissions. The economic implications of alternative treatments of land-use change emissions are large and their treatment was one of the most hotly debated issues in the

Kyoto Protocol negotiations. The size and treatment of changes in regional carbon stocks can have a substantial impact on regional costs of meeting a national emissions limitation goal in a budget period. However, this is a short-term consideration. In the long term, land-use emissions mitigation potential is limited. Eventually all forestry programs approach steady-state carbon-to-land ratios, though these ratios could change with climate change. If a given plot of land is to continue to provide carbon uptake services, the existing biomass must be removed, but the associated carbon must be isolated from the atmosphere. Since the biomass resources can be used to replace fossil fuels, forestry programs can mature into biomass energy programs.

Commercial biomass production is also limited. At present the technology is immature. It suffers from the disadvantage that harvested energy must be employed to move the crop, with its high water content, from the field to a central processing facility. Further, land is scarce and has multiple uses in addition to the production of commercial biomass fuels including crops, pasture, forestry, urban, and parks and unmanaged systems.

The present heated debate over soil carbon can be understood as primarily a debate over two issues, the initial emissions allocation (accounting plays a significant role in determining initial emissions and therefore emissions mitigation obligations) and real, near-term options for carbon removal. Not that these technologies are not valuable – Edmonds et al. (1999) estimate the value to range from tens of billions of present discounted US dollars to hundreds of billions of present discounted US dollars; see Figure 7.11. But, there are legitimate issues that exist which surround the practical applications of capturing that potential. Monitoring and verification loom large as does intertemporal responsibility and accountability.

Carbon Capture in Commercial Energy Systems and Geologic Disposal

CO_2 can be captured in various ways – after combustion, or before combustion during a transformation of the fuel, or directly from the atmosphere by, for example, enhancing natural sinks for carbon as discussed above. The main carbon capture and disposal technology categories are listed in Table 7.4.

If carbon is to be captured on a large scale, numerous issues need to be addressed including the need for transport and temporary storage facilities. The nature of the temporary facilities will depend, at least in part, on the technologies being employed to remove the CO_2 and the nature of the long-term storage technologies.

Using CO_2 to produce desirable byproducts may offset some or all of the cost of capture and storage. For example, CO_2 can be used to produce coalbed methane while simultaneously storing the CO_2 in the coal.[15] Similarly, CO_2 is

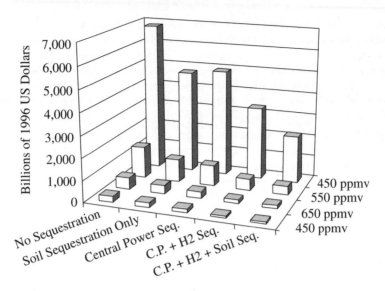

Notes:
CP = Carbon capture and sequestration from fossil fuels used to generate electric power.
H2 Seq. = Fossil fuels used as feedstocks for hydrogen production with carbon capture and sequestration.

Source: Battelle (2000).

Figure 7.11   *Cost of stabilizing CO₂ concentrations with and without carbon capture and sequestration technologies (billions of 1990 US$)*

currently extracted and shipped via pipeline for use in enhanced oil recovery. It would then be a product with a positive economic value, but while the potential for positive externalities exists, this potential is limited. If CO₂ were captured at scale, the quantities that would be available on the market would drive the sale price of a ton negative.

Carbon capture and disposal technologies could also be used to enable the transition to hydrogen-based transport and/or distributed energy systems. For example, the decarbonization of natural gas to produce hydrogen would be competitive with large-scale use of many of the renewable energy sources (Audus et al., 1996); storage of the CO₂ would avoid most of the GHG emissions.

System costs include the cost of capture (that is, capital costs, efficiency loss, operation and maintenance), the cost of transport and temporary storage, the cost of sequestration, and the costs of monitoring and verification.

Table 7.4   Carbon capture and disposal technology options

CO₂ capture	CO₂ storage	Carbon sequestration
From the energy system Central plant such as power plant, refineries, etc.	*Geological storage* • Depleted oil or gas fields • Deep saline reservoirs • Unminable coal seams • Basalt formations	*Terrestrial carbon capture and sequestration* • Soils • Trees
In production of energy carriers for example, hydrogen	*Ocean storage* • Mid-depth dispersion • Deep lake • Hydrates	*Ocean carbon capture and sequestration* • Fertilization
	As a solid • Carbon • Solid CO₂ • As a mineral carbonate	*Direct recovery from the atmosphere*

The International Energy Agency's Greenhouse Gas R&D Program recently re-examined the cost of capturing CO_2 from power plant and other sources. Typical cost of electricity and the cost of avoided CO_2 emissions with state of the art plant are illustrated in Table 7.5 (Audus, 2000) for natural gas costing $2 per gigajoule (GJ) and coal at $1.5 per GJ, at a 10 percent discount rate; these figures include compression of CO_2 to 110 bar for transmission.

Edmonds et al. (1999) produced estimates of the cost of introducing carbon capture and disposal options for power generation and hydrogen production under a global limit to the concentration of atmospheric CO_2. This study found that in a carbon control regime, carbon capture and disposal technologies are cost-competitive with other modes of power generation. Geologic reservoirs appear to be available in quantities that would be comparable to potential emissions during the twenty-first century on a global scale, but their geographic distribution and integrity remains an issue for further research. Table 7.6 gives the range of estimates of available capacity.

In contrast, Table 7.7 shows cumulative carbon capture and geologic disposal during the twenty-first century for various CO_2 concentrations and against two alternative reference energy system backgrounds, OGF[16] and CBF.[17] These values are well within the range of the available geological reservoirs. But disposal reservoir requirements could be greater for some technology and policy regimes (Edmonds and Wise, 1998) – up to twice the values presented in Table 7.7.[18]

It is worth noting that the combination of commercial biomass with carbon capture and geologic disposal technologies opens the door for negative emis-

Table 7.5 Costs and efficiency of CO_2 capture with natural gas and coal-fired plant

Process	Efficiency (%)	Specific investment ($/kW)	Cost of electricity (c/kWh)	CO_2 emission (g/kWh)	Cost of CO_2 avoided ($/t$CO_2$)
Gas combined cycle					
● No CO_2 capture	56	410	2.2	370	Reference
● Post-combustion capture	47	790	3.2	61	32
● Pre-combustion capture	48	910	3.4	65	39
Pulverized coal fuel					
● No CO_2 capture	46	1020	3.7	722	Reference
● Post-combustion capture	33	1860	6.4	148	47
IGCC					
● No CO_2 capture	46	1470	4.8	710	Reference
● Pre-combustion capture	38	2200	6.9	134	37

Source: Edmonds, Freund and Dooley (2001).

171

Table 7.6   Estimates of global capacity of storage reservoirs

Carbon storage reservoir	Range (PgC)
Deep ocean	1,391–27,000
Deep saline reservoirs	87–2,727
Depleted gas reservoirs	136–300
Depleted oil reservoirs	41–191
Unminable coal seams	>20

Sources: Herzog et al. (1997); Freund and Ormerod (1997).

Table 7.7   Cumulative carbon capture (PgC) from 2000 to 2095 for various CO$_2$ concentration ceilings

Reference case	450 ppmv	550 ppmv	650 ppmv	750 ppmv
OGF	374	281	221	195
CBF	279	203	168	157

sion energy use. Because the carbon contained in commercial biomass fuels was originally removed by the plant from the atmosphere, it is generally considered to be carbon neutral. That is, the amount of carbon released when the crop is oxidized to release its energy is exactly offset by the carbon uptake by the plant during growth. If that carbon were captured rather than released and permanently removed from the atmosphere, the use of commercial biomass would in effect 'scrub' the atmosphere. Of course, it is also technically possible to directly scrub the atmosphere as discussed by Lackner et al. (1999).

In the long term, it may be necessary to remove carbon in the form of a solid, a potentially more expensive proposition, but technically feasible. Steinberg and Grohse (1989) and Steinberg (1991) discuss technologies that remove carbon in the form of elemental carbon. Elemental carbon could be stored in coalmines without capacity problems if the original source of the carbon were coal.

Butt et al. (1998), Goff and Lackner (1998), Lackner et al. (1995, 1997a,b,c, and 1999) discuss taking a stream of CO$_2$ and reacting it to calcium carbonate. The general approach is sufficiently flexible that it could be used either with a waste gas stream, or applied to open air scrubbing. The approach is more expensive than capturing and disposing of CO$_2$ as a gas, because the first step in the process is capturing CO$_2$ as a gas. Exactly how much more expensive than capture and disposal of CO$_2$ as a gas remains for future research to determine. On the other hand, the final product is not subject to escape to the atmosphere, and could potentially be employed as a bulk material, for example, to dike vulnerable coastal zones subject to sea-level rise.

Hydrogen and Fuel Cells

Fuel cells can produce electricity using a variety of fuel inputs at a wide range of scales. The transportation sector is a major source of CO$_2$ emissions that is characterized by high capital costs and low energy costs for delivering energy services. As a consequence, with the present suite of technologies, transportation energy demand is relatively price insensitive to carbon taxes. Like batteries, fuel cells using hydrogen as their fuel make it possible to provide energy services without releasing CO$_2$ into the atmosphere. Technical prospects for fuel cells look promising, but require a low-cost source of hydrogen. Fossil fuels, particularly natural gas, are the least expensive sources of hydrogen presently available (Edmonds et al., 2000; Kinzey et al., 1998). Combined with carbon capture and geologic sequestration technologies, fuel cells could be a major factor in a carbon control regime. The technology must overcome present technical and economic obstacles. These include their present high cost, the need for a viable, cost-effective technology for carbon capture and geologic disposal, and the need for a completely new infrastructure for the large-scale refining of hydrogen, its storage and distribution.

The Value of Carbon Capture and Disposal Technology

It is clear from the calculations presented in Edmonds et al. (1997) shown in Figure 7.11 that there is exceptional value in the successful development and deployment of these technologies in a regime to limit CO$_2$ concentrations. The difference in cost between regimes that have a full suite of carbon capture and disposal and hydrogen using technologies available and a regime that has none is a factor of three or more in overall cost. If successful these technologies could allow fossil fuels to continue to provide the core of the global energy services, yet provide a mechanism by which cumulative carbon emissions could be limited.

What is less clear is the path by which these technologies would come into common practice. Further, the ability of these technologies to participate in programs to control net carbon emissions to the atmosphere will be limited without adequate associated programs for monitoring and verification. In addition, local transport, storage, and health and safety issues must be addressed.

Virtually all storage systems will require monitoring. If CO_2 storage is to be an important technology for emission mitigation, then significant quantities of carbon can be expected to accumulate. After 50 or more years, leakage rates of only 1 percent per year could amount to more than a billion tonnes of carbon released to the atmosphere annually. This in turn could be a significant share of the global annual emissions budget. While there is currently no reason to believe that any significant quantities of CO_2 would be released to the atmosphere, monitoring will be important if the technology is to be deployed.

There Is No 'Silver Bullet'

While some technologies, such as for example, carbon capture and disposal show great promise for controlling the cost of limiting cumulative emissions of carbon to the atmosphere, no single technology, or subset of technologies will ultimately be adequate everywhere, for all applications, over all time. The inability of humans to foresee the development of future science and engineering breakthroughs, the variety of regional technology needs and institutions, and the changing global and regional circumstances argues for a portfolio of technologies. There is a role for renewable energy supplies, nuclear and fusion power, improved fossil-fuel performance, conservation, fuel cells and hydrogen systems, as well as carbon capture and disposal in a cost-minimizing technology portfolio. Many of these technologies either are not presently deployed at scale but have the potential to evolve dramatically. Such changes to the global energy system will require investments in energy R&D ranging from basic science, such as for example the biological sciences and biotechnology, to technology enhancements that will enable technology to deploy widely. There is a role for both the public and private sectors in developing and deploying these technologies.

14   UNCERTAINTY AND RISK MANAGEMENT

While an analytical model can develop some hypothetical emissions control trajectory assuming perfect knowledge for a 100-year time-scale, the real world cannot. Knowledge is continually being acquired, and decisions taken are continually being revised. There is no real-world policy autopilot. In fact, in the real world, policy development must proceed under a paradigm of 'act then learn then act again'. The relevant question is not 'what is the best course of action for the next 100 years' but rather 'what is the best course for the near-term given the long-term objective, as we currently understand it?'.

The problem of how best to analyze the problem of decision making under uncertainty has vexed many researchers. One approach is to frame the problem of selecting a path over a period of time as a situation in which there are a range of concentration ceilings, any of which could be chosen, but with different *a priori* probabilities. While this approach is appealing on the surface, when combined with the irreversibility of the carbon accumulation assumption, the result of the analysis depends completely on an interaction between the length of time until the true ceiling is revealed and the rate at which carbon is accumulating. If the correct value is not known for some time and the model must always preserve the option to remain below the 'correct' ceiling, pushing the time at which the correct ceiling is known into the future means that regardless of how low the probability that the lowest ceiling will be chosen, the model must preserve that option and will increasingly gravitate toward the lowest emission trajectory the further in time the true ceiling is revealed.

A more fruitful approach is to employ a decision tree structure in a cost–benefit analysis. This was the approach taken by seven models participating in an EMF exercise on climate-change decision making under uncertainty (Manne, 1995). The EMF study assumed that uncertainty would not be resolved until 2020. The study focused on a hedging strategy for a low-probability, high-consequence scenario. Two parameters were varied: the mean temperature sensitivity factor and the cost of damages associated with climate change. The unfavorable high-consequence scenario was defined as the top 5 percent of each of these two distributions. Two surveys of expert opinion were used for choosing the distribution of these variables (Morgan and Keith (1995) for climate sensitivity, and Nordhaus (1994) for warming damages).

Seven modeling groups participated. Three cases were examined. The first case assumed that the high-consequence event occurs with certainty. In that case models immediately begin to reduce emissions. The second or reference case assumed that the high-consequence did not occur. In this case emissions grew monotonically. The third case was the one in which the future state of the world is unclear until 2020. In 2020 the high-consequence is revealed to either occur, or not, with certainty. Only the relative probabilities of the two outcomes are known before 2020. The high-consequence nature of the undesirable outcome must be balanced against its low, 0.25 percent, probability of occurrence. The research question is, what is the optimum hedging strategy? How much emissions mitigation should be undertaken prior to 2020? On the one hand it could be costly to follow the reference case too closely if in 2020 a bad outcome was revealed and the economy would have to make rapid changes. On the other hand, it could also be costly to depart too far from the reference case because in the more likely event that the bad outcome did not eventuate, extra emissions mitigation would have economic costs that were lost forever.

The seven modeling groups (see IPCC (2001, p. 613) and Figure 10.2) reported that the optimal hedging strategy in the face of a high-consequence, but low-probability outcome, entailed only very modest departures from the reference emissions path prior to the year 2020 when the true state of the world was hypothesized to be revealed. This research finding was qualitatively reproduced by seven models. Of course, the nature of the result will be determined by the specific situation under consideration, and as Peck and Teisberg (1993a, b) demonstrated, by the absence or existence of non-linear impacts and the date at which they could be expected to occur.

15   SUMMARY AND CONCLUSIONS

The literature on the cost of stabilizing the concentration of CO_2 is already rich. A substantial body of research has already been conducted that sheds light on the issue. Much of this work was facilitated, coordinated, and motivated by the Stanford Energy Modeling Forum.

The problem of stabilizing the concentration of CO_2 is fundamentally different from the problem of stabilizing the concentration of a conventional pollutant or even other non-CO_2 GHGs. Anthropogenic emissions of carbon from the terrestrial biosphere and the fossil-fuel resource reservoirs are partitioned between the atmosphere and ocean reservoirs. Over very long periods of time, 1,000 years, the distribution is stable. As a consequence, a fraction of any net anthropogenic emission is permanently committed to the atmosphere and in the very long term, 1,000 years, net anthropogenic emissions must cease if atmospheric CO_2 concentrations are to be stabilized. Cumulative net anthropogenic emissions govern very long-term concentrations, while transient processes determine concentrations over shorter periods.

All anthropogenic emissions pathways that stabilize the concentration of atmospheric CO_2 at levels up to 750 ppmv imply dramatic changes in the global energy system over the course of the twenty-first century. During that period, global net emissions of carbon to the atmosphere must both peak and then decline.

The cost of bringing such a transition to pass depends on many factors, all of which are difficult to predict. These include the way the world energy system would unfold in the absence of concern about climate – itself governed by a wide array of factors such as population growth and economic productivity around the world – and the evolution of energy technologies. The range of plausible futures that can be constructed looking forward across the next century encompasses scenarios that vary from those in which emissions rise to 50 billion tonnes of carbon per year or more to those in which emissions decline to zero independent of any concerns for climate change. Costs also depend on the emissions control policies and institutions put into effect around the world as well as the technology options available to provide the energy services anticipated in the century ahead.

Most cases that have examined the lowest cost to society of stabilizing the concentration of CO_2 in the atmosphere find that it is associated with a value of carbon that rises overtime. In the simplest 'Hotelling' model it rises at the rate of interest so as to equate the present discounted cost of reducing the last tonne of carbon everywhere and over all time – a feat accomplished more easily in models than in the real world. Alternatively stated, this means that everyone must value carbon equally regardless of where they live and the value of that tonne must rise over time at the rate of interest. Of course, the initial value of the global tax will be higher the smaller the concentration. The physical implication is a gradual transition. That is one that begins with a slight departure from present trends and gradually moves toward a dramatically different future.

There are four reasons why a gradual transition reduces costs. A gradual transition:

- minimizes premature retirement of capital stocks,
- makes most emissions reductions in the future when technology has lowered costs,
- takes advantage of the positive marginal value of capital, and
- takes advantage of a greater cumulative emissions allowance during the first 100 years.

Regardless of whether the value at which emissions are to be stabilized is 350 ppmv or 750 ppmv (pre-industrial values being near 275 ppmv), global emissions in the twenty-first century must peak and then begin a long-term decline toward zero. Dates at which the gradual transition begins are near at hand. For a concentration of 550 ppmv the date at which the gradual transition begins is 2013 and the date at which global carbon emissions peak is 2033.

Under special circumstances the gradual transition rule may be violated. That is, if a dramatic, and costly, early reduction in emissions stimulates technological change that lowers costs so fast that it more than compensates for other inefficiencies such as inefficiencies in the time value of money, premature retirement of capital stock, and the tighter century-scale cumulative emissions constraint. Much of the literature suggests that parameter values needed to effect this result are not likely to be obtained in fact.

Both the cost and effectiveness of policies to limit emissions of GHGs are uncertain. This uncertainty is often used as either a reason to take dramatic action immediately (the precautionary principle) or a reason to take no action at all (an alternative application of the same precautionary principle). In fact, tools have been developed to manage risk. Work undertaken to date suggests that when properly framed, the appropriate strategy of emissions mitigation is one of gradual transition from a reference case.

One of the most important findings of recent work is the result that the cost of stabilizing the concentration of CO_2 declines very rapidly as the concentration rises from 450 ppmv to 550 ppmv.

All of the strategic analysis that has been published to date is constructed on the assumption that the world is monolithic. All nations act together and are coordinated. There may be strong real-world impediments to this occurring. One problem is that in a program that allocates emissions rights between countries there is more at stake in the allocation of emissions rights than there is in solving the climate problem. That is, the value of the emissions rights being distributed among nations is significantly larger than the expected value of benefits from the controlling climate change. As a consequence, negotiations concerning the problem of defining a 'fair and equitable' allocation of allowances may be protracted, and it will be a very long time before any emissions mitigation occurs.

Most of the analysis to date has focused on the minimum possible cost. These analyses are helpful in that there is a unique solution to the problem. There is only one least-cost strategy and there are an infinite number of ways and degrees in which to be inefficient. Unfortunately, we cannot know *a priori* which of the multitude of inefficient mechanisms will ultimately be deployed. But, there is every likelihood that realized costs of achieving any particular concentration target will be higher, and potentially very much higher, than least-cost.

On the other hand, technology is one of the largest levers available to control costs, regardless of the mechanism employed to create the credible commitment to limit cumulative global carbon emissions. Many of the technologies that could play a large future role in limiting cumulative carbon emissions are minor elements in the present energy system. There is no reason to believe that any single technology will be able to control the cost of limiting cumulative global carbon emissions adequately. Rather, a portfolio of technologies including renewable energy supplies, nuclear and fusion power, improved fossil-fuel performance, conservation, fuel cells and hydrogen systems, as well as carbon capture and sequestration will all be needed to address the variety of technology needs across the world's regions and over time.

NOTES

* This research was made possible in part, by funding from the Integrated Assessment program, Biological and Environmental Research (BER), U.S. Department of Energy, under contract DE-AC06-07RLO1830, and by support from the Integrated Assessment program at EPRI. In addition, the authors are grateful to John Clarke, Jim Griffin, Richard Richels and John Weyant, for comments on earlier versions of this manuscript.

  This chapter is based on a report, prepared by Battelle Memorial Institute (Battelle) as an account of sponsored research activities. Neither Client nor Battelle nor any person acting on behalf of either: MAKES ANY WARRANTY OR REPRESENTATION, EXPRESS OR IMPLIED, with respect to the accuracy, completeness, or usefulness of the information contained in this report, or that the use of any information, apparatus, process, or composition disclosed in this report may not infringe privately owned rights; or assumes any liabilities with respect to the use of, or for damages resulting from the use of, any information, apparatus, process, or composition disclosed in this report. Reference herein to any specific commercial product, process, or service by trade name, trademark, manufacturer, or otherwise, does not necessarily constitute or imply its endorsement, recommendation, or favoring by Battelle. The views and opinions of authors expressed herein do not necessarily state or reflect those of Battelle.

1. India, Germany, United Kingdom, Ukraine, Canada, Italy, South Korea, Mexico, and France.

2. The Oak Ridge National Laboratory Carbon Dioxide Information Analysis Center (CDIAC), http://cdiac.esd.ornl.gov/ftp/ndp030/nation97.ems: G. Marland, T.A. Boden, and R.J. Andres, 2000, 'Global, Regional, and National CO₂ Emissions', in Trends: A Compendium of Data on Global Change. Carbon Dioxide Information Analysis Center, Oak Ridge National Laboratory, US Department of Energy, Oak Ridge, TN, USA.

3. CO_2 is the most important greenhouse gas released in quantity by humans. It is has the largest influence of present and anticipated future climate of any greenhouse-related gas released by humans. Its principal sources of emission are the combustion of fossil fuels (80 percent), cement manufacture (1 percent), and land-use emissions such as deforestation. Land-use emissions rates are estimated to be 1.7 billion metric tons of carbon per year in the 1990s, but this number is highly uncertain ranging from 0.6 to 2.5 billion metric tons of carbon per year in the 1990s (Technical Summary of the Working Group 1 report of the Intergovernmental Panel on Climate Change, taken from, http://www.meto.govt.uk/sec5/CR_div/ipcc/wg1/WGI-TS.pdf).

4. A petagram is 10^{15} grams or 1 billion metric tons. A petagram of carbon (PgC) is therefore a billion metric tons of carbon.

5. Some indirect release of greenhouse gases may be associated with these technologies, though generally not in their operation. For example, CH_4 may be released in the process of creating a hydroelectric facility and carbon may be released in the manufacture of cement used in the construction of nuclear power reactors.

6. Most research has focused on removing carbon in the form of CO_2. CO_2 could be stored in sites that include depleted oil and gas wells, coal seams, or deep brine reservoirs. Storing the carbon in the oceans has also been suggested and Japanese researchers have explored this option. If the carbon is removed as a solid, either as carbon black or as calcium carbonate, other sites such as mines become options.

7. See, for example, IPCC (1996) and IPCC (2000), though the latter gives only emissions and cumulative emissions calculations.

8. Arrow (1962) first emphasized this in his article 'The economic implications of learning by doing'. Nakićenović (1996) discusses the importance of learning by doing in energy technology, and Messner (1995) endogenizes the learning process in energy models. The learning-by-doing component of change is significant, too. Kline and Rosenberg (1986) discuss industry studies that indicate that learning-by-doing type improvements to processes in some cases contribute more to technological progress than the initial process development itself.

9. Learning-by-doing models are not only highly non-linear systems and therefore poten- tially sensitive to input assumptions, but quantitative values employed by modelers are typically drawn from the successful historical examples. Furthermore, the empirical foun- dations of learning by doing are drawn from observations of the relationship between cumulative deployment and/or investment in new technology and cost. This relationship is equally consistent with the hypothesis that a third factor reduced costs, in turn leading to increases in demand.
10. The difference between the WRE and WG1 pathways can imply a maximum difference of 0.2°C in global-mean temperature and 4 cm in global-mean sea level despite the fact that both pathways stabilize the concentration of CO_2 at 550 ppmv.
11. The US Energy Information Administration provided the first set of results, shown in Table 7.3. This analysis ignores effects on countries other than the United States, but it is useful in that it compares the results for six domestic US analyses for the years 2010 and 2020.
12. Numerous studies have examined this issue, including Babiker and Jacoby (1999), Bernstein et al. (1999), Bollen et al. (1999), MacCracken et al. (1999), and McKibbin et al. (1999).
13. This is not to deny the fact that there are not secondary implications for energy substitu- tion, resource depletion, and economic feedbacks. But these are the direct consequence of differences in exogenously specified technology opportunities.
14. For example, global generation of power is 75 percent non-carbon emitting in the year 2100 because the non-carbon-emitting technologies are simply more cost competitive than emitting technologies in many instances. Similarly, the commercial biomass industry is the largest occupation of farmers in the year 2100, larger than all other crops combined. It produces more energy in the year 2100 than world oil and gas production combined in the year 1985, and more than world oil and gas production combined in the IS92a scenario in 2100.
15. The methane could be utilized as an energy resource or sold as an energy product. If the methane, itself an extremely potent greenhouse gas, were to escape into the atmosphere, it would potentially negate any climate-change mitigation associated with the storage of CO_2.
16. OGF stands for 'Oil and Gas Forever' a case in which oil and gas resources are sufficiently abundant to maintain present oil and gas prices indefinitely.
17. CBF stands for 'Coal Bridge to the Future', a case in which conventional oil and gas resources are limited and unconventional oil and gas resources are expensive. In contrast, coal resources are abundant and inexpensive.
18. For example, Edmonds et al. (1997) estimate that in the OGF case a technology mandate to deploy carbon-neutral technology in new investments after the year 2020 would stabi- lize the concentration of carbon at about 550 ppmv in the OGF case, requiring the capture and sequestration of 342 PgC by the year 2095.

REFERENCES

Alcamo, J., A. Bouwman, J. Edmonds, A. Grübler, T. Morita and A. Sugandhy (1995), 'An evaluation of the IPCC IS92 emission scenarios', in IPCC (1995), pp. 247–304.

Arrow, K. (1962), 'The Economic Implications of Learning by Doing', *Review of Economic Studies*, **29**: 155–73.

Audus, H., O. Kaarstad and M. Kowal (1996), 'Decarbonisation of fossil fuels: hydrogen as an energy carrier', in *Hydrogen Energy Progress XI, Proceedings of the World Hydrogen Energy Conference*, T.N. Veziroglu, C.-J. Winter, J.P. Baselt and G. Kreysa (eds), Stuttgart, Germany.

Audus, H. (2001), 'Leading Options for the Capture of CO_2 at Power Stations', in

Proceedings of the Fifth International Conference on Greenhouse Gas Control Technologies, D.J. Williams, R.A. Durie, P. McMullan, C.A.J. Paulson and A.Y. Smith (eds), CSIRO Publishing, Collingwood, Australia, pp. 91–6.

Babiker, M. and J. Jacoby (1999), 'Developing country effects of Kyoto-type restrictions', in Pan et al. (eds), pp. 153–68.

Battelle (2000), *Global Energy Technology Strategy Addressing Climate Change*, Battelle Memorial Institute, Washington, DC 20024.

Bernstein, P.M., W.D. Montgomery, T. Rutherford and G.-F. Yang (1999), 'Effects of restrictions on international permit trading: the MS-MRT Model', in Pan et al. (eds), pp. 27–56.

Bollen, J., T. Manders and H. Timmer (1999), 'The IPCC-SRES stabilization scenarios', in Pan et al. (eds), pp. 27–56.

Butt, D.P., K.S. Lackner, C.H. Wente, K. Nomura and Y. Yanagisawa (1998), *The Importance of and a Method for Disposing of Carbon Dioxide in a Thermodynamically Stable Form*, LA-UR-98-1108, Los Alamos National Laboratory, Los Alamos, NM.

Cole, V., C. Cerri, K. Minami, A. Mosier, N. Rosenberg and D. Sauerbeck (1996), 'Agricultural options for mitigation of greenhouse gas emissions', in IPCC (1996), pp. 744–71.

Dooley, J. (1998), 'Unintended consequences: energy R&D in a deregulated energy market', *Energy Policy*, **26** (7): 547–55.

Edmonds, J. and J. Reilly (1985), *Global Energy: Assessing the Future*, Oxford University Press, New York.

Edmonds, J. (1999), 'Beyond Kyoto: toward a technology greenhouse strategy', *Consequences*, **5** (1): 17–28.

Edmonds, J., D. Barns and M. Ton (1993), 'Carbon coalitions: the cost and effectiveness of energy agreements to alter trajectories of atmospheric carbon dioxide emissions', in Y. Kaya, N. Nakićenović, W.D. Nordhaus and F.L. Toth (eds), *International Workshop on Costs, Impacts, and Possible Benefits of CO$_2$ Mitigation*, Institute for Applied Systems Analysis (IIASA), Laxenburg, Austria (June), pp. 291–314.

Edmonds, J., J. Dooley and S.H. Kim (1999), 'Long-term energy technology: needs and opportunities for stabilizing atmospheric CO$_2$ concentrations', in *Climate Change Policy: Practical Strategies to Promote Economic Growth and Environmental Quality*, Monograph series on tax, trade and environmental policies and US economic growth, American Council for Capital Formation, Center for Policy Research, Washington, DC, pp. 81–97.

Edmonds, J., P. Freund and J. Dooley (2001), 'The role of carbon management technologies in addressing atmospheric stabilization of greenhouse gases', in D.J. Williams, R.A. Durie, P. McMullan, C.A.J. Paulson and A.Y. Smith (eds), *Greenhouse Gas Control Technologies, Proceedings of the Fifth International Conference on Greenhouse Gas Control Technologies*, CSIRO Publishing, Collingswood, VIC, Australia, pp. 46–51.

Edmonds, J., J.M. Roop and M.J. Scott (2000), *Technology and the Economics of Climate Change Policy*, The Pew Center for Global Climate Change, Arlington, VA.

Edmonds, J. and M. Wise (1998), 'The economics of climate change: building backstop technologies and policies to implement the Framework Convention on Climate Change', *Energy & Environment*, **9** (4): 383–97.

Edmonds, J., M. Wise and J. Dooley (1997), 'Atmospheric stabilization and the role of energy technology', in C.E. Walker, M.A. Bloomfield and M. Thorning (eds), *Climate Change Policy, Risk Prioritization and U.S. Economic Growth*, American Council for Capital Formation, Washington, DC, pp. 71–94.

Edmonds, J. and M. Wise (1997), 'The international distribution of costs and benefits of alternative global emission control proposals', Paper presented to the Energy Modeling Forum 14, Tokyo, Japan.

Freund, P. and W.G. Ormerod (1997) 'Progress toward storage of carbon dioxide', *Energy Conversion and Management*, **38**, Supplement: S199–S204.

Goff, F. and K.S. Lackner (1998), 'Carbon dioxide sequestrating using ultramafic rocks', *Environmental Geosciences*, **5** (3): 89–101.

Goulder, L.H. (1995a), 'Effects of carbon taxes in an economy with prior tax distortions: an intertemporal general equilibrium analysis', *Journal of Environmental Economics and Management*, **29**: 271–97.

Goulder, L.H. (1995b), 'Environmental taxation and the double dividend: a reader's guide', *International Tax and Public Finance*, **2**: 157–83.

Goulder, L.H. and K. Mathai (2000), 'Optimal CO_2 Abatement in the Presence of Induced Technological Change', *Journal of Environmental Economics and Management*, **39**: 1–38.

Goulder, L.H. and S. Schneider (1999), 'Induced technological change, crowding out, and the attractiveness of CO_2 emissions abatement', *Resource and Environmental Economics*, **21** (3–4): 211–53.

Grubb, M. (1997), 'Technologies, energy systems, and the timing of CO_2 abatement: an overview of economic issues', *Energy Policy*, **25**: 159–72.

Grubb, M.J., M. Ha Duong and T. Chapuis (1995), 'The economics of changing course', *Energy Policy*, **23** (4/5): 417–32.

Grübler, A. and S. Messner (1998), 'Technological change and the timing of mitigation measures', *Energy Economics*, **20**: 495–512.

Ha-Duong, M., M.J. Grubb and J.-C. Hourcade (1997), 'Influence of socioeconomic inertia and uncertainty on optimal CO_2-emission abatement', *Nature*, **390**: 270–273.

Hahn, R.W. and R.N. Stavins (1999), 'What has Kyoto wrought? The real architecture of international tradable permit markets', Electric Power Research Institute Global Climate Change Research Seminar, Columbus, OH, September 27–29.

Herzog, H., E. Drake and E. Adams (1997), *CO_2 Capture, Reuse, and Storage Technologies for Mitigation Global Climate Change*, MIT Energy Laboratory, MIT, Cambridge, MA.

Hotelling, H. (1931), 'The economics of exhaustible resources', *Journal of Political Economy*, **39**: 137–75.

IEA (International Energy Agency) (1997), *IEA Energy Technology R&D Statistics: 1975–1995*, International Energy Agency, Paris.

Inter-laboratory Working Group (2000), *Scenarios for a Clean Energy Future: Appendices*, Prepared by the Inter-laboratory Working Group on Energy-Efficient and Low-Carbon Technologies for the Office of Energy Efficiency and Renewable Energy, US Department of Energy.

IPCC (Intergovernmental Panel on Climate Change) (1995), *Climate Change 1994: Radiative Forcing of Climate Change and An Evaluation of the IPCC IS92 Emissions Scenarios*, J.T. Houghton, L.G.M. Filho, J. Bruce, H. Lee, B.A. Callander, E. Haites, N. Harris and K. Maskell (eds), Cambridge University Press, Cambridge, UK.

IPCC (Intergovernmental Panel on Climate Change) (1996), *Climate Change 1995:*

Impacts, Adaptation, and Mitigation of Climate Change: Scientific-Technical Analysis. The Contribution of Working Group II to the Second Assessment Report of the Intergovernmental Panel on Climate Change, R.T. Watson, M.C. Zinyowera and R.H. Moss (eds), Cambridge University Press, Cambridge, UK.

IPCC (Intergovernmental Panel on Climate Change) (2000), *Special Report on Emissions Scenarios*, N. Nakićenović and R. Swart (eds), Cambridge University Press, Cambridge, UK.

IPCC (Intergovernmental Panel on Climate Change) (2001), *Climate Change 2001: Mitigation*, B. Metz, O. Davidson, R. Swart and J. Pan (eds), Cambridge University Press, Cambridge, UK.

Jorgenson, D.W. and P.J. Wilcoxen (1993), 'Reducing U.S. carbon emissions: an econometric general equilibrium assessment', *Resource and Energy Economics*, **15**: 7–25.

Kinzey, B.R., M.A. Wise and J.J. Dooley (1998), 'Fuel cells: a competitive market tool for carbon reductions', *Proceedings of the 21st Annual Conference of the International Association of Energy Economics*, Montreal, Canada, May.

Kline, S.J. and N. Rosenberg (1986), 'An Overview of Innovation', in *The Positive Sum Strategy: Harnessing Technology for Economic Growth*, National Academy Press, Washington, DC, USA.

Lackner, K.S., D.P. Butt and C.H. Wendt (1997a), 'Magnesite disposal of carbon dioxide', *Proceedings of the 22nd International Technical Conference on Coal Utilization and Fuel Systems*, Clearwater, FL, March: 419–30.

Lackner, K.S., D.P. Butt, C.H. Wente, F. Goff and G. Guthrie (1997b), *Carbon Dioxide Disposal in Mineral Form – Keeping Coal Competitive*, LA-UR-97-2097, Los Alamos National Laboratory, Los Alamos, NM.

Lackner, K.S., D.P. Butt, C.H. Wente and D.H. Sharp (1997b), 'Carbon dioxide disposal in solid form', *Proceedings of the 21st Internatinal Conference on Coal Utilization and Fuel Systems*, Clearwater, FL, LA-UR-96-598, Los Alamos National Laboratory, Los Alamos, NM.

Lackner, K.S., C.H. Wente, D.P. Butt, E.L. Joyce Jr. and D.H. Sharp (1995), 'Carbon dioxide disposal in carbonate minerals', *Energy*, **20** (11): 1153–70.

Lackner, K.S., H.J. Ziock and P. Grimes (1999), 'Carbon dioxide extraction from air: is it an option?', *Proceedings of the 24th International Technical Conference on Coal Utilization and Fuel Systems*, Clearwater, FL, March: 885–96.

Lecocq, F., J.-C. Hourcade and T. Lepesant (1999), 'Equity, uncertainty and the robustness of entitlement rules', IIASA, EMF, IEA Conference on Energy Modeling, Paris, June 16–18.

Leggett, J., W.J. Pepper and R.J. Swart (1992), 'Emission Scenarios for the IPCC: an Update', in *Climate Change 1992: The Supplementary Report to the IPCC Scientific Assessment*, J.T. Houghton, B.A. Callander and S.K. Varney (eds), Cambridge University Press, Cambridge, UK.

MacCracken, C.N., J.A. Edmonds, S.H. Kim and R.D. Sands (1999), 'The economics of the Kyoto Protocol', *The Energy Journal*, Special Issue: 25–73.

Manne, A.S. (1995), *Hedging Strategies for Global Carbon Dioxide Abatement: A Summary of Poll Results*, EMF-14 Subgroup, Analysis for Decisions under Uncertainty, Stanford University, Stanford, CA.

Manne, A.S. and R.G. Richels (1997), 'On stabilizing CO₂ concentrations – cost-effective emission reduction strategies', *Environmental Modeling & Assessment*, **2** (4): 251–66.

McKibbin, W., M.T. Ross, R. Shackleton and P.J. Wilcoxen (1999), 'Emissions trading, capital flows and the Kyoto Protocol', in Pan et al. (eds), pp. 61–90.

Messner, S. (1995), 'Endogenized technological learning in an energy systems model', Working Paper WP-95-114, International Institute for Applied Systems Analysis (IIASA), Laxenburg, Austria.

Morgan, M. and D. Keith (1995), 'Subjective judgement by climate experts', *Environmental Science and Technology*, **29**: A468–A476.

Morita, T. and H.-C. Lee (1998), IPCC SRES Database, Version 0.1, Emission Scenario Database prepared for IPCC Special Report on Emissions Scenarios, http:www-cger.nies.go.jp/cger-e/db/ipcc.html.

Nakićenović, N. (1996), *Technological Change and Learning*, International Institute for Applied Systems Analysis (IIASA), Laxenburg, Austria.

Nakićenović, N. (1999), 'Energy perspectives for Eurasia and the Kyoto Protocol', Paper presented to the International Conference on Sustainable Future of the Global System, 23–24 February United Nations University, Tokyo; International Institute for Applied Systems Analysis (IIASA), Laxenburg, Austria.

Nakićenović, N., N. Victor and T. Morita (1998), 'Emissions scenarios database and review of scenarios', *Mitigation and Adaptation Strategies for Global Change*, **3** (2–4): 95–131.

Nordhaus, W. (1994), 'Expert opinion on climate change', *American Scientist*, **82** (1): 45–51.

Pan, J., N. van Leeuwen, H. Timmer and R. Swart (eds) (1999), *Economic Impact of Mitigation Measures*, Central Planning Bureau, The Hague, The Netherlands.

Peck, S.C. and T.J. Teisberg (1993a), 'CO_2 emissions control: comparing policy instruments', *Energy Policy*, **21** (3): 222–30.

Peck, S.C. and T.J. Teisberg (1993b), 'Global warming uncertainties and the value of information: an analysis using CETA', *Resource and Energy Economics*, **15** (1): 71–97.

Richels, R., J. Edmonds, H. Gruenspecht and T. Wigley (1996), 'The Berlin Mandate: the design of cost-effective mitigation strategies', in N. Nakićenović, W.D. Nordhaus, R. Richels and F.L. Toth (eds), *Climate Change: Integrating Science, Economics and Policy*, CP-96-1, International Institute for Applied Systems Analysis, Laxenburg, Austria, pp. 29–48.

Rogner, H.-H. (1997), 'An assessment of world hydrocarbon resources', *Annual Review of Energy and Environment*, **22**: 217–62.

Rose, A., B. Stevens, J. Edmonds and M. Wise (1998), 'International equity and differentiation in global warming policy', *Environmental Resource Economics*, **12**: 25–51.

Schneider, S.H. and L.H. Goulder (1997), 'Achieving carbon dioxide emissions reductions at low cost', *Nature*, **389**: 13–14, 4 September.

Stavins, R.N. (1997), 'Policy instruments for climate change: how can national governments address a global problem?', in *Workshop on Design of International Emissions Trading Systems*, National Bureau of Economic Research, W. Nordhaus and R. Stavins, organizers; Snowmass, CO, August 13–14.

Steinberg, M. (1991), *Biomass and Hydrocarb Technology for Removal of Atmospheric CO_2*, BNL-4441OR (Rev. 2/91), Brookhaven National Laboratory, Upton, NY 11973.

Steinberg, M. and E.W. Grohse (1989), *The Hydrocarb Process for Environmentally Acceptable and Economically Competitive Coal-derived Fuel for the Utility and*

Heat Engine Market, BNL-43554, Brookhaven National Laboratory, Upton, New York.

United Nations (1997), *Kyoto Protocol To The United Nations Framework Convention On Climate Change*, United Nations, New York.

United States Department of Energy (1997), *Scenarios of U.S. Carbon Reductions: Potential Impacts of Energy Technologies by 2010 and Beyond*, Office of Energy Efficiency and Renewable Energy, 1000 Independence Avenue, S.W., Washington, DC 20585.

Weyant, J.P. and T. Olavson (1999), 'Issues in modeling induced technological change in energy, environment, and climate policy', *Environmental Modeling and Assessment*, **4** (2/3): 67–86.

Wigley, T.M.L., R. Richels and J.A. Edmonds (1996), 'Economic and environmental choices in the stabilization of atmospheric CO₂ concentrations', *Nature*, **379** (6562): 240–43.

APPENDIX 7A   MEASURING COSTS

While everyone knows intuitively what is meant by cost, it is interesting to ask what modelers are reporting under that heading. The marginal cost that is reported is perhaps the simplest and most comparable of measures. It is the cost in currency of the last, most expensive, activity undertaken in the economy to limit emissions. It is the tax rate when taxes are used to limit emissions. It is the market-clearing price when emissions are capped and allowances can be freely traded.

Total costs are a bit more complex. Modelers employ several different measures when they report the total cost of carbon mitigation. Of these, the simplest measure is called direct cost, which can be defined as the area under the marginal abatement curve for carbon. Marginal abatement curves specify the relationship between carbon price and the quantity of emissions reduction relative to a reference case. Direct cost is approximately equal to one-half of the carbon price times the reduction in carbon emissions.

For cases where emissions permits are traded between regions, direct cost is adjusted by the value of transfer payments required to purchase or sell permits. This measure is useful because it is simple to construct and is comparable across models. To provide a sense of scale to the rest of the economy, direct cost can be expressed as a percentage of GDP.

Another common measure of cost is the percentage change in model-generated GDP between a reference and control case. There are many reasons why a change in GDP may differ from direct cost. In addition to direct cost, indirect cost components include the effects of pre-existing taxes, changes in terms of trade, and the way tax revenues are recycled. Also, measurement of GDP depends on the choice of index and base year used to construct that index. This reflects real-world problems in constructing a quantity index when relative prices are changing. It may also include macroeconomic feed-back effects. When taxes are used, revenues are generated, and depending on how those revenues are used, GDP can be different. Similarly, when emissions are capped and emissions permits are distributed, the distribution of those permits (wealth) can have an effect on the GDP as well.

Determining the size of the indirect cost components has proved difficult, and is a topic of study for modeling groups participating in Stanford University's Energy Modeling Forum. Some modeling groups have chosen to report only direct costs net of sales of emissions rights. Other groups have reported overall changes in GDP, or some other measure of economic welfare, but without an indication of the relative sizes of the indirect cost components. Costs can be reported period by period, or as the present value of a future stream of costs. As it turns out, defining and measuring cost is more difficult, even in the relatively simple world of economic models, than one might otherwise have anticipated.

8. Energy, the environment and the economy: hedging our bets

Alan S. Manne*

1 INTRODUCTION

Global climate change is a controversial area, and its analysis draws on many disciplines. Much of the initial work was done by atmospheric scientists. Then ecologists joined the debate, and then other physical scientists. Economists were latecomers. It was easy for everyone to agree on 'win–win' strategies, for example, energy conservation measures that reduce carbon emissions and also reduce costs. The economists made it clear, however, that it would be much more difficult to reach agreement on 'cost–benefit' strategies – those in which near-term costs are incurred by one group of nations so that future benefits might be obtained by others. This is a central issue in integrated assessment modeling.

In this brief survey, I shall not attempt to cover the many integrated assessment papers that have followed after the pioneering work by Nordhaus (1994). Instead, I shall use a very simple model to convey some of the key ideas that are central to dynamic benefit–cost analysis. Despite its simplicity, this model displays some of the most controversial features in this debate. It provides an economist's perspective on emissions and on taxes to restrain these emissions. It shows how the price mechanism may be employed to separate equity from efficiency issues.

The basic structure is that of a general equilibrium model. In form, it is identical to that used in a paper written jointly with Gunter Stephan (1999), but several of the numerical parameters have been modified. One element remains constant – the focus on discount rates. The lower the discount rate, the more it pays to incur present costs in order to obtain future benefits.

In designing any model, there is an inherent conflict between transparency and realism. Engineers and physical scientists tend to favor a detailed 'bottom-up' approach, but it can be extremely difficult to implement this type of model and to cross-check the results. There are many pitfalls in designing an integrated assessment model. The essential feature is that there are both privately consumed goods and also a 'public good' – the global commons. A realistic model would include many greenhouse gases, many time periods, many regions and many technologies for energy supply and conservation. For transparency, however, I shall focus on just one greenhouse gas – energy-related carbon dioxide. This is by far the most important of the greenhouse gases. See Houghton et al. (1996, p. 17).

Many of the costs of abatement might be incurred over the next few decades, but the benefits are likely to extend over the twenty-first and twenty-second centuries. Accordingly, it is convenient to measure time in decades rather than in terms of individual years. For internal consistency, anticipations of the future are represented in terms of perfect foresight rather than myopic vision. This type of general equilibrium model is termed *intertemporal*.

I shall distinguish just two regions: the wealthy Organization for Economic Cooperation and Development (OECD) nations (North) and the rest of the world (South). These regions could be viewed in terms of overlapping generations, but here they will each be treated as an infinite-lived single representative agent. Like almost all integrated assessments, this one contains several modules: one for the energy sector, one for the global environment and one for the economy in each region. These modules are linked through domestic goods balances and through international trade. The model will first be presented in algebraic form, and then in terms of sensitivity to key parameters. The chapter will conclude with an example of a 'hedging' strategy. A copy of the GAMS input file is available upon request.

2   THE ENERGY SECTOR

To keep things simple, there are only two energy supply technologies: low-cost carbon-emitting fuels (coal, oil and gas) and high-cost carbon-free fuels (nuclear, hydroelectric, wind power, solar and others). In each region r and each point of time t, there is a decision to be made with respect to $F_{r,t}$ (fossil fuels) and $N_{r,t}$ (non-fossil fuels). These are viewed as perfect substitutes in the supply of aggregate energy $E_{r,t}$ (measured in exajoules of total primary energy):

$$E_{r,t} = F_{r,t} + N_{r,t}. \tag{8.1}$$

Alternatively, one could subdivide energy supplies into two or more groups that are partial substitutes for each other. For a bottom-up model of the energy supply sector but with just two demand groups (electric and non-electric), see the website of the MERGE model undertaken jointly with Richard Richels: www.stanford.edu/group/MERGE/, and for a bottom-up model with many individual categories of useful energy demands, see the website of MARKAL: www.ecn.nl/unit_bs/etsap/.

Both MERGE and MARKAL represent the fixity of capital by including constraints on the rates of increase and decline of individual technologies. In the absence of such constraints, there would be penny-switching. That is, small differences in costs could lead to discontinuously large changes in quantities of energy produced and consumed.

Over the next few centuries, our illustrative model is based on virtually inexhaustible supplies of fossil fuels, but eventually it may become necessary to limit their cumulative use. As a precaution to avoid an excessive increase in the mean global temperature, we shall probably have to cut back on carbon emissions. If this phase-out is to be accomplished in an orderly fashion, it cannot be too rapid. Energy-producing and -consuming devices (for example, power plants, buildings and transport systems) are replaced only gradually. Here it is supposed that fossil energy in each region, $F_{r,t}$, cannot be reduced more rapidly than 20 percent per decade. That is:

$$F_{r,t+1} \geq 0.8 F_{r,t}. \tag{8.2}$$

There are also expansion constraints on the backstop technology – new, carbon-free forms of energy ($N_{r,t}$). Here it is assumed that no more than 1 percent of total energy supplies can be provided by these technologies during the first period of their introduction. Thereafter, carbon-free energy cannot grow much faster than doubling every decade. This is expressed as:

$$N_{r,t+1} \leq 0.01 E_{r,t+1} + 2 N_{r,t}. \tag{8.3}$$

Carbon emissions in each region are proportional to the use of fossil fuels. Here there is a global carbon coefficient (gcc), rather than an individual coefficient associated with the use of coal, oil and gas. This coefficient translates fossil-fuel use into carbon emissions ($Z_{r,t}$):

$$Z_{r,t} = gcc F_{r,t}. \tag{8.4}$$

It is a typical feature of an integrated assessment model that global carbon emissions are a jointly determined decision variable, ZG_t. We assume that international negotiations take place in an ideal world, and that these negotiations result in a property right for each region in the global commons. This right takes the form of a fractional share, and these shares may vary from one period to the next. Initially, they might be oriented toward each region's fractions of the global emissions total, but they might tend over time toward a more egalitarian criterion, for example, equal per capita emission rights.

Clearly these shares are contentious parameters, but so are all other aspects of international negotiations. In order to move toward economic efficiency, each region would be allowed a carbon quota that may be utilized at home, or may be traded in an international market. With this structure of the problem, quota rights depend both on the negotiated shares and on the global decision with respect to emission quantities in each period. Below, we shall see that when there is free trade in emission rights, the shares do not have a significant effect upon the global quantity of emissions.

Internationally tradeable carbon rights are abbreviated *crt*. The export quantities are termed $X_{r,crt,t}$. (Negative values of these quantities would denote imports.) Many forms of restriction might be imposed upon these trades, and such restrictions could raise the global costs of abatement. With the option of international trade, regional and global carbon emissions are linked by equations of the following type for the quota of each region in each time period:

$$Z_{r,t} + X_{r,crt,t} = shares_{r,t} ZG_t. \tag{8.5}$$

3   THE GLOBAL ENVIRONMENT

Carbon emissions are measured as a *flow* – in billion tons of carbon annually. But the greenhouse effect (radiative forcing) depends upon a *stock* variable – the concentrations of greenhouse gases in the atmosphere. Typically, the concentrations of greenhouse gases are measured in parts per million by volume (ppmv). With these units, the following 'two-box' difference equation is employed to translate global emissions in period t (ZG_t) into concentrations in period $t + 1$:

$$CS_{t+1} = 2.9ZG_t + 0.92CS_t. \tag{8.6}$$

Equation (8.6) is an approximation to the carbon cycle relationship described in Chapter 2 of this volume by Schlesinger. The stock concentration variable CS_t is defined to be zero in 2000. That is, it is measured in terms of the increase over the level in 2000. The model is calibrated so as to give results that are typical of many integrated assessment models. If there is zero abatement (business as usual), concentrations will rise from 370 ppmv in 2000 to about 550 ppmv by 2080. This would be twice the mid-nineteenth-century pre-industrial level of 275 ppmv. Equation (8.6) is based upon a carbon half-life of about a century. It implies that if the global flow of emissions (ZG_t) dropped to zero, carbon would be absorbed from the atmosphere into carbon sinks at the rate of 8 percent per decade. Eventually, concentrations would return to their level in 2000. With minor modifications, we could modify equations (8.6) so as to ensure that zero emissions would eventually lead back to the pre-industrial level. Or we could use a 'five-box' difference equation to track empirical concentration levels more closely. See Maier-Reimer and Hasselmann (1987).

In any integrated assessment model, damages are perhaps the most difficult value to estimate. There are impacts upon goods that are sold in markets (for example, agricultural products and timber), and there are non-market impacts (for example, changes in the habitat of individual species). Because of the difficulties of quantification, many analyses are therefore based upon cost-effectiveness – the minimum cost required for limiting concentrations (or alternatively, mean global temperature) to a specific level. But this begs the question of whether the benefits of reducing emissions outweigh the costs.

Here, the benefit–cost paradigm will be retained. It is supposed that damages in 2000 were negligible, and that they are a quadratic function of the increase over the concentration level in 2000. We ignore the fact that the oceans induce a thermal inertia lag between global concentrations and climate change. We also ignore the cooling effects of aerosols and the heating effects of greenhouse gases other than carbon dioxide. The damage factors DAM_t are then related as follows to the increase over the concentration level in 2000:

$$DAM_t = 1 - \left(\frac{CS_t}{1800}\right)^2 \tag{8.7}$$

in the 'low-damage' case. That is, no damages are discernible at 370 ppmv, the concentration level of 2000. With an increase of 180 ppmv, concentrations would be twice the pre-industrial level (370 + 180 = 550). The damage factor is 99 percent, and losses are 1 percent of GDP. For the 'high-damage' case, the denominator in equation (8.7) becomes 600 (instead of 1800). With this scenario, at twice the pre-industrial level of concentrations, losses rise to 9 percent of GDP. This is far higher than the damage levels usually estimated for climate effects upon market-oriented activities such as agriculture and forestry. High damage levels could, however, be associated with low-probability, high-consequence scenarios such as catastrophic changes in the Gulf Stream current.

4   THE DOMESTIC AND THE INTERNATIONAL ECONOMY

In an integrated assessment, the economy may be represented through a multisector interindustry model, but this leads to considerable complexity without any obvious gain in insights. Here instead, all the non-energy sectors are aggregated into a single homogeneous unit of output within each region. The output of this single sector is a numéraire good (num). Its level is determined by a nested constant elasticity of substitution (CES) production function. There are Cobb–Douglas tradeoffs between capital and labor. Labor is expressed in 'efficiency' units. It is perfectly inelastic in supply within each region and at each point in time. Physical capital is accumulated as in a typical Ramsey model. The demands for energy are generated at a second level in the production function, where $\rho(r) = 1 - [1/\sigma(r)]$, and $\sigma(r)$ is the elasticity of substitution between energy and capital-labor in region r.

When the value of energy is a small share of output, the elasticity of substitution is virtually the same as the absolute value of the price elasticity of demand for energy. Here it is taken to be 0.50 in the North and 0.35 in the South. With these values, we obtain results that are consistent with those of many of the models analyzed by the Energy Modeling Forum (EMF). See Weyant (1999). In this way, the nested production function allows us to account for low-cost energy conservation through the price mechanism:

$$Y_{r,t} = \left\{ \left[a_{r,t} K_{r,t}^{\alpha(r)} L_{r,t}^{1-\alpha(r)} \right]^{\rho(r)} + \left[b_{r,t} E_{r,t} \right]^{\rho(r)} \right\}^{\frac{1}{\rho(r)}}. \tag{8.8}$$

The parameters $a_{r,t}$ and $b_{r,t}$ are also chosen so as to replicate many of the EMF results. Specifically, if the prices of capital, labor and energy remain constant, capital and labor will grow at the annual rate of 1.3 percent in the North and 3.3 percent in the South during the twenty-first century. This scenario would lead to a marked reduction in today's per capita income differences, but would not lead to equalization until well after the twenty-second century. Energy grows at a slower rate than GDP. This may be described as zero-cost energy conservation or as 'autonomous energy efficiency improvements'. It may also be described as the income elasticity of demand. To obtain projections that fit with the conventional wisdom, this elasticity is taken to be 0.45. That is, for every percentage point increase in GDP, there is an increase of only 0.45 percent in energy demand.

Capital accumulation is driven by annual investment $I_{r,t}$, and it is subject to depreciation at a geometric annual decay rate of 5 percent. Since time is measured in ten-year periods, the accumulation process is written as the following first-order difference equation:

$$K_{r,t+1} = 5I_{r,t+1} + (1 - depr)^{10}(K_{r,t} + 5I_{r,t}).$$ (8.9)

In equation (8.9), the annual investment rates are multiplied by factors of 5 in order to allow for the fact that the time periods are each a decade long, and investment–output time lags are only a fraction of this length.

The value of domestic output is determined by the following 'green GDP' equation. The left-hand side shows that $Y_{r,t}$, the value of each region's conventional domestic output, is reduced by the global damage factor, DAM_t. For example, in the 'low-damage' case, this factor would be 99 percent when carbon concentrations rise to twice the pre-industrial level. The right-hand side represents the uses of green GDP: consumption C_t, investment I_t, net exports (or imports) of the numéraire good $X_{r,num,t}$ and energy costs:

$$DAM_t Y_{r,t} = C_{r,t} + I_{r,t} + X_{r,num,t} + cfosF_{r,t} + cbakN_{r,t}.$$ (8.10)

cfos, the unit cost of fossil fuels, is taken to be \$3 per GJ (\$18 per barrel of crude oil) and *cbak*, the unit cost of the backstop carbon-free fuels, is equal to the cost of fossil fuels plus a premium of \$500 per ton (a total of about \$12 per GJ). This is typical of the cost levels that are presently believed to be required for future technologies. One such technology might be photovoltaic cells. Another would be the capture and long-term sequestration of carbon dioxide, and then the conversion of energy carriers from hydrocarbons to hydrogen fuels.

The regions are linked not only by global carbon dioxide concentrations, but also by international trade. Here there are only two tradeable goods, *trd*. One is carbon emission rights, *crt*, and the other is the numéraire good, *num*. The basic equilibrium condition of international trade is that net exports of each good sum to zero in each time period:

$$\sum_r X_{r,trd,t} = 0 \quad \text{(for all } trd \text{ and all } t).$$ (8.11)

Finally, there is an objective function. Each region is viewed as an infinite-lived agent. It chooses time paths of consumption and savings so as to maximize the discounted utility of the region's consumption over time subject to an intertemporal wealth constraint. There is a unitary elasticity of substitution between consumption in each period. The utility discount factor $udf_{r,t}$ may vary over time – and between regions.

It is convenient to solve this problem through the sequential joint maximization procedure proposed by Rutherford (1999). This entails assigning an arbitrary set of positive Negishi weights, nw_r, to each region and solving the non-linear programming problem of maximizing global Negishi welfare, *NWEL*, subject to constraints (8.1)–(8.11):

$$NWEL = \sum_r nw_r \sum_t udf_{r,t} \log C_{r,t}. \tag{8.12}$$

The numerical process is terminated if each region's consumption expenditures are consistent with its wealth constraint. Otherwise, we modify the Negishi weights – increasing the weights of regions that have not used their entire wealth on consumption, and decreasing the weights of other regions. Typically, this process converges, and it leads to an intertemporal general equilibrium solution. A similar approach may be employed if there are overlapping generations and more than two regions.

The choice of Negishi weights is straightforward, but not the choice of the utility discount factors. Note that these factors represent discount rates on *utility* – not on goods. They are subject to as much controversy as the damage parameters. One can take either a prescriptive or a descriptive approach. See the conflicting essays on this topic in Portney and Weyant (1999). With a *prescriptive* approach, one can arbitrarily assign a very low utility discount rate and place a high weight on distant future damages. This approach is favored by environmental activists. It leads to immediate action on carbon abatement, but it also leads to immediate difficulties in other areas. Not only does this imply a strong reluctance to deplete the world's environmental capital, but it also leads to an unrealistically strong immediate incentive to accumulate conventional physical capital in each of the regions.

Rather than build in this outcome, I tend to favor a *descriptive* approach: one ensuring that the utility discount rate is consistent with the rate at which goods are discounted in today's markets. With unitary elasticity of intertemporal substitution, it can be shown that the optimal growth rate of consumption ($grow_r$) is related as follows to the utility discount rate (udr_r) and to the marginal productivity of capital (mpc_r):

$$mpc_r = grow_r + udr_r. \tag{8.13}$$

Now if international markets determine the rate of capital transfers between regions, there cannot be big interregional differences in the marginal productivity of capital. Following the empirical estimates of Nordhaus (1994, pp. 125–9), I have taken the mpc_r to be 5 percent in both regions. Accordingly, the utility discount rate (udr_r) is adjusted up or down so as to offset the differences in growth rates. If consumption is to grow at the same rate as the GDP, the discount rates must then be 3.7 percent in the North and 1.7 percent in the South. That is, North's utility discount rate must be 2 percent higher than that in the South. This is the basis for determination of the utility discount factors in the objective function (8.12).

With this approach, the model generates a virtually constant discount rate on the numéraire good over time. Investment and consumption expand in parallel with the GDP. From a modeling perspective, there is the further advantage that there are only minor capital flows. Inflows are under 2 percent of the South's GDP in any one year during the next two centuries. This is our base case assumption. As an alternative, we shall explore what happens when the utility discount rate is fixed at 3 percent in both regions.

5 SENSITIVITY TO THE DAMAGE PARAMETER

Figure 8.1 shows three alternative scenarios for carbon emissions. The top line shows how these might evolve under a BAU (business-as-usual) scenario – no international restrictions on carbon. Emissions grow by a factor of about 3 during the twenty-first century – during a period in which global GDP grows by a factor of nearly 10. There is a low income elasticity of demand for energy, but there is no price-induced conservation, and there is no incentive for introducing the carbon-free forms of energy. This is a scenario in which global concentrations exceed twice the pre-industrial level in 2080, and damages could begin to be significant.

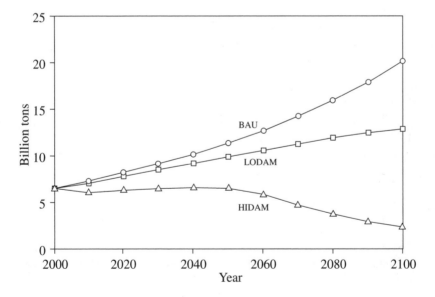

Figure 8.1   Carbon emissions

Now suppose that we know the damage factor from 2000 onwards, and that we are in a low-damage world (LODAM). This is the case in which there is a denominator of 1800 ppmv in equation (8.7). In this situation, there is only a small incentive to engage in low-cost, price-induced conservation during the early years. The carbon-free backstop is not introduced until 2080. The backstop is expensive, and the global GDP is slightly reduced from its BAU level. By 2100, global carbon emissions are about two-thirds their BAU level.

With the high-damage scenario (HIDAM), there is a much more pressing early incentive to engage in price-induced conservation, and the carbon-free backstop is introduced in 2020. By 2100, this supplies about 80 percent of the global total. Carbon emissions never increase above their level in 2000, and they begin to decline significantly after 2050. This is the good news, but what is the bad news? In order to control damages, there is a significant cost in terms of 'green GDP'. Both abatement and damage costs are expensive. From 2050 onward, green GDP in the HIDAM scenario is almost 5 percent below LODAM, and this in turn lies several percentage points below conventionally defined GDP in the BAU scenario. (See Figure 8.2).

Another way to compare LODAM and HIDAM is to look at the carbon taxes (or efficiency prices) that they imply. (See Figure 8.3.) In both scenarios, the carbon taxes rise throughout the twenty-first century, but they tend

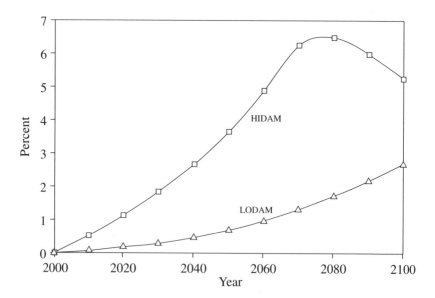

Figure 8.2   Percent GDP reductions from BAU

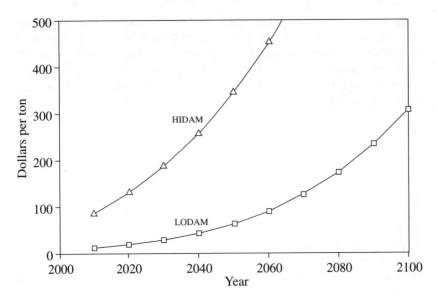

Figure 8.3   Carbon taxes

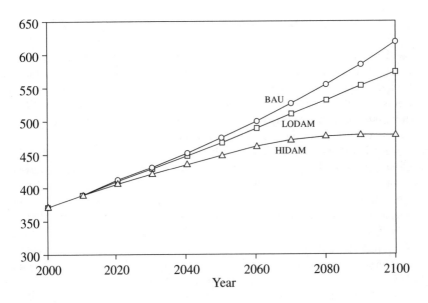

Figure 8.4   Carbon concentrations (ppmv)

to be six or seven times higher in HIDAM than in LODAM during the early decades. In HIDAM, it is the *expectation* of these high prices that makes it profitable to introduce the carbon-free backstop as early as 2020.

For the record, Figure 8.4 shows the carbon concentrations under the three alternative scenarios. Concentrations represent a cumulative decision variable, and this does not respond rapidly to changes in emissions. Note that the two top scenarios (BAU and LODAM) do not differ significantly until 2050. The HIDAM scenario is barely distinguishable from the two others in 2030, but thereafter is noticeably different.

6   SENSITIVITY TO CARBON SHARE ALLOCATIONS

Fortunately for integrated assessment analysts, not all parameters are crucial to the results. Much of the work of international negotiators has been focused on issues of equity. There is broad agreement that the wealthy nations must bear most or all of the costs of abatement during the first decades of the twenty-first century. Eventually, however, the nations of the South must take on some share of the global burden. Beyond these general principles, there is little agreement on the specifics.

Figures 8.1–4 illustrate the outcome under a specific sharing rule: that North's share in 2010 is only 30 percent of global carbon emissions, and that within a few decades it must decline to just 10 percent. This allocation lies considerably below North's 50 percent share of global emissions in 2000, but it does *not* mean that North's emissions must be immediately reduced to 30 percent of the global total. The model incorporates the option of international trade in emission rights. In this way, there is the possibility of separation between equity and efficiency issues. With international trade in emission rights, North has the option of purchasing these rights from the South. This turns out to be less expensive than some price-induced conservation in the North, and it reduces the immediate burden of abatement.

But what if there were a different sharing rule – one that allocates all of the global emission rights to the South and none to the North? It will come as no surprise that this lowers North's green GDP, and that it raises South's. But on a global basis, green GDP is virtually unchanged. Global and regional carbon emissions are also unchanged. All that happens is that this alternative sharing rule leads to an increase in North's imports of carbon rights from the South. With international trade in emission rights, there is virtually complete separation of equity and efficiency. Global and regional carbon emissions may be determined on efficiency criteria, but there is no simple way to determine an equitable arrangement for the distribution of carbon emission rights. This is where skillful negotiators can still make a difference. The results are consistent with the Coase theorem – the proposition that wealth transfer effects are too small to influence the Pareto-optimal level of provision of the public good. For more on the topic of alternative burden-sharing schemes, see Manne and Richels (1995). That paper also includes material relating to our two concluding topics – time discounting and hedging under uncertainty.

7   SENSITIVITY TO TIME DISCOUNTING

Time discounting is closely connected with the choice of each region's utility discount rates. Up to this point, we have adopted a descriptive view of this choice. That is, each region chooses these rates so as to maintain a constant marginal productivity of capital over time – 5 percent per year. Now what if the integrated assessment were based upon a prescriptive principle? I have already described my objections to the proposition that each region *ought* to govern its actions by a very low discount rate – possibly zero. In this case, there is a strong incentive to immediate action on abatement, and there is a strong incentive for immediate accumulation of physical capital. Moreover, near-term actions are highly sensitive to distant-future parameters such as the costs of carbon-free backstops that might be invented in two or three centuries.

But what if each region's annual utility discount rate were chosen uniformly – and at some positive level like 3 percent? This avoids implausible outcomes such as rapid immediate accumulation of physical capital, but it leads to still another difficulty. There are different GDP growth rates in the different regions, but there are international capital flows that tend to equalize the costs of capital between these regions. If capital flows are unlimited, the global marginal productivity of capital is close to the initial values of 5 percent. But if capital flows are initially limited to, say, 5 percent of the South's GDP – rising by 2050 to 10 percent of its GDP – then there are initially two distinct rates of return. There will be a lower one in the North and a higher one in the South. (See the two lines in Figure 8.5.) Eventually, the rate of return becomes equalized in the two regions, but during the transition period there is a foreign exchange shortage in the South, and there is a significant premium on this foreign exchange. Figure 8.5 is based on the LODAM scenario, but the results are quite similar in the case of HIDAM.

So ... what is my conclusion with respect to discount rates? It is instructive to compare alternative philosophical views within an integrated assessment model, but the most transparent results – those that can easily be explained to policymakers and to the public – are ones in which the model is constructed so as to replicate market rates of return. When much lower rates are employed, an intertemporal model produces paradoxical results. Either constraints must be imposed on physical capital formation, or there will be an implausi-

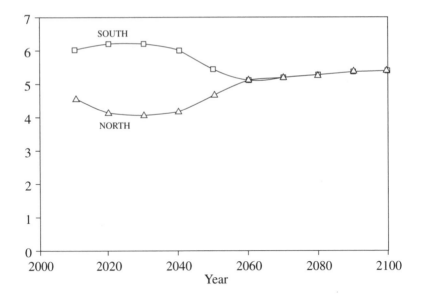

Figure 8.5   Marginal productivity of capital (annual percent)

ble buildup of physical capital during the immediate future. There will also be excessive sensitivity to cost and benefit parameters that will be unknown for several centuries. And when much higher rates are employed, we rule out the possibility of taking near-term actions to avoid distant-future environmental disasters.

8   HEDGING STRATEGIES

Each of the preceding calculations was based on a paradigm that can be abbreviated as LTA: learn, then act. First one learns the value of the uncertain parameter(s), and then one acts. Now it is time to consider an alternative view of decisions under uncertainty. This is abbreviated ATL: act, then learn. ATL emphasizes the idea that it takes time to resolve uncertainties, and that meanwhile we are constrained to take one or another form of action. For example, BAU is a form of action. It represents complete disregard for the future, and this makes sense only if future damages are negligible. Instead, let us see what might be involved in an ATL (hedging) strategy.

Both ATL and LTA focus on uncertainty with respect to key parameters, but ATL differs in two important respects from the LTA perspective. First, it requires that one specify the probability of the various uncertain outcomes.

This is needed in order to compute the *expected* discounted utility for each agent in the system. And second, ATL requires that one specify a date of resolution of one or more of the key uncertainties.

To illustrate the idea of hedging within this type of integrated assessment model, consider the controversy over the damage parameter in equation (8.7). Right now, we cannot be sure whether we shall end up in a LODAM or a HIDAM world. Science provides no objective way to reach agreement on which of these worlds will occur. For concreteness, suppose that we assign a subjective probability of 95 percent to the low-damage, high-probability case LODAM and 5 percent to HIDAM. When are we likely to find out which of these scenarios is going to prove true?

It is reasonable to expect some progress in our understanding of climate impacts over the next few decades. This means that there could be a resolution of the damage uncertainties shortly after 2020. Until 2020, there is no easy way to distinguish whether we are in a LODAM or a HIDAM world. Even in the HIDAM case, a BAU emissions path implies that damages would be just 0.4 percent of conventionally measured GDP. It is only from the next decision point onward (2030) that damages from the BAU path would rise to 1.0 percent of GDP. These HIDAM costs could well be noticeable, and might be sufficient to lead to concerted international actions.

By contrast with the LTA perspective, ATL incorporates foresight, hedging and precautionary strategies. It allows for limits on the rate of decline of carbon fuel emissions and on the rate of increase of carbon-free fuels. The ATL format also allows for uncertainties in the form of subjective probabilities. Figure 8.6 compares carbon emissions from both the LTA and the ATL perspectives. The LTA results are plotted as dashed lines, and the ATL results as solid lines. The two LTA scenarios provide bounds on the ATL carbon emission path. With only a 5 percent chance of HIDAM, the optimal global emissions scenario remains remarkably close to the LTA path for the LODAM scenario.

It is a misrepresentation to describe this as a do-nothing strategy. It just does not make sense to undertake large-scale precautionary strategies based on the rule of thumb that the worst possible outcome (HIDAM) will surely occur. The hedging strategy entails preparations for the eventual deployment of one or more carbon-free backstops. A modest carbon tax, say $5–10 per ton (the LODAM scenario), will begin to limit emissions, and to point the economy toward a low-carbon future.

Fortunately, policymakers do not have to commit today to a global emissions path for a long period of time, say, the next century. There will be ample opportunities for learning and for mid-course corrections. The challenge facing today's negotiators is to arrive at a prudent hedging strategy – one that balances the risks of waiting with the risks of premature action. The

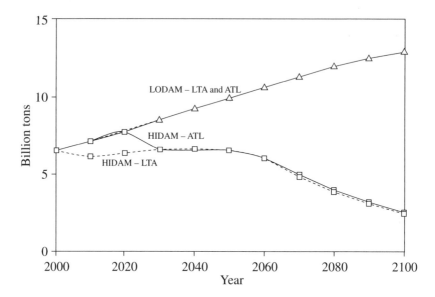

Figure 8.6   Carbon emissions LTA versus ATL

longer it takes to resolve uncertainty, the greater the need for immediate precautionary action. This underscores the importance of scientific research among the portfolio of options for dealing with global climate change.

NOTE

*   Helpful comments have been received from James Griffin and Richard Richels. For research
     assistance, the author is indebted to Charles Ng.

REFERENCES

Houghton, J.T., L.G. Meira Filho, B.A. Callander, N. Harris, A. Kattenberg and K. Maskell (1996), *Climate Change 1995: The Science of Climate Change*, Intergovernmental Panel on Climate Change, Cambridge University Press, Cambridge, UK.

Maier-Reimer, E. and K. Hasselmann (1987), 'Transport and storage of carbon dioxide in the ocean: an inorganic ocean-circulation carbon cycle model', *Climate Dynamics* **2**, pp. 63–90.

Manne, A.S. and R. Richels (1995), 'The greenhouse debate: economic efficiency, burden sharing and hedging strategies', *The Energy Journal*, **16** (4), pp. 1–37.

Manne, A.S. and G. Stephan (1999), 'Climate-change policies and international rate-of-return differentials', *Energy Policy*, **27**, pp. 309–16.

Nordhaus, W.D. (1994), *Managing the Global Commons: The Economics of Climate Change*, MIT Press, Cambridge, MA.

Portney, P.R. and J.P. Weyant (1999), *Discounting and Intergenerational Equity*, Resources for the Future, Washington, DC.

Rutherford, T. (1999), 'Sequential joint maximization' ch. 9 in J.P. Weyant (ed.), *Energy and Environmental Policy Modeling*, Kluwer Academic Publishers, Norwell, MA, pp. 139–75.

Weyant, J.P. (1999), 'The costs of the Kyoto Protocol: a multi-model evaluation', *The Energy Journal*, Special Issue.

9. International agreements and the struggle to tame carbon

David G. Victor

1 INTRODUCTION

My task is to comment on the role of international agreements for controlling carbon. I undertake this effort at a time, summer 2001, when the attempt to build an international regime to manage carbon is in disarray. The US government has abandoned any pretense of ratifying and implementing the Kyoto Protocol while most nations in Europe are leading a coalition that will attempt to bring the Protocol into legal force even without US participation. The US is leading an effort to think about alternatives to (or radical reform of) the Kyoto Protocol, perhaps even scrapping the idea of a new treaty altogether. The European Union is leading an effort to finalize agreement on the many detailed issues, such as accounting rules, that are necessary if the Kyoto Protocol is to serve as the architecture for international efforts to slow global warming. These nations are establishing two separate paths with potentially two competing architectures and conflicting rules. Now is an opportune time to step back and explore the fundamentals – what are we trying to achieve with an international agreement on carbon, and what are the architectural options? This chapter offers some answers.

First, a brief review of the main findings from the previous chapters in this book suggests some attributes of the climate change problem that must be taken into account when attempting to design an effective international agreement to combat the problem. Chapter 2 by Schlesinger and Chapter 3 by North underscore that there is little direct, immediate relationship between carbon emissions over a particular period in time and the climate of that period. Rather, human-caused changes in climate are a function of the growing concentrations of carbon dioxide and other greenhouse gases that accumulate in the atmosphere over long periods of time. Yet many of the proposals under discussion in the international diplomatic efforts to address global warming, including the Kyoto Protocol, envisage imposing high costs from controlling emissions over the short term and do not set long-term goals (see Edmonds and Sands, Chapter 7). This approach contrasts sharply with the results from the economic model presented by Manne in Chapter 8, which suggests that a more efficient strategy would involve much more modest control policies in the first few decades, which would send long-term signals to the economy and, over long periods of time (five decades and beyond) have a significant impact on atmospheric concentrations of greenhouse gases.

Over the long term, the benefits of controlling emissions could be substantial since it could prove especially difficult to adapt to large, unchecked changes in climate (see Mendelsohn, Chapter 5). The studies in this book also underscore the tremendous uncertainty in the shape of the marginal damage function from this growing concentration of CO_2 and other greenhouse gases. The uncertainties stem, in part, from incomplete knowledge about the relationship between CO_2 concentrations and climate (see North, Chapter 3) and particularly from the difficulties in linking changes in climate to particular damages (see Mendelsohn, Chapter 5 and Smith et al., Chapter 6).

Taken together, these findings suggest the need for an international strategy based on long-term goals and commitments as well as one that is adaptive to new information. Those two criteria – adaptive to new information and long term – are not completely compatible. The international system is highly adaptive because treaties, the main instruments of international governance, require the consent of governments to have force. Thus treaties are relatively easy to adjust in response to changing interests and information. Indeed, every major international environmental agreement is explicitly designed for change – in some cases, changes in commitments occur through conferences at which governmental representatives agree to adjust rules, and in other cases the treaties themselves are rewritten or amended and then subjected to re-ratification by their members.

While it is relatively easy to design agreements that can adapt to changing circumstances, the very flexibility of international law makes it much harder to create agreements that send credible long-term commitments. It is hard for states to bind themselves, collectively, to long-term commitments when international law allows those very states to change or abandon their commitments. This fact can lead to particularly unstable agreements when addressing problems, such as climate change, that require interdependent commitments. The level at which one state is willing to control its emissions depends on the level of others' efforts, in part because costly emission controls affect economic competitiveness. The defection of a single large player alters the calculus for all others, leading to a much less ambitious equilibrium in level of control that governments are willing to codify into international treaties.

Much of the controversy today about the Kyoto Protocol between economists and activists is, in part, a controversy about the best solution to this difficult task of setting credible long-term commitments. Economists have been particularly mindful of the long-term nature of the climate-change problem and the short-term costs of controlling emissions. Activists have been more concerned about the need to get some short-term commitment, even if it is inefficient, that sends a credible signal for the longer term. For economists, the troubles with the Kyoto Protocol offer an opportunity to rethink the architecture for the collective effort to slow global warming. For activists, rethinking the architecture is particularly threatening because it is the source of still further delays in sending a credible signal.

Thus we are dealing with a problem that is particularly ill suited for the instruments available under international law because it spans long time periods and is marked by short-term costs with benefits that accrue only over long time periods. To examine the types of agreements that will be stable and effective, we must look closely at the interests of each potential member of the treaty since each must ratify the deal. Thus Section 2 starts by focusing on the advanced industrialized nations because they are the only ones willing to pay for any significant abatement in greenhouse gases. Any viable framework for controlling carbon dioxide and the other greenhouse gases must start with them. I am mindful that Mendelsohn in Chapter 5 suggests that some of those nations may actually benefit from some global warming. Thus even with these nations, it may be hard to gain agreement on an effective emission control program. I examine four options and dismiss all but one. What is left is known as the 'hybrid' approach to regulating pollution, and I explore why it is superior to the others in delivering an agreement that will be economically efficient as well as matched to the interests of the major participants.

In Section 3, I examine the incentives at work in the developing world and conclude that the current efforts to force developing countries to undertake emission targets will lead either to deadlock or to an agreement that does little to slow global warming. Finally, in Section 4, I comment on the prospects for solving the problem of greenhouse gas emissions directly – through massive investment in new technology. Section 5 concludes.

Throughout, my treatment is sparse and focused on the political and institutional issues that arise, especially, in the international system. That system operates in ways that are very different from national law, but the differences are often not well appreciated. The key difference, as will become clear, is the voluntary nature of international law and the weakness of enforcement mechanisms – those twin problems are severe, and they lead to some unusual advice. For simplicity, I also focus on carbon dioxide emitted from fossil fuels. Other gases, in particular methane, also contribute to global warming; but fluxes of methane are hard to measure accurately and have much shorter lifetime in the atmosphere and are much less important to the long-term global warming problem than the accumulation of carbon dioxide in the atmosphere.

2   A FRAMEWORK FOR CONTROLLING CARBON: THE INDUSTRIALIZED COUNTRIES

The centerpiece of any international strategy for addressing global warming over the long term must be a system that puts a price on carbon. So long as it costs nothing to emit carbon, there will be only weak incentives to innovate and apply technologies to reduce carbon.

The core of that effort must begin with countries that have the highest willingness to pay for carbon controls – the advanced industrialized nations. Some argue that these nations must lead because they are responsible for most of the problem – only if they lead will an agreement be 'fair', and fair international agreements (it is assumed) are more effective than those that are unjust.[1] The evidence that fairness leads to more effective agreements is actually pretty weak, especially when commitments require governments to implement costly actions.[2] In the past, governments have adopted many agreements that appear to be 'fair' and appear to work. For example, the Montreal Protocol, adopted in 1987 and amended several times since, which requires the industrialized countries to phase our their use of chlorofluorocarbons and other ozone-depleting substances rapidly while giving the less wealthy developing countries a longer timetable for compliance. This treaty also requires the industrialized countries to pay for the 'agreed incremental cost' of compliance by the developing countries. This treaty appears to be the quintessential 'fair' bargain. In reality, this and all the other examples of effective treaties are actually examples of a different principle at work: willingness to pay. It so happens, that for most of the international environmental problems on the world agenda – including global warming – willingness to pay is highly correlated with income and liberalism. The advanced industrialized democracies contribute most to the problem at hand, but they also have the highest willingness to pay. In contrast, treaties such as the 1994 Convention on Desertification have been largely symbolic, because the countries that have the resources to address the problem at hand are not willing to pay much for a solution. Most of the variation in the ability of international law to influence behavior is explained by this phenomenon.

The cause of this phenomenon will become a familiar refrain in this chapter: it is difficult to impose an obligation on a reluctant country. One can compensate (bribe) another state to participate, as in the Montreal Protocol's arrangement for paying the 'agreed incremental costs' of compliance. Exactly that is done today under the Framework Convention on Climate Change, the only multilateral treaty on global warming that is in force under international law. But compensation can probably go only so far before the industrialized countries will want the developing nations to shoulder some of the burden. Or, one can coerce reluctant countries to join. One can lean on allies, threaten retaliation, and generally be nasty in international politics to force the reluctant to play, but those efforts only go so far. Studies on the influence of economic sanctions, for example, show that they are often blunt and ineffective (Hufbauer et al., 1990). I see only one way to coerce reluctant countries into participation in a climate-change regime and that is by coupling participation in the regime to the benefits of membership in the World Trade Organization (WTO). Yet integrating global warming and trade is fraught with danger – it could severely upset the world trading system, it poses novel legal and technical problems, and it is politically impossible in the foreseeable future. Today, the WTO membership is large and the majority of nations are developing countries, nearly all of which have been hostile to linking trade with environmental protection.

Thus any effective global warming treaty must be largely in the interest of the signatory country – either because it wants to undertake controls on carbon or because it is paid to do so. That is a hard test to satisfy, and it is why the Kyoto Protocol is in such trouble today. The treaty imposes costs on economies that far exceed what they are willing to pay. What would a viable treaty look like? In this section, I examine that question from the vantage point of the industrialized countries – those nations that have a non-zero willingness to pay. In the next section I examine the developing countries – those where willingness to pay is approximately zero. These two groups have different incentives and they must be examined separately. For the former, the question is, 'How to put a price on carbon?'; for the latter, the question is, 'How to control carbon while avoiding a price?'.

The Kyoto Protocol

Of course, there is already an international agreement that seeks to control carbon – the Kyoto Protocol. It requires 38 industrialized countries to control their emissions, on average, 5 percent below 1990 levels by the years 2008–2012. Each country has its own emission target, set forth in Annex B of the Protocol. The Protocol envisages creation of an emission trading system that would let countries trade portions of their targets, which would give them flexibility. The model for this system is the sulfur dioxide emission trading system under the 1990 Clean Air Act in the United States. The theory of emission trading is well established, although in practice the many countries emission trading have delivered uneven results because markets are often poorly designed (Tietenberg, 1985; Hahn and Hester, 1989).

At the time of writing (March 2001), the Kyoto Protocol is in the midst of a slow motion meltdown. The proximate cause of its troubles is the Bush administration's announcement that it would not control carbon dioxide emissions at the levels mandated in the Kyoto Protocol.[3] With the world's largest emitter not limiting its effluent (about 25 percent of the world's total emissions), other countries will find it hard to justify subjecting their economies to costly emission controls when the US does not. The need to preserve a 'level playing field' in the world economic competition will make that scenario hard to swallow.

The intermediate cause of Kyoto's troubles is that the targets set in Kyoto were too ambitious. They envisaged achieving significant reductions in emissions below the level at which the world's major economies would otherwise grow, over a short period of time (barely a decade after the ink was dry on the Kyoto accord). Yet the lifetime for technologies that are responsible for most emissions – such as electric power plants, houses and factories, and automobiles – is relatively long. The time set for the Kyoto emission caps is not commensurate with the time scale for technological change. I shall return to technology at the end of the chapter, since that offers one way forward.

The troubles are immediately evident in Figure 9.1, which shows historical emissions of carbon dioxide for the three most important political units among the countries that have some willingness to pay for slowing global warming – the United States, the European Union, and Japan. None is on track to comply with the Kyoto targets; yet the clock is ticking. When President George W. Bush announced that the US would not implement the targets, he was merely stating a position that reflects the situation in most other advanced industrialized nations. It is just that no other nation dares publicly declare that it will not comply with the target for fear of political crucifixion. The Kyoto Protocol has become a symbol for efforts to slow global warming, and one crosses the symbol only at peril.

There are at least three scenarios by which the advanced industrialized nations could comply with the targets, but none is attractive. First, diplomats might make it easier to comply with the Kyoto caps on emissions by playing accounting tricks. Notably, the Protocol includes language that allows countries to take credit for 'sinks' that remove CO_2 from the atmosphere. When plants grow they accumulate carbon in their trunks, stems, roots and leaves, as well as in surrounding soils. Agricultural soils are important sinks. In the United States, for example, starting in about 1910, when tractors made it easier for farmers to plow deeper, intensive tilling has reduced the carbon content of soils. Since the 1950s, farmers have shifted to 'no till' techniques that have helped slow soil erosion while also fortuitously increasing the carbon content of soils. Trees are especially important. Forests are growing larger and denser in all the advanced industrialized countries, in part because efficient farming is reducing the need for cropland and some of the abandoned land reverts to forest.[4]

Luck and clever accounting could deliver large credits for these sinks. One data set suggests that the US could offset about 14 percent of its current

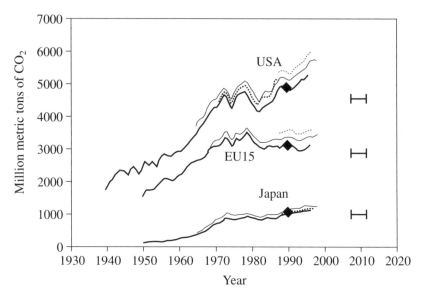

Note: The figure shows historical data from four semi-independent data sources and thus indicates the low uncertainty in the data. The large diamonds show the official data reported by countries for 1990, the base year for determining compliance with the Kyoto targets, which are shown as bars from 2008–12. US emissions have continued to rise steeply since the early 1990s, but emissions in Europe and Japan are more flat. Data exclude carbon sinks (for example, forests and soils) as well as non-CO_2 greenhouse gases.

Sources: Oak Ridge National Laboratory (solid heavy lines), IIASA/WEC (International Institute for Applied Systems Analysis/World Energy Council) (dashed heavy lines), BPAmoco (solid light lines), EIA (Energy Information Administration) (dashed light lines).

Figure 9.1   Trends in CO_2 emissions from combustion of fossil fuels

emissions if it were awarded full credit for 'land-use change and forestry' – a significant downpayment that could amount to nearly half of the required reduction during 2008–2012.[5] The more credit awarded for CO_2 that plants and trees are already absorbing, the easier it is for nations to comply with the Kyoto Protocol targets without actually changing behavior.

But this strategy founders on the lack of widely accepted methods and data for counting sinks.[6] Even if nations could agree on the necessary procedures, there would still be enormous potential for cooking the books. Only a monitoring program larger and more intrusive than anything ever attempted under international law could settle the inevitable disputes. In temperate and boreal regions, where all the advanced industrialized nations are located, most carbon in forests and in the soils varies naturally. Decades of monitoring would be needed to be certain that a 'sink' was not merely transient and deserved full credit.[7] Yet the commitment periods under international law are typically much shorter, such as the five-year 'budget period' of the Kyoto Protocol.

A second dead end is for nations in deficit to earn credits overseas in developing countries through the Clean Development Mechanism. Diplomats still have not been able to agree on the rules that would govern the Clean Development Mechanism. Thus investors are still not sure whether and how they could earn credits through these mechanisms. Years of preparation, testing, and learning will be required to build a pipeline of sensible projects. Time has run out for firms and governments to earn large quantities of credits by investing in emission-reducing projects through the project-by-project, Clean Development Mechanism.

Emission trading is a third way to ease compliance, but it also leads to a dead end. At the time of writing, negotiations on the rules to govern emission trading had broken down in The Hague in November 2000 and were patched together in the summer and fall of 2001. Even if governments solve considerable technical and political problems, such as how to enforce compliance, emission trading under the Kyoto Protocol still poses a significant political problem. Russia and Ukraine are by far the cheapest source of emission credits – not because the Russians and Ukrainians have had an epiphany about the risks of global warming, but rather because their negotiators got an emission target in Kyoto that far exceeds their likely level of emissions. Russia and Ukraine agreed in Kyoto to freeze emissions at 1990 levels, but the collapse of the Soviet economy in the early 1990s means that their emissions are already far below that target and unlikely to recover fully by 2008. Selling the windfall to nations in emissions deficit – notably the US – could earn Russia and Ukraine about $100 billion.[8] About four-fifths of that windfall would flow to Russia. Since the windfall is free – completely an artifact of the luck and skill of the diplomats in Kyoto rather than the result of any effort to control emissions – these extra credits would squeeze out bona fide efforts to control emissions. That buys paper compliance, but no reduction in global warming. No Western legislature will ratify a deal that merely enriches Russia and Ukraine while doing nothing to control emissions and slow global warming.

My interpretation of these events – that the advanced industrialized world is not on track to comply with the Kyoto Protocol and there is no attractive scenario for fixing the problem – is that the Kyoto Protocol will collapse. What next?

After Kyoto

One option 'after Kyoto' is to do nothing to create additional international law and institutions. The Framework Convention on Climate Change will still be in place, requiring all countries to report data and requiring industrialized countries to make some effort to control emissions. Such a 'best-efforts' regime could promote experimentation with different policies for controlling emissions (Hahn, 1998), and as nations learn which systems work, they might codify them into stricter treaties later on. Indeed, one problem with the Kyoto framework is that governments attempted to codify specific, stringent commitments into international law before they had much shared knowledge about how to implement such commitments.

Whether the best-efforts approach makes sense depends on how much one is willing to pay today to slow global warming. The troubles with the Kyoto Protocol may lead the world to a best-efforts policy for a few years, perhaps longer, as nations figure out what to do next. However, there are two reasons why the analysis should not stop here. First, it would be unwise to let a best-efforts approach flourish without some vision for how more stringent controls on emissions might be codified in the future. As Jacoby and Reiner (2001) warn, there are great dangers that as each nation goes its own way it will be hard to stitch their efforts back together into a coherent, rigorous international system for limiting emissions of greenhouse gases. Second, a best-efforts approach will not be adequate for those who feel that global warming is a severe problem that merits stringent action. The concerns over economic competitiveness require a tighter coordination between countries to ensure that each does its proper share – that coordination requires negotiation over the *allocation* of the effort among nations and also requires mechanisms for *enforcement* to ensure that each does its agreed part. The best-efforts system is poor on both those criteria because, by design, it does not require quantifying and codifying exactly what each country will do; nor does it envisage holding a country's feet to the fire if it fails to comply. Indeed, the chief benefit of 'best efforts' is that it allows flexibility for learning – including failure. My sense is that, especially in Europe, the willingness to pay for policies that will help slow global warming is greater than can be justified by a best-efforts approach alone.

What are the options for a regulatory system that moves beyond Kyoto and beyond 'best efforts?'. When thinking about the options it is useful to return to Weitzman's (1974) insight. Broadly, we can control the quantity of emissions and let the market determine price. That, more or less, is the approach in the Kyoto Protocol, which sets a cap on total emissions. Or, we can control the price (for example, a coordinated carbon tax) and let the quantity fluctuate with the market. Without perfect information, the architects of an international treaty cannot do both. I evaluate both – quantities and prices – with an eye to the three criteria that have already been suggested. First, which approach makes the most economic sense? Second, can nations find a way to allocate commitments under international law? Third, which is easier to enforce?

On the economic attractiveness, the choice is easy. Carbon dioxide, the main cause of global warming, is a 'stock' pollutant. The processes that remove carbon dioxide from the atmosphere operate mainly on long time-scales (five decades and longer), and thus the concentration of carbon accumulates slowly in the atmosphere. Thus the benefits from controls on this growing stock in the form of less global warming also rise slowly and steadily. Short-term variations in the quantity emitted, such as over a few years or a decade, do not have much effect on the total stock of carbon dioxide that is accumulating in the atmosphere. Although the benefits of emission control only emerge gradually, the cost of efforts to limit emissions could be very sensitive to their exact timing. If governments commit to regulate emission quantities but misjudge future costs they could force early premature retirement of carbon-intensive equipment (for example, coal-fired power plants) – a waste of resources that could be invested elsewhere in the economy. By that logic, outlined by Weitzman (1974) and applied by Pizer (1999) to the global warming problem, prices are the best instrument. They send a signal to firms to control carbon dioxide, but they do not require compliance with specific emission targets during specific timetables.

Under international law, a 'price' approach could take the form of an international tax on emissions that would funnel into an international fund. That option is politically impossible for the simple reason that few nations would agree to send 'their' money to a huge international fund. Thus most visions for a price instrument imagine a coordinated carbon tax (Cooper, 1998, 1999). Each country would set and enforce the tax on its own and collect and spend the revenues. The tax might be set at a common level ($ per ton of emissions) to reflect a common willingness to pay to control carbon. However, it is conceivable that nations could negotiate on an allocation of effort that was not uniform – some that have a higher willingness to pay might impose stiffer taxes. To offset the effects on competitiveness – known as 'leakage' because carbon-intensive production would migrate from high-tax to low-tax jurisdictions – nations might also impose border tariffs to offset the effect of different tax levels. Such border measures would probably run foul of the WTO today, but perhaps they could be permitted in the future. The tax scheme might also allow countries to claim a credit for projects that they fund outside their borders.

Thus the tax approach does well on two criteria – it makes economic sense, and it makes it relatively easy for nations to allocate the effort by negotiating over tax rates. Allocation would not be a trivial process, just as it was not trivial for nations to agree how to allocate tariff reductions and other rules that are the mainstay of international trade rounds. But the tax approach makes the level of effort transparent, and nations may be willing to agree on differential tax rates even without offsetting border tariffs if only because the worries about 'leakage' will not be severe except at high tax levels.

Unfortunately, the tax approach fails on the count of enforcement. There is no way to know the effective tax level in an economy because governments will impose carbon taxes on top of existing distortions. Also, they may use revenues from carbon taxes to create new subsidies that blunt the effect of the tax. It would be easy to spot the nominal level of the tax, but the real level would be quite hard. This problem is not completely novel to international law; for example, in WTO disputes, complex economic models are used to estimate the effect of illegal trade measures and to quantify the level of retaliation that is allowed when a nation persistently violates its commitments. But the state of economic modeling on energy taxes is far from where it must be to allow such calculations for a carbon tax. Moreover, even if nations could agree on a procedure for enforcement, how could judgments be imposed? In the WTO, which has the most effective enforcement system in international economic law,[9] retaliation is available because trade is inherently a bilateral activity and in relatively open international markets, there are numerous opportunities for retaliation. No such lever sits ready and available in a system of coordinated carbon taxes – unless, of course, that system is integrated with the WTO, which is an option I have already suggested is highly unlikely.

The score for 'quantity' measures – notably the 'cap and trade' approach that is the hallmark of the Kyoto Protocol – is exactly the reverse. Its economic logic is dubious, unless one posits that certain dangerous thresholds of climate change must not be crossed and one should 'cap' emissions to avoid those thresholds. I note that scholars have argued that such thresholds may exist (for example, Broecker, 1987; Stocker and Schmittner, 1998; Still et al., 1999), but nobody knows where the thresholds lie or even whether they exist. Rather, there is a whole series of long-tailed distribution functions around poorly characterized risks. In that situation, even though thresholds may objectively exist in the real world, the economic logic for abatement is more or less the same as for a simple 'stock' problem. The benefit of lowering the risk that the world will slip across some (unknown) dangerous threshold rises gradually as the accumulation of the stock of greenhouse gases in the atmosphere is slowed. The existence of non-linear threshold effects is what worries me most about global warming, but since we do not know which thresholds and effects will be most dangerous, we are still dealing with a stock problem. A quantity instrument is not the best way to address such a problem.

I note that there is a particular danger in the use of quantity instruments in international environmental law. The political dynamic in negotiating international environmental treaties often rewards bold but symbolic promises. In a negotiation such as the one leading to the Kyoto Protocol, the political benefits of bold promises are immediate, and the costs are a decade or more distant in the future. That leads to ambitious caps that cause one of two outcomes – neither of which leads to sensible policy. One outcome, now evident, is that as the elixir of symbolism wears off, countries find that they cannot meet their caps and they simply refuse to join the treaty. That, more or less, is the problem of the Kyoto Protocol today. A different outcome is that governments ratify the agreement and then find that they have imposed the quantity nightmare on their economies. They are forcing their firms to meet emission targets during specific time periods that cannot be met except at extreme cost. For evidence of the cost of such constrained markets one need look no further than the electric power exchange in California, where prices periodically skyrocket because demand is rising and supply is constrained. Similarly, if the supply of carbon credits is constrained because technologies in the energy sector are long-lived and the pace of technological change is relatively slow and the demand growth is robust, then prices (and costs) will skyrocket. That should be a real worry for those nations that are still contemplating imposing the Kyoto limits on their economies. What will they do in 2012 if the books do not balance?

The cap and trade approach also scores poorly on the criterion of allocation. Schelling (1997) and Cooper (1998) have argued, correctly in my view, that they do not see any viable way to allocate enormously valuable emission credits under international law. I agree. Elsewhere (Victor, 2001), I estimate that the implied value of the permits issued in Kyoto was over $2 trillion. One could imagine creating such assets within a system of strong law, such as exists inside nation states and now exists, more or less, across the European Union (EU). Indeed, we do that already. For example, states auction licenses for the wireless spectrum ($100 billion worth in the EU alone in 2000, thanks to the auction of the 'third generation' of wireless licenses). But under international law it is especially hard to create secure assets because countries can refuse to join (or withdraw from) the treaties that are the instruments of international law.

Allocation of emission permits is particularly difficult not only because the assets at stake are extremely valuable but also because the future demand for permits is highly uncertain. Countries are often risk averse when they contemplate whether to join treaties (Stein and Pauly, 1993). In the case of global warming, they will focus on the downside danger that future emissions and abatement costs will be higher than anticipated, and they will demand additional permits accordingly. Uncertainty exists because governments try to make allocations for a decade or more into the future (as in Kyoto, which in 1997 sought to set targets for 2008–12) and techniques for projecting emissions and costs are contested. Governments could attempt to shorten the lag by negotiating targets for only a few years in the future, but they cannot shorten by much because of the long delays in ratifying and implementing international agreements. Uncertainty also exists, fundamentally, because the cap and trade system is a quantity instrument. It offers no surety about cost.

This uncertainty creates a destructive dynamic that, in my view, is fatal for the pure quantity approach. When governments attempt to allocate permits they create, in essence, a *negative sum* negotiating dynamic. Each new country brought into the negotiation over allocating emission permits will, like the others, demand additional permits as compensation just in case costs are higher than expected. Yet the countries cannot simply issue additional permits because, like inflation, the extra permits dilute value and lead to additional emissions. This problem is especially severe for countries that are reluctant to undertake any costly emission controls at all and is best seen in the behavior of Russia and Ukraine at Kyoto. Neither country had any willingness to pay for carbon control because, understandably, they had other economic priorities and (with very few exceptions) scientists from the Soviet Academy of Sciences have concluded that some warming would actually be good for these cold countries. It is not surprising, then, that the emission targets allowed for Russia and Ukraine almost exactly equal the highest credible projections for emissions from those countries during the years 2008–12 (Nakićenović et al., 1998; Victor et al., 2001).

One may wonder why, with these fatal weaknesses, the cap and trade approach is today's anointed king. Part of the reason is that alternatives – 'best efforts' or a coordinated carbon tax – are even worse. And part of the reason is political. For the environmental community, emission caps are superior because they are easy to explain and ensure a particular environmental outcome – a particular level of emissions that will not be exceeded.[10]

The one area where the cap and trade approach does very well, in principle, is enforcement. If buyers are liable for the integrity of the permits then they will be sure that they purchase from sellers that comply. More accurately, the concept might be termed 'issuer liability' since the burden of compliance is on the government that issues tradeable emission permits, not necessarily the particular firm that sells the permit in the market. This approach forces the market to price the risk of default and creates a built-in incentive for compliance. That is an important advantage for emission trading since enforcement is the Achilles' heel of international law. I note, in passing, that a strange thing has happened on the road from Kyoto – the countries that are most enthusiastic about emission trading have become equally enthusiastic about 'seller liability', which would seem to undercut the chief advantage of their favorite instrument. In the negotiations at The Hague in November 2000, which were slated to tie up the loose ends of the Kyoto Protocol (but ended famously in deadlock), slightly different terms were used. The idea there was to create a 'Commitment Period Reserve', which would require countries to hold a certain fraction of the emission permits ('allowances') allocated in Kyoto in their national registers, untraded, until the end of the 2008–12 commitment period. When the books are balanced after 2012, the true excess in each country's register can be sold or banked. If the Commitment Period Reserve is set at a high level (for example, 100 percent) then the system functions almost identically to a buyer liability regime – a country will have valuable tradeable credits only if it remains inside the system and beats its target. If the Commitment Period Reserve is set at a lower rate then some of its permits can move under, in essence, a seller liability rule. The major advocates for emission trading – Australia, Canada, Japan, Russia and the United States – favor lower Commitment Period Reserve rates (60 to 70 percent) because that is the best way to ensure that the large quantities of excess Russian and Ukrainian permits can trade quickly and without penalty, ensuring that the buying countries can comply with their targets.[11] In short, the severity of the Kyoto targets has driven the countries that have the strongest long-term interest in a viable emission trading system to push for rules that would undercut one of the chief advantages of emission trading in the international legal system. We live in strange times.

A Best Option?

The message from above is unsettling. There is no presumptive best instrument for dealing with the global warming problem. The best-efforts approaches fail on the grounds that they cannot be codified in ways that allocate specific commitments and reassure all the participants that they are pulling an appropriate share; and, for that same reason, it is hard to enforce a best-efforts approach. Best efforts helps nations get started, but it is not a viable framework for the long run. The prices approach, or carbon tax, makes good economic sense but runs afoul on enforcement. Cap and trade runs significant economic risks, is hard to get started because allocation is a very difficult task, but with issuer liability is relatively easy to enforce. Table 9.1 summarizes the results.

It is worth considering a fourth alternative, also shown in Table 9.1: a 'hybrid' system that combines both the price and quantity. Countries would set emission targets and allow trading, as in the Kyoto Protocol. But governments would also be allowed to sell additional emission permits at an agreed price. In effect, that provision would put a ceiling on the price and make it much easier to estimate the cost of compliance. Economists are familiar with the mechanism from the work of Roberts and Spence (1976); work by McKibbin and Wilcoxen (1997), Kopp (1999) and his colleagues at Resources for the Future, and Victor (2001) have explored its application to the climate problem.

Table 9.1   Four regimes compared

Regime	Criterion		
	Economic logic	Allocation	Enforcement
'Best efforts'	OK for first steps only	Hard to codify	Very hard
Coordinated taxes	Excellent	Relatively easy	Very hard
Cap and trade	Poor	Very hard	Relatively easy (in principle)
Hybrid approach	Good (if price cap is set low enough)	Medium	Medium

The hybrid approach greatly reduces the worst features of the three systems examined above. It forces clear choices about allocation of commitments and prices – in contrast with the best-efforts approach, it makes each nation's effort clear and allows each nation to assess whether its competitors have agreed to undertake a comparable effort. If the trigger price is set near the level where countries expect to be trading permits anyway then the economic effects of the hybrid mechanism are similar to those of a coordinated tax, which makes the hybrid an attractive mechanism for addressing a 'stock' problem like the buildup of greenhouse gases. The hybrid approach greatly (but not fully) eases the problem of allocation because it eliminates many of the 'worst-case' scenarios that make it hard to get reluctant countries on board. (I return to this in the next section, where I address issues related to developing countries.) Finally, because the hybrid system is based, in part, on trading of emission rights it is easier to enforce than a pure tax system, for at least two reasons. First, buyer liability is available as a way to price the risk of non-compliance. Second, unlike in a pure tax system, a market inside each country is available to put a price on the 'real' marginal cost of carbon, which makes it easier (but not trivial) for outsiders to spot whether governments have adopted countervailing policies that lower the effective price of carbon.

More work is needed to flesh out how the hybrid system might operate. My top candidate for research topics in this area is to examine the problem of tax substitution that causes such trouble for the pure tax systems. Governments will have revenues from selling permits at the agreed price; what kind of rules will be needed to keep them from using those revenues (or other payments and policies) to distort the effect of the hybrid trading/tax system? We need answers to this question before the hybrid approach is ready for prime time. My suspicion is that those rules will need to become more demanding as the stringency of the regulatory effort increases; I also suspect that two interesting findings will result. First, the rules will not be much different in their intrusiveness from rules that already exist in the WTO – on food safety, on technical regulations, on intellectual property protection, and so on. This is not a watershed for the intrusiveness of international law, as Rabkin (1998) has suggested in his critique of international efforts to slow global warming. Second, similar rules will be needed for *any* of the four systems evaluated here, and thus the hybrid approach is not much worse than the pure cap and trade or the best-efforts options. That leads to an intriguing possibility: perhaps the pure carbon tax, which is based on the most sound economic logic, is also workable with such rules in place. I suspect that the pure tax approach will remain unworkable because it delivers *all* of its incentive through the tax, whereas a well-designed hybrid system relies heavily on the permit trading market to generate prices that reflect the real marginal cost of controlling carbon. Economically, the hybrid approach and the pure tax system may be identical; administratively, the hybrid approach may be easier to monitor and enforce because price discovery occurs in a permit market rather than in the distortion-prone tax code. We need to work all this out in more detail.

The hybrid is not an ideal choice but it is probably better than all the alternatives, as suggested in Table 9.1. I close by underscoring that we are in a pivotal period today. What lesson will be learned as the Kyoto Protocol collapses? In part, the right lesson is that the targets set in Kyoto were too ambitious and the work plan of unfinished elements was too ambitious. In addition, however, the very architecture of the Kyoto Protocol is flawed. The pure cap and trade system creates an architecture in which it will be nearly impossible to allocate emission permits in the future, especially as the trading system is expanded to include additional countries that are less willing to pay for carbon controls. That is probably a bad idea since almost everyone agrees that the big political challenge for the future will be how to incorporate the developing countries, to which I turn now.

3   THE DEVELOPING COUNTRIES

I have little to say about the problem of dealing with the developing countries because I think the essential contours of the problems are fairly simple to understand. The developing countries do not want to spend much, or any, resources on dealing with this problem. I am sure that they are worried about droughts and floods in the future, but they are more worried about droughts and floods and economic development today (Schelling, 1997). Their will-

ingness to pay is low, and they will not accept commitments that require them
to change behavior, unless compensated or coerced.

This simple fact leads down one (or more) of at least three pathways. One
pathway would simply leave the developing countries out of any effort. That
is unwise because the developing countries are the sites of many low-cost
opportunities for controlling emissions. It is also unwise because these nations must be engaged in some way so that they have built up the experience
needed to participate when they are willing to pay for carbon controls in the
future and, in the interim, as they implement carbon controls that are paid for
by others.

A second pathway is to allow these countries to opt in to emission controls
on a project-by-project basis. That is more or less the system envisaged in the
Kyoto Protocol under the Clean Development Mechanism, in which investors
who pay for 'clean' projects that are more expensive than would have occurred anyway can earn credits for the difference between the emissions that
would have occurred and those that actually result. The system is cumbersome and will have high transaction costs and that will discourage investment,
just as the high transaction costs of the pollution offsets program under the
1977 Clean Air Amendments in the US discouraged investment in offsets
(Hahn and Hester, 1989). But I do not see much alternative.

A third pathway is more worrisome: set emission targets for these countries and allow them to participate in an emission trading program. It seems
to me that those who complain that the developing countries are 'exempt'
from the Kyoto Protocol have in mind that these countries should agree to
targets. But taking that argument a few steps further leads to a dead end. How
will we set the targets? One approach, for example, is to set generous 'head-
room' targets that more or less equal the likely emission path of the country.
But it strikes me that this logic will lead to a repeat of the 'hot air' experience
with Russia and Ukraine. If the developing countries are reluctant participants then they will demand permits to cover the worst-case scenario, and
that will lead to demands that probably exceed their actual emission pathway
– all those excess permits are a form of 'inflation' that will lead to greater
emissions and lower permit prices in the emission trading program. The
hybrid approach can dampen that incentive by eliminating the worst of the
worst-case scenarios, but the developing countries are still willing to pay a
price that, presumably, is much lower than the agreed price in the hybrid. The
result, again, is inflation of permits and greater emissions.

Thus, ironically, I think we shall find upon close inspection that our interests are probably not well served by forcing developing countries to accept
targets. If we do force them, then the value of our own emission permits will
erode through inflation, and these new entrants to the trading system, ironically, will undermine our collective effort to control emissions (remember,

that is the goal of this whole enterprise). There is a great hope that it would be possible to create growth or index targets for emissions in these countries, perhaps using data such as shown in Figure 9.2. But I think we shall find as we look closely at these data that they are quite soft – probably too soft, for now, to be used inside an emission trading system in which the underlying assets are worth trillions and tens of billions of dollars move across borders.

So I conclude that the cumbersome Clean Development Mechanism is the only real option for developing nations. But more effort should be made to embed that option into larger programs to identify projects in developing countries that are in the host country's own interest and then back those – in part because they generate emission credits at low cost and mainly because they help the host country solve problems like urban air pollution. China's remarkable drop in carbon intensity over the last decade (Figure 9.2) is the result of such efforts, mainly driven by China itself, to solve a local problem (particulate and SO_2 emissions from coal) that is highly correlated with a global problem (CO_2 emissions from coal). Over the long run, the developing countries will probably shoulder some burden for slowing global warming – not mainly because we force them to but because rising incomes and democratization will bring value systems and interests that include protection of climate. During the short run, I would focus on self-interest – and the China case shows that a lot can be achieved that way. The other countries shown in Figure 9.2 (Brazil and India) have not seen such a decline, and efforts are needed to explore how to help them move in that direction. In Brazil, it may prove difficult to squeeze much carbon from the economy because so much of the Brazilian electric power system is based on zero-carbon hydroelectricity; in India, however, coal is king and inefficiency reigns.

Thus I doubt that imposing binding emission targets on the developing countries is in the interest of the advanced industrialized nations, but we are hardly helpless when faced with the need to regulate emissions in the developing world. We can do a lot to find projects that correspond with their interests and also help to reduce carbon. Already, industrialized nations have funded many such projects through the Global Environment Facility and through bilateral programs. The advent of a credible Clean Development Mechanism would help to spur those efforts. We should not count on them to bend down, permanently, the trajectory of emissions from the developing countries, which will rise under every scenario for the foreseeable future. But we can help put them on a lower track. To expect more is to produce an agreement that is laden with hot air permits or totally unacceptable to the developing countries.

Finally, at some stage it will become necessary to require the developing countries to join whatever binding emission control scheme is established for the industrialized world. More thinking is needed on the provisions for 'gradu-

(a) Brazil

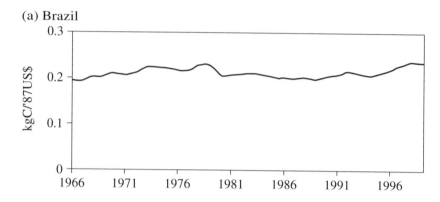

(b) China

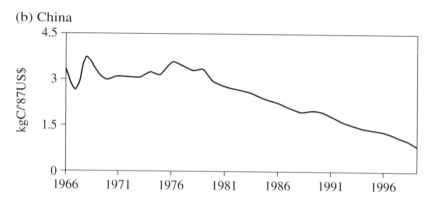

(c) India

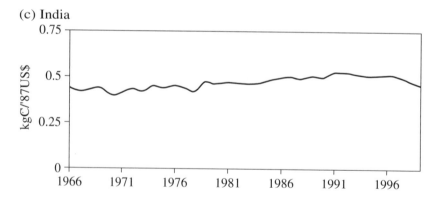

Note: Units: kilograms of carbon per unit GDP (constant 1987 US$).

Sources: Carbon emissions calculated from *BP Statistical Review of World Energy* (converted with high heating values coefficients) and income from World Bank *World Development Indicators*.

Figure 9.2   Carbon intensity for (a) Brazil, (b) China and (c) India

ation' into the tighter regulatory system. Back in 1992, when the Framework Convention on Climate Change (FCCC) was finalized, membership in the Organization for Economic Cooperation and Development (OECD) was the criterion for membership in the club of nations that had the tightest obligations to control emissions – the list of 24 members of Annex II of the FCCC was identical to the OECD membership at the time.[12] Since then, the OECD criterion has not fared well. Mexico and South Korea have joined the OECD but remain 'developing countries' for the purposes of controlling greenhouse gas emissions, and they refused to accept emission targets under the Kyoto Protocol. Turkey has remained a member of the OECD but has sought to exit Annex II of the FCCC and also refused to accept a target under the Kyoto Protocol.

One alternative approach to 'graduation' is to set a particular threshold income level. Countries would be required to impose emission controls above the threshold and to impose even more costly obligations at higher income levels, perhaps through a system of emission targets indexed to income. This approach is attractive in theory but hard to implement in practice since countries may refuse to join even as their incomes pass the threshold. In principle, one could hold other benefits of international cooperation – such as membership in the WTO – hostage to participation in the scheme to control emissions. In practice, that could be hard to implement, not least because today most members of the WTO are developing countries and are understandably wary of linking the immediate benefits from trade liberalization through the WTO to other issues about which they care much less, including long-term protection of the climate.

4   A TECHNOLOGY STRATEGY

The above will seem like a counsel of despair, and indeed many will wonder whether a robust international treaty for addressing the global warming problem is feasible at all. One alternative path, gaining currency today, is a 'technology strategy'. We owe much to Edmonds et al. (2001) for quantifying the large potential for reducing emissions of greenhouse gases through technological change. Others have also shown that assumptions about technological change are the single most important factor in driving projections for future emissions of greenhouse gases. Perhaps if we focus on technology then, eventually, controlling carbon will be cheaper (or even free). A bill is working its way through the US Senate, sponsored by Senator Frank Murkowski, that seems to envisage just that. The Global Climate Coalition, chief among the US critics of efforts to control carbon, also advocates investment in technology. Many fossil-fuel firms have lined up in support. Is this a good idea?

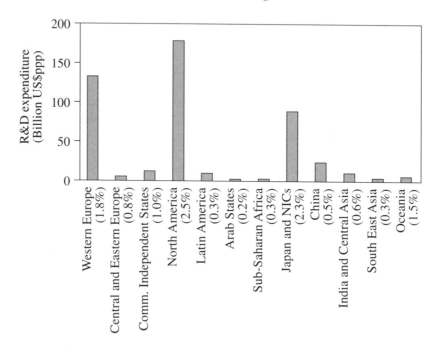

Note: NICs = newly industrialized countries.

Source: UNESCO (1999).

Figure 9.3   Geographical distribution of spending on R&D

A technology strategy has much to recommend it. A concerted effort now can make steep cuts less costly in the future. And for scholars of international relations a technology strategy requires the cooperation of many fewer nations when compared with emission controls that must, eventually, involve every nation on Earth. Most investment in research and development (R&D) occurs in a small number of countries (see Figure 9.3), and thus to increase world investment in technology it is necessary to gain the agreement of only a few countries – and those same countries are the ones whose publics care most about global warming. Moreover, the rapid rise of private investment in developing countries (Figure 9.4) means that private markets increasingly carry technologies into use throughout the world. Finally, many scholars have lamented the decline in energy R&D funding in the advanced industrialized nations (for example, Dooley, 1998; Margolis and Kammen, 1999); a technology strategy for global warming could help to reverse that problem as well. All that seems to be good news.

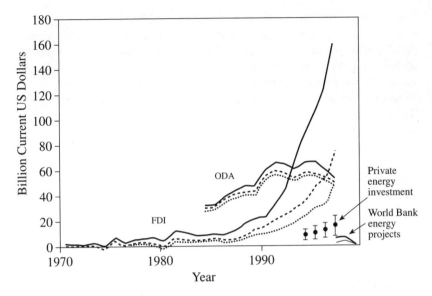

Note: ODA (official development assistance) includes concessionary loans and official aid (grants). FDI (foreign direct investment) is net inflows. Also shown are ODA and FDI for when removing the top 5 recipients of FDI (heavy dashed lines) and top 10 recipients (light dashed lines); even when removing those countries the basic trends are the same. For comparison, estimates of energy-related FDI are shown (based on assumption that 5 to 15 percent of FDI is focused on the energy sector) and also tabulations of energy-related World Bank projects.

Source: ODA and FDI data from World Bank, *World Development Statistics* (CD-ROM series).

Figure 9.4   Official development assistance and foreign direct investment in developing countries (current dollars)

We should be cautious about a technology strategy, however. One reason for caution is that the biggest failures of technology policy have occurred when there is no market for the technology being created. Thus a technology strategy is not an alternative to putting a price on carbon – rather, such a strategy will work only if carbon is priced. The need for an international framework for limiting carbon is especially great because only then will there be incentives on large world markets to install carbon-reducing technologies. A lot of the basic upstream research can be done without a strong incentive for carbon control, but as soon as technologies reach the stage of demonstration projects and niche market deployment, the lack of any price signal will deter commercial investment. Second, we should be careful in developing a technology strategy, also, to pursue the strategy on an international level. Some of the technologies to be developed are so risky or expensive that no nation will fund them entirely on its own; some new technologies, such as the next generation of safe and affordable nuclear power, are (partially) international public goods. This suggests the need, in parallel with the process leading from the Framework Convention, for a more active form of international collaboration on technology development. The style of that cooperation should take as its precedent not international environmental diplomacy but, rather, the cooperative technology and science programs such as those coordinated through the OECD and the International Council of Scientific Unions (ICSU). Some of this is already under way, such as through the International Energy Agency's Greenhouse Gas R&D Program, but an intensive effort will require closer coordination. The effort will require agreements and goals – in the form of non-binding, flexible memoranda of understanding rather than binding targets and timetables.

5   CONCLUSIONS

Part of the problem with efforts to slow global warming is that they have not been realistic. Most notably in the Kyoto Protocol, diplomats have set ambitious targets and timetables without a plan for implementation. And they have not given adequate attention to whether the architecture they were creating is viable. The weakness of international law poses severe challenges for any effort to develop an effective climate-change treaty. It is hard to allocate commitments under international law because countries must not feel aggrieved by their allocation – or then they can simply refuse to join the agreement. And it is hard to enforce obligations once they enter into force. Add to this the fact that developing countries – which account for most nations on Earth, most people, and most of the expected growth in emissions over the next few decades – do not care much about global warming, and we have recipe for a deadlock.

   I do not offer an elegant solution to the deadlock, but I do suggest one – the hybrid approach – that is likely to work better than the alternatives. I also suggest that America's obsession with what is wrong with the Kyoto Protocol – namely that it exempts the developing countries – is misplaced. Forcing the developing countries to impose costly obligations will not be successful, and forcing targets on these nations and bringing them prematurely into an emission trading program will actually harm our interests over the long run. It so happens that on this one point – the one hated most by Kyoto's most vocal critics – the Kyoto Protocol got it right. We should exempt the developing countries, let them opt in on a project-by-project basis, and encourage technology partnerships to identify win–win opportunities.

NOTES

1. For a statement of this view, a review of the literature, and the main arguments about the importance of fairness (against which I shall argue in this chapter) see the relevant IPCC chapter: T. Banuri, K. Göran-Mäler, M. Grubb, H.K. Jacobson, and F. Yamin, 'Equity and social considerations', in James P. Bruce, Hoesung Lee and Erik F. Haites (eds), *Climate Change 1995: Economic and Social Dimensions of Climate Change* (Cambridge: Cambridge University Press), Chapter 3. My chapter is not intended necessarily as a critique of the IPCC authors – their task was to review the literature. Rather, it is a critique of the assumptions and concepts in the literature. Moreover, I shall not consider here the relevance of fairness as expressed in decisions by the International Court of Justice (ICJ) and through liability schemes, though the IPCC chapter does address those issues. In my view, neither the ICJ nor liability schemes are relevant to the adoption and implementation of international agreements to slow global warming. Liability schemes are rarely used and require proving harm, which cannot be done for global warming impacts in the foreseeable future (see the final section of this chapter). The ICJ resolves disputes, which are mainly bilateral in nature; ICJ decisions have little if any sway on multilateral environmental negotiations; and, the dispute resolution procedures of multilateral environmental agreements have never been invoked and are unlikely to be in the future.
2. See Victor (1999) for a detailed review of the evidence. I do not address so-called 'procedural fairness' concepts, such as the need for a policy-making process that is highly participatory, access to information, minority rights and so on.
3. Letter from President George W. Bush to Senators Hagel, Helms, Craig and Roberts, 13 March 2001, Washington, DC.
4. For an inventory showing that all temperate and boreal forests are increasing in size and density, see UNECE/FAO (2000).
5. That figure is based on statistics compiled by US EPA (2000); 14 percent is computed as the fraction of the most recent US emissions (1998).
6. There are also some legal problems. Article 3.3 of the Kyoto Protocol states that only sinks 'resulting from direct human-induced land use change and forestry activities' can earn credit; at the time of writing (summer 2000) there is no agreed scheme for discerning 'direct' sinks from other factors that also cause trees to grow and sequester carbon (for example, warmer climates and higher CO_2 levels). Nor is it clear if trends such as rebounding of forests on abandoned agriculture lands, which long pre-date global warming policies, would qualify. Article 3.4, which concerns other land-use sinks (for example, agriculture soils) suggests that credits could be deferred until the second budget period (that is, after 2012); no decisions have been reached on how those credits would be measured or awarded. For the best summary of the issues that surround accounting rules for land use, see Schlamadinger and Marland (2000).
7. For a theoretical treatment and some application of data see Jonas et al. (2000). To my knowledge, no other studies have quantified the 'verification times' for carbon sinks.
8. Chapter 3 describes calculations behind these numbers in more detail.
9. Arguably, the International Monetary Fund's enforcement system is even more effective since the IMF can threaten to withdraw support from deviant countries. However, the IMF system is not a relevant precedent for the global warming problem since I doubt that there will be an international climate fund whose revenues could be made conditional upon compliance by the recipient. Here I am focusing on compliance with commitments by the advanced industrialized nations; in the IMF, enforcement is most effective against vulnerable, small developing nations.
10. Some have also argued that this approach should be the presumptive favorite in international law because it allows governments to give generous caps to reluctant countries and thus compensate them for their participation (Wiener, 1999), although I do not subscribe to that view for the reasons noted above.
11. For more detail, see http://www.cfr.org/kyoto and my commentary on the 'Pronk text', which was the chief negotiating text for the meeting at The Hague.

12. The European Union is also a member of Annex II, bringing the total to 25 members. The OECD does not have similar provisions to allow the EU to become an OECD member, and thus but for that technical difference the lists are identical.

REFERENCES

Broecker, Wallace S. (1987), 'Unpleasant surprises in the greenhouse', *Nature*, **328** (6126), (9 July): 123.

Cooper, R.N. (1998), 'Toward a real treaty on global warming', *Foreign Affairs*, **77** (2): 66–79.

Cooper, R.N. (1999), 'International approaches to global climate change', Paper 99–03, Cambridge, MA: Weatherhead Center for International Affairs, Harvard University.

Dooley, J.J. (1998), 'Unintended consequences: energy R&D in a deregulated energy market', *Energy Policy*, **26**: 547.

Edmonds, J.A., Wilson, T. and Rosenzweig, R. (2001), *A Technology Strategy for Slowing Global Warming*, Palo Alto, CA: Electric Power Research Institute.

Hahn, R.W. (1998), *The Economics and Politics of Climate Change*, AEI Studies on Global Environmental Policy, Washington, DC: American Enterprise Institute.

Hahn, R.W. and Hester, G.L. (1989), 'Where did all the markets go? An analysis of EPA's Emission Trading Program', *Yale Journal on Regulation*, **6**: 109–53.

Hufbauer, G.C., Schott, J.J. and Elliott, K.A. (1990), *Economic Sanctions Reconsidered*, 2nd edn, Washington, DC: Institute for International Economics.

Jacoby, Henry and Reiner, David M. (2001), 'Getting climate change on track after The Hague', *International Affairs*, **77** (2).

Jonas, M., Obersteiner, M. and Nilsson, S. (2000), *How to Go from Today's Kyoto Protocol to a post-Kyoto Future that Adheres to the Principles of Full Carbon Accounting and Global-scale Verification? A Discussion Based on Greenhouse Gas Accounting, Uncertainty and Verification*, IIASA Interim Report IR-00-061, Laxenburg, Austria: International Institute for Applied Systems Analysis.

Kopp, Raymond (1999), 'Definitions of Kyoto compliance: reducing uncertainty and enhancing prospects for ratification', Washington, DC: Resources for the Future (November).

Margolis, Robert M. and Kammen, Daniel M. (1999), 'Underinvestment: the energy technology and R&D policy challenge', *Science*, **528**: 690–92.

McKibbin, W.J. and Wilcoxen, P.J. (1997), 'A better way to slow global climate change', Brookings Policy Brief No. 17, Washington, DC: Brookings Institution.

Nakićenović, N., Grübler, A. and McDonald, A. (1998), *Global Energy Perspectives*, Cambridge: Cambridge University Press.

Pizer, William A. (1999), 'Choosing prices or quantity controls for greenhouse gases', Climate Change Brief No. 17, Washington, DC:Resources for the Future.

Rabkin, Jeremy (1998), *Why Sovereignty Matters*, Washington, DC: AEI Press.

Roberts, M.J. and Spence, M. (1976), 'Effluent charges and licenses under uncertainty', *Journal of Environmental Economics and Management*, **5**: 193–208.

Schelling, Thomas C. (1997), 'The cost of combating global warming', *Foreign Affairs*, **76** (November/December): 8–14.

Schlamadinger, J. and Marland, G. (2000), *Land use and Global Climate Change: Forests, Land Management, and the Kyoto Protocol*, Arlington, VA: Pew Center on Global Climate Change.

Stein, Janice Gross and Pauly, Louis W. (eds) (1993), *Choosing to Co-operate: How States Avoid Loss*, Baltimore, MD: Johns Hopkins University Press.
Still, Christopher J., Foster, Prudence and Schneider, Stephen H. (1999), 'Simulating the effects of climate change on tropical montane cloud forests', *Nature*, **398**: 608–10.
Stocker, Thomas F. and Schmittner, Andreas (1998), 'Influence of CO_2 emission rates on the stability of the thermohaline circulation', *Nature*, **388**: 862–5.
Tietenberg, T.H. (1985), *Emission Trading: An Exercise in Reforming Pollution Policy*, Washington, DC: Resources for the Future.
UNECE/FAO (United Nations Economic Commission for Europe, Trade Division/ Timber Section) (2000), *Temperate and Boreal Forest Resource Assessment: An International System for Collecting, Processing, and Disseminating Information on Forest Resources*, Geneva: United Nations.
UNESCO (United Nations Educational Scientific and Cultural Organization) (1999), *World Science Report*, Paris: UNESCO.
Victor, David G. (1999), 'The regulation of greenhouse gases: does fairness matter?', in F.L. Tóth (ed.), *Fair Weather? Fairness Concerns in Climate Change*, London: Earthscan, ch. 12.
Victor, David G. (2001), *The Collapse of the Kyoto Protocol and the Struggle to Slow Global Warming*, Princeton, NJ: Princeton University Press.
Victor, D.G., Nakićenović, N. and Victor, N. (2001), 'The Kyoto Protocol emission allocations: windfall surpluses for Russia and Ukraine', *Climatic Change* (in press).
Weitzman, M.L. (1974), 'Prices vs. quantities', *Review of Economic Studies*, **41**: 477–91.
Wiener, Jonathan B. (1999), 'Global environmental regulation: instrument choice in legal context', *The Yale Law Journal*, **108**: 677–800.

10. Five letters to the President

A LETTER TO PRESIDENT GEORGE W. BUSH BY LENNART HJALMARSSEN*

Global Climate-change Policy: A European Perspective

Mr President, from a European Union (EU) perspective, Kyoto is not dead. Many Americans would have been startled to see the newspaper headlines and the rage and alarm in Europe caused by the recent statements from your administration. Even if – as David Victor has shown here – there are good reasons to reject the Kyoto accord as it stands, because the targets are almost literally unachievable, and the instruments suggested not cost-effective, a withdrawal from the issue of global warming altogether would be inexcusable. I want to use my time with you to discuss the issue of global warming from an EU perspective. Since I know that you have a positive attitude towards nuclear power and because of my extensive experience from work in Eastern Europe and my experience from European panels of experts on nuclear power issues, I shall also address the development in Eastern Europe and the future role of nuclear power in climate policy.

Present trends

The EU accounts for about 15 percent of global energy consumption. According to the commitments undertaken at the Kyoto conference in 1997, the EU should reduce its greenhouse gas (GHG) emissions in the 2008–12 period to a level that is 8 percent below their level in 1990. This commitment has then been allocated into national targets ranging from +27 percent for Portugal to –28 percent for Luxembourg. These huge divergences among EU countries reflect a large number of factors including economic growth and changing market structures. They also highlight the difficulties involved in devising an equitable scheme for allocation of reductions in GHG emissions.

So far, between 1990 and 1998, the EU has reduced its GHG emissions by 2 percent, to some extent due to methane reductions caused by new regulations for waste disposal, but especially due to CO_2 reductions in the UK and Germany, where natural gas has been replacing coal in electricity generation, outweighing the increase in all other countries' CO_2 emissions. Thus, there has been an increase compared to the 2008–12 commitments even in 'high-profile' countries[1] such as:

- Austria: +6% achieved vs –13% commitment;
- Belgium: +6.5% achieved vs –7.5% commitment;
- Denmark: +9% achieved vs –21% commitment;
- Sweden: +6% achieved vs +4% commitment.

Because the energy and transport sector is responsible for 80 percent of all emissions in the EU, I shall focus on this. The EU energy system is – and will over the next 25 years remain – dominated by fossil fuels. Renewables, including hydropower, biomass and waste, wind and geothermal power, cover less than 5 percent of energy supply. Again, the variation among countries is large:

- For electricity generation, carbon-free nuclear and/or hydro power dominate in France, Sweden and (non-EU) Norway, while the UK has rapidly expanded natural gas – combined cycle and, to some extent, nuclear power generation.
- For heating, Germany, Finland, Denmark and Sweden have developed extensive cogeneration-district heating systems in urban areas with large shares of biomass and waste as fuels.

In general, electricity has gained market shares during the 1990s. The change between 1994–1999 for the whole of Western Europe was (see Enerdata 2000):

- total energy: +7%
- electricity: +12%
- nuclear: +9%
- hydro: +6%
- thermal: +15%
    natural gas: +74%
    coal: –9%.

According to the most recent comprehensive EU-wide study, *The Shared Analysis Project,*[2] the share of fossil fuels is projected to increase marginally over the projection period, 1995–2020, from its present 80 percent share, despite significant expected increase in renewables, energy conservation, and the rate of technical progress. If extensive decommissioning of nuclear power takes place, even coal consumption for power generation is projected to increase. Moreover under the baseline assumptions, EU CO_2 emissions by 2010 will exceed those of 1990 by more than 7 percent.

My conclusion is that the EU is not going to meet the Kyoto targets without extensive use of flexible mechanisms. Extensive use of such mechanisms, Mr President, seems also to be consistent with your own view. This is not, however, the EU view. According to this, flexible mechanisms should not account for more than 50 percent of emission reductions. Let me then briefly review the current policy issues related to the EU climate-change policy.

Deregulation of energy markets

The deregulation of the electricity and gas markets will enhance competition and lower prices, especially for electricity, in which case there is a large capacity locked in due to regulation, the release of which will depress electricity prices for an extended period of time. Low electricity prices will slow down investments in new capacity and make life extensions of existing capacity (coal and nuclear in particular) relatively more profitable. This will slow down the rate of fuel switching from coal to natural gas, but it will also extend the life of nuclear power.

Waste-disposal regulations

New waste-disposal regulations in several countries will enhance fuel switching in co-generation from coal to waste, but also investments in new capacity. This will further reduce emissions of non-CO_2 GHG emissions.

Subsidized renewables

All EU countries promote renewables and cogeneration by different kinds of subsidies, involving subsidization of capital costs, preferential electricity selling prices and electricity tax exemptions. This is most evident in the case of wind power, the expansion of which is solely driven by large subsidies. Still, except for Denmark, the share of renewables in total energy use is small and, according to *The Shared Analysis Project*, it will grow slowly as a share of final energy use in the EU.

Green taxation

There is no common EU tax policy to implement any EU-wide CO_2 taxation. For other reasons, Sweden and the UK vehemently oppose such a common tax policy. Therefore, there are large differences in tax structures and tax levels across the EU. While taxation of household energy consumption is extensive, industrial energy use is usually not taxed outside Scandinavia. Several countries outside Scandinavia, however, plan to implement taxation of energy or CO_2 emissions in industry. Thus, switching taxes on industry from labor to energy is high on the political agenda, although more in the debate than in actual policy.

A lot of research has been devoted to the double dividend hypothesis in order to find out whether green taxation may both improve environment and enhance employment. The results are ambiguous and rather model dependent. Since taxation of labor is high in the EU, even if there is a double dividend the impact would be small. Take Sweden, for example: a 100 percent increase in CO_2 taxation would reduce the labor tax distortion by 1 to 2 percentage points. Only in Eastern Europe, where energy prices are extremely high relative to labor, will tax switching have a substantial impact.

While proponents of green taxation refer to the double dividend, opponents refer to the erosion of competitiveness of energy-intensive industries in our small open economies. In order not to force these industries to close down or relocate to low-tax countries, tax exemptions are frequent in countries with CO_2 taxation. The problem with this is that, in principle, tax exemptions are regarded as subsidies according to both the World Trade Organization rules and the EU rules. The most prominent high-tax country, Sweden, has a pending case in the EU, concerning its tax exemptions for energy-intensive industries.

Thus, for several reasons one should not expect CO_2 taxation to play a major role in climate policy of the EU in the near future, although a few countries may develop their own policies. This means that the most efficient instrument to achieve lower emissions will not be utilized to anywhere near its full potential. A caveat holds for gasoline and diesel taxation.

Transport policy
The transportation sector is of serious concern from the point of view of GHG emissions. In the EU it accounts for about 30 percent of final energy demand. It has been consistently the fastest growing final energy demand sector, exceeding 3 percent per year since 1985, compared to 1 percent per annum growth in total energy use. It has proved to be quite insensitive to a number of measures to reduce consumption, including, huge investments in rail systems and mass transit and, compared to the US, very high fuel taxation.

The last EU-driven fuel-tax increases in France in 2000, caused violent protests, spreading to several other countries. As an effect of those, France, Spain, Belgium and the UK decreased their fuel taxes.

Thus, it is hard to imagine much higher fuel taxation as an important policy instrument in the EU in the short term. Fuel taxes may increase further, especially during periods of falling world market prices – at a pace accepted by public opinion – and mainly for fiscal reasons and not primarily as an instrument to reduce fuel consumption. Instead, the main policy option seems to be wishful thinking, involving hope for more energy-efficient vehicles and hope that, despite ever-rising incomes, individuals will start approaching saturation levels for their personal travel.

On the other hand, Mr President, Europeans would like to see much higher fuel taxes in the US. European governments discovered long ago that gasoline taxes are optimal from a fiscal point of view, causing very small economic distortions. Therefore, not only to finance your large tax cuts but also to finance investments in public transport, I strongly recommend that you introduce a low CO_2 tax on gasoline as a first step towards a more energy-efficient transportation system.

Energy conservation

Among all the instruments available, energy conservation measures would seem to be one of the most important and most promising. The *potential* for energy conservation appears very large in almost all energy conservation studies for different countries. Because of the often large gap between best-practice and average-practice technology, the impression from such studies is that at least 50 percent of energy use could be *avoided* in most countries, by closing this gap. But there is very little empirical evidence of significant *realized* energy savings even in modern market economies with well-informed agents and efficient bureaucracies, in spite of the enormous amount of money spent on energy conservation and demand-side management programs. Why is this so?

In my view there are two main reasons for the disappointing results of energy conservation programs:

- Since most programs are optional, there is an important *selection effect*. Many or most participants participate just because they were anyway, in the near future, going to implement the measures for which they now get paid or subsidized.
- Because technical progress does not come to a halt just because we have installed best-practice equipment, there is also an important *dynamic vintage effect*. The gap between our now modern equipment will again widen every year until we invest next time. If we do not renew all equipment every year, there will always be a gap between best-practice and average-practice technology. Energy conservation programs will therefore to a very large extent only have a temporary effect on reducing the gap between average-practice and best-practice technology.

Thus, energy conservation efforts are based on the illusion that it is possible to reduce long-term energy consumption by permanently closing the gap between best-practice and average-practice technology. My view is that higher energy efficiency will mainly be achieved through the gradual improvement of capital stocks in industry and households and not through large government-directed energy conservation programs. Thus, the uncertainty about the efficiency of energy conservation programs is huge, making such programs high-risk projects.

An exception is Central and Eastern Europe, where there is a large gap between its existing best-practice and worldwide best-practice technology. Although efficient implementation of energy conservation programs in this part of the world is difficult to achieve, the potential for Joint Implementation and Clean Development Mechanisms to decrease the 'gap' could be substantial, depending on the design of these mechanisms.

Central and Eastern Europe
The development of energy consumption in the Central and Eastern European (CEE) countries reflects the general economic development in these regions. The economic transition has made a large share of the existing capital stock obsolete. In all countries concerned, the energy sectors are undergoing structural reforms. Market liberalization and regulatory reforms are in different stages in different countries, but in general the process is slow. Because of lack of maintenance and investments, a large share of the conventional thermal electricity-generating capacity is obsolete from an economic point of view and even more so from an environmental one. Many plants are old and in different stages of decay. It is difficult to know exactly how much of the old thermal capacity should be regarded as economically and environmentally obsolete, but it may be a substantial share.

In general, the nuclear part of the electricity sector is in much better physical and economic condition than the conventional thermal part. Thus, nuclear power (and hydro power) has gained market shares in all countries which have nuclear power. Today nuclear power has an electricity production share close to 50 percent in the Slovak Republic and close to 40 percent in Bulgaria and Hungary. The development of the energy sector during 1994–99 may be summarized as follows:

- total energy: –9%
- electricity: –3%
    nuclear: +14%
    hydro: –5%
    thermal: –6%
        natural gas: –15%
        coal: –1%.

In most countries final energy demand has declined since its peak during the late 1980s. The drop in demand has mainly been at the expense of solid fuels, gas and distributed heat, while oil (transport) and electricity have increased their market shares.

In general, energy intensity has decreased in most countries during the 1990s in terms of energy/GDP and energy/capita. To a large extent this is caused by the relative decline in heavy industry output and a worsening standard of living in the household sector. Industry modernization, reduction of heat losses, and other energy conservation measures have also contributed to lower energy intensity, measured in terms of total energy input per dollar of GDP; the energy intensity is very high in most of these countries. Yet, in terms of per capita energy consumption in the household sector the pattern is quite different.

Even if the energy prices are still below world market prices in some countries, the energy prices are actually *extremely high*, that is, from the point of view of purchasing power and relative price. In Ukraine, for example, about one-third of monthly earnings goes to household energy bills compared to about 3 percent in Sweden and even less in many EU countries. Thus, the relative cost of energy within households is at least 10 times higher than in the West. Correspondingly, the relative price of industrial electricity relative to labor or capital is even more extreme. The price of one GWh of electricity relative to the monthly wage rate is about 400 in Ukraine and Romania. In Sweden it is about one and in the EU the average is somewhat higher than one. This means that, in the future, we should expect the price of energy to *decrease* substantially relative to labor and capital in industry and relative to other goods and services in households. Thus, there will be a demand-enhancing effect from these relative price changes when the economy starts to grow.

However, the argument for energy prices at world market levels is still valid. From an overall nationwide point of view, world prices converted at the equilibrium exchange rate represent the social opportunity costs to the economy of utilizing tradeable goods. If the signals provided by such prices are distorted, the economy will not use its comparative advantage in its most efficient way, that is, we get a less efficient pattern of production and consumption. This is the economic argument for world market prices on energy.

Industry restructuring, from heavy industry to light manufacturing and services, might cause a decline in future energy demand. However, there is a lot of uncertainty about this component for at least two reasons. First, energy demand in general and electricity demand in particular is strongly correlated with changes in plant utilization. In many countries the capacity utilization in heavy industry is very low today even if the plants have not yet been closed. Thus, most of the impact on energy demand of industry restructuring may already be realized. Second, even if the prospects for heavy industry in Central and Eastern Europe seem gloomy today with a lot of uncertainty surrounding the future comparative advantages of those countries, nevertheless, some countries must have comparative advantages in heavy industry. Some CEE countries are indeed going to produce all the steel and cement required for the reconstruction and future growth of Central and Eastern Europe even if we today do not know exactly which ones.

According to the Kyoto Convention, the CEE countries agreed to reduce emissions of six greenhouse gases by 8 percent by 2008–12 using 1990 as the base year.[3] Between 1990 and 1999, CO_2 emissions in the CEE countries decreased by 40 percent. With slow economic growth most CEE countries are likely to meet their targets by a significant margin. But if economic growth takes off at 2–3 percent per year, most of them would probably have to undertake actions to avoid exceeding their emissions target. Thus, even if Eastern Europe, and especially Russia and Ukraine, may positively contribute to the achievement of the Kyoto target in the short run, the stock of unused emissions will gradually disappear in the long run.

Is there a future for nuclear power?

Imposing limitations on greenhouse gas emissions will have a fundamental impact on the comparative advantages of different energy production technologies and their relative costs, because the energy sector in most countries is responsible for a large share of GHG emissions. Considering the politically feasible potential for emissions reductions in the transport sector, a heavy burden will rest on the electricity, hot water and steam-generating sectors. This would require an extensive increase in the production of electricity from renewables – hydro-, wind, biofuels and geothermal energy – and nuclear power. Because of a rather limited potential supply of renewables at an economically viable level in most countries, extending the life of existing plants and even investments in new nuclear power provides an economically attractive activity.

In comparison with many other countries, and with the United States in particular, the cost of nuclear power is very low all over Western Europe. The most important reasons seem to be:

- a successful choice of reactor technology;
- efficient management during construction and operation and short (about 5 years for the most recent and largest units) construction periods;
- an efficient nuclear safety regulation and an efficient licensing process; and
- low estimated costs of decommissioning and spent fuel treatment in an international comparison and much lower than US estimates. Moreover, the costs of already built deposits for medium-radioactive waste, confirm those estimates.

In spite of all the cost advantages, nuclear power is very controversial in several European countries, mainly now with regard to the unsettled issue of reprocessing or long-term storage of spent fuel. Thus, Sweden and Germany have decided to phase out nuclear power. When this will occur – or whether it actually will take place – is very uncertain. To illustrate the uncertainty, Sweden (where nuclear power has a market share above 50 percent) provides an excellent example.

After the Three Mile Island accident, the Swedish parliament (the Riksdag) in 1980 decided to hold a non-binding national referendum on the future of nuclear power in Sweden. As a result of the referendum, the Riksdag took two steps. First, it was decided that no more nuclear power reactors would be licensed, but the ones under construction (a capacity increase of about 50 percent) would be finished. Second, it was decided that the existing nuclear reactors should not be allowed to operate beyond the expected lifetime of the youngest reactor, often taken to be the year 2010.

Much has happened in the 21 years since the nuclear referendum. The debate faded, was revived by the Chernobyl accident, and was once again swept under the political carpet. In 1997, however, the government decided to close down the two reactors at Barsebäck, located opposite Copenhagen, the first one before July 1, 1998, and the second one before July 1, 2001. One reactor at Barsebäck was in fact closed down in 1999, while the other one is still operating in the summer of 2002, and it is highly uncertain when or if it will be closed down in the foreseeable future.

For the moment, nuclear power has strong support from the Swedish public. Moreover, analyses indicate that it would be extremely costly for Sweden to simultaneously phase out nuclear power and stabilize CO_2 emissions; see Andersson (1997)[4] and Nordhaus (1995).[5] According to Andersson (1997), the present value cost of a *combined* nuclear power phase-out and fulfillment of the CO_2 commitment is about $7000 per capita, while an isolated nuclear power phase-out or fulfillment of the CO_2 commitment would cost 'only' about $2000 per capita. Therefore in my view, it is highly unlikely that Sweden (or any EU country) will phase out nuclear power before the reactors are obsolete.

The same conclusion holds for Central and Eastern Europe. Here, nuclear power is clearly cheaper than any foreseeable alternative. The operating costs, including an allowance for decommissioning, are low – at about the same level as in Scandinavia. Even the figures available for investment costs indicate that new nuclear power is also cheaper than any alternative, including natural gas. Hydropower may be an alternative, but in most cases only as a load-topping capacity since non-exploited hydro resources are limited and in any case are generally of small unit size and hence relatively high cost.

The large comparative advantages of nuclear power in the CEE countries raises a concern for the safety of nuclear power in this region. Nuclear safety is of primary importance when considered within the context of European

Union enlargement: the Agenda 2000 agreement emphasizes that nuclear safety is a priority. In the Report to the European Commission from a Panel (of which I was a member) of High Level Advisors on Nuclear Safety in Central and Eastern Europe and in the New Independent States (1998), the following conclusions emerged:

- After the revolutions in 1989, extensive reactor safety improvement programs had been realized in all countries. At least in those CEE countries that had nuclear power, the utilities had been able to finance their own investments (even in Bulgaria) for safety and performance improvements. Thus, the need for direct financial support from the EU for reactor improvement projects was regarded as rather limited.
- Regarding the oldest reactors of conventional (VVER 440 and 230) and Chernobyl (RBMK) designs, these have safety deficiencies primarily concerning their ability to cope with accidents, which are normally safeguarded against in Western designs. They can be operated for a short time without excessive risk, but life extension is highly undesirable.
- Regarding the later (VVER type reactors 213 and 1000 and later RBMK) designs, these can be upgraded by means of improved instrumentation and control, maintenance, testing, operational safety improvements and the inclusion of mitigative features, enough to justify their continued operation.
- The most important area for future EU support lies in those parts of the infrastructure that are publicly funded and play an important role in guaranteeing all aspects of nuclear safety. The most obviously important aspect of publicly funded activities is that of the nuclear regulatory bodies themselves. But it also concerns the clean-up of uranium mining activities, radioactive waste and spent fuel management, the improvement of safeguard capabilities, the care of research reactors and a general need to support nuclear safety research activities.

Meeting limitations on GHG emissions according to the Kyoto accord and its future extensions may have a major impact on the cost of a closure, since alternative options may be much more costly. This may be less relevant for Russia and Ukraine, where emissions are far below 1990 levels and economic growth is slow. But it is very relevant for the CEE countries. In 1995, Slovenia had already exceeded the 1990 CO_2 emission level by 8 percent, while Poland was close to the 1990 level. Without the nuclear power option or with reductions in nuclear power generation, meeting the Kyoto agreement could be very costly for most CEE countries.

Concluding remarks

While change of fuel mix in electricity and steam generation may be the cheapest solution in most European countries for the period to 2010, the importance of this effect will probably decline in the longer term. One set of policy analyses in *The Shared Analysis Project* calculated the necessary levels of general EU-wide CO_2 taxation to achieve different emission targets in the most cost-effective way. The results suggest a tax level of about $50 per ton of carbon just to stabilize the emissions at the 1990 level and a tax level about $100 per ton of carbon to achieve a reduction of 6 percent. Carbon tax levels in the range of $50 to $100 per ton of carbon would make nuclear power least costly in most European countries. Substituting nuclear power for conventional thermal electricity generation is one of the few economically attractive options to GHG reductions, and indispensable in the long term. Therefore Mr President I strongly support your efforts to revitalize the nuclear power sector in your own country.

So far the progress to meet the Kyoto targets has also been slow in Europe. To meet these, the EU needs less rhetoric and more policy implementation based on cost-effective measures. A new architecture for the Kyoto framework is needed. Without the support of the country with the biggest emissions, a global GHG policy is doomed to fail. With American support, it would become not only forceful but also much more cost-effective than the present one, which does not ensure that the economic burden is supportable. Therefore, Mr President your leadership on this issue is vital.

A LETTER TO PRESIDENT GEORGE W. BUSH BY PAUL PORTNEY

Mr President, you were absolutely right to reject the targets and timetables in the Kyoto Protocol. Everyone around the world knew that the United States, and probably some countries in Europe, were not going to meet their targets in the given time frame. Getting this protocol out of the way clears the deck for something meaningful on climate change. But having indicated what you are *not* going to do, you now have a responsibility to indicate what you *will* do.

I do not have to tell you that this problem is extraordinarily complicated on a number of dimensions – scientifically, economically, politically, diplomatically and philosophically. Such noted scientists as Bill Schlesinger and Gerald North have indicated the dimensions of scientific uncertainty. Distinguished economists such as Larry Goulder, Robert Mendelsohn, Jae Edmonds and Ron Sands, Alan Manne and Joel Smith have suggested how complicated and uncertain this issue is economically. People like David Victor have indicated how complicated it is diplomatically and politically, both domestically and internationally.

In the international arena, a number of the countries with whom we negotiate on climate issues have been occasionally duplicitous in expressing their concern for the environment. In fact, they have been at least partially motivated by an interest in leveling the playing field economically with the United States, which has reigned supreme at least over the last decade. This issue is also quite complicated philosophically. It affects the way we are viewed by other countries in the world – which may affect your ability, Mr President, to negotiate treaties on things that you really do seem to care about, such as free trade, intellectual property, the expansion of NATO and other matters. So for these reasons this is an issue that is worth thinking about.

Finally, by way of introduction we need to realize that some warming appears to be inevitable, whether or not we choose to take mitigation measures. We should help prepare for the warming that will occur both in the United States and in other countries.

What could you do then? There many possible policy responses, ranging from doing nothing to undertaking things like the Kyoto Protocol. I have suggested that the latter would be too much and much too soon for the United States to undertake. Let me raise for your consideration one particularly interesting proposal put forward by four of my colleagues at Resources for the Future. It would establish a mandatory domestic cap-and-trade program for CO_2 emissions, in which one would choose both the cap at which CO_2 emissions would be limited in the United States, as well as one other parameter I will talk about subsequently. Most or all of the permits would be auctioned off by the federal government. Some of these permits could be distributed on the basis of historical emissions – and there are reasons why 'grand fathering' at least some permits would make this program more politically palatable. It is important for other reasons that most of the permits be auctioned off. However, neither you nor I believe that Washington should have still more revenues to hold. Therefore, the revenues from the CO_2 permit auction should be returned to the public on a dollar-for-dollar basis. Furthermore, over time and provided we are able to do this, we would negotiate ways to both trade out of carbon reduction obligations or to allow carbon sinks to take the place of the carbon reduction obligations that we have.

The other wrinkle in my colleagues' proposal is that the price of the permits would be capped at some so-called 'safety-valve' level. In other words, it would be a permit trading system but there would be a guarantee that the price of the permits would go no higher than some level that would be set legislatively. There is reasonably broad interest in a program like this, attracting the support of some environmental groups who have never before been willing to support an incentive-based approach to environmental policy. There is also support from many in the business community who fear a world in which there is no certainty whatsoever on what they might have to pay for carbon emission reductions in the future.

How much would such a program cost? Clearly, that depends on the quantitative cap that you put on emissions, and also on the safety-valve price. For purposes of discussion, suppose we decided to cap US CO_2 emissions at 1990 levels and establish a safety-valve price (or a maximum permit price) of $50 per ton of carbon. According to my calculations, I believe that this would increase the price of gasoline by ten to fifteen cents a gallon and increase the price of electricity by perhaps one cent a kilowatt-hour in those parts of the country where average prices are on the order of six cents a kilowatt-hour. But I need to point out to you that we have been wrong estimating the cost of various environment regulatory programs in the past – most notably the expected cost of controlling sulfur dioxide emissions from coal-fired power plants – so we could be wrong here.

Who is going to be hit hard by this? The coal industry would take a big hit, and that has serious implications in turn for the railroad industry. Rural areas will be harder hit because they depend more on gasoline than urban areas do. Large parts of the Midwest will feel a pinch because much of their electricity comes from coal. And western parts of the United States, where the distances that people drive are greater, will be much harder hit than the East.

If you paid careful attention to the television on election night, as I know you did, this prediction has a special implication for you. It suggests that it is those 'red' parts of the country where you did very well that will be hit the hardest from this climate-change proposal. It will have the least impact on those areas from Seattle to San Diego and Maine to Maryland where the Democrats tended to do very well, clustered along the coast as they are. Needless to say, you would have to pay careful political attention to a proposal that would have such political ramifications. Even small changes in electricity or other energy prices can have significant electoral impacts.

What would such a proposal like this get you? What would its benefits be? First of all, in addition to slowing the accumulation in the atmosphere of CO_2, my colleagues' proposal would also result in reduced emissions of volatile organic compounds, nitrogen oxides, and particulate matter. This in turn would translate into improved air quality – and, therefore, less acute chronic and acute morbidity, less premature mortality, improvements in visibility, reductions in materials damage, and possibly reduced acidification in aquatic ecosystems that we care about. We would also reduce our oil imports, which would have favorable consequences for trade and possibly even macroeconomic and military well-being.

Truth be told, the reduction in carbon dioxide emissions in the United States alone would have an absolutely meaningless impact on atmospheric concentrations of CO_2 from this program. However, if you choose to undertake such a program it would demonstrate to the other countries of the world that this is a problem that we take seriously, and might induce them to take action whereas otherwise they would be disinclined to do so.

What should you do? You were elected President of the 280 million people in the United States to work with Congress in making such choices. As you think about what to do, keep in mind that it would be best to take what is sometimes called an 'options' approach. In the same way that you would never commit yourself to a ten-year tax cut when assumptions about future revenues are highly speculative, you need to think about a carbon policy in which any commitments you make now would be reviewed on a fairly short periodic basis. The policy should be reviewed in the light of both the economic impacts that climate mitigation measures are having, as well as the accretion of future scientific evidence. Anything other than an options approach, which you continually revisit, would be sure folly, because of the tremendous scientific, economic and other types of uncertainties that we have talked about. There is absolutely no way the US should commit itself to any kind of inflexible long-term climate policy that cannot be revisited.

Thank you for the opportunity to speak with you, Mr President.

A LETTER TO PRESIDENT GEORGE W. BUSH BY JOHN P. WEYANT

Mr President, I would like to give you my suggestions regarding climate-change policy. The bottom line on my advice is to not forgo the good and useful alternatives in hopes of finding pure and perfect solutions that are unattainable. I shall start by giving you an overview of what the climate problem seems to be, then discuss some desirable characteristics for a climate-change policy, and end with a discussion of how to get started with or without the Kyoto Protocol structure.

Human-induced climate change will most likely become a big problem and could become a very big problem during this century. Human influences on the climate system have already been detected and the problem will probably worsen gradually, but steadily over time. There is, however, some possibility of abrupt climate change or abrupt climate-change impacts at some point along the way and that possibility will probably increase over time as well.

At present it is impossible to predict exactly when and how bad the climate-change problem will become because of significant and pervasive uncertainties concerning at least the following factors: (i) the science of climate change, (ii) the science of climate-change impacts, including the evaluation of market and non-market impacts, (iii) the policies other countries might implement, (iv) the policies we in the US will want to and be able to implement, and (v) how undeveloped countries will participate in climate-change policies in the future.

Despite these uncertainties, however, there is now enough evidence to justify preparing to avoid some of the worst possible outcomes we can envisage. Some of these measures could be designed to reduce greenhouse gas emissions, while others might simply prepare us to do so, or prepare us to adapt to or compensate others who are adversely impacted by any climate changes that might occur.

Given the long-term nature of the climate-change problem and in light of these uncertainties, a prudent course of action might include the adoption of a tentative long-term limit on the concentration of greenhouse gases in the atmosphere. Whatever shape an international agreement on limiting greenhouse gas emissions might take, we know that there are several ways (often referred to as flexibilities) by which the total cost of achieving our objectives can be reduced. Fully exploiting each of these flexibilities has the potential to reduce the cost of achieving any emission limitations by a factor of two or more relative to not exploiting them at all, and combined they could reduce costs by more than an order of magnitude.

Since greenhouse gas emissions everywhere cause climate changes everywhere we should try to make greenhouse gas emission reductions wherever it is cheapest to do so regardless of who pays for them. Since climate change is related to the stock of greenhouse gases in the atmosphere rather than the much smaller annual flow into it, we should reduce greenhouse gases at a rate that is gradual enough to allow the existing stock of energy-producing and -using equipment to reach the end of its useful economic life, focusing the substitution of less carbon-emitting equipment on new installations to satisfy new or replacement demands. We should reduce emissions of all greenhouse gases in a way that minimizes the cost of slowing climate change, that is, so that the marginal cost of reducing climate change by one unit via reductions of one greenhouse gas is the same as for any other greenhouse gas. Finally, we should use a portfolio of policies covering emission reductions (taxes, cap and trade, subsidies), research on the nature of the problem to refine our understanding of its likely timing and magnitude, and implement measures designed to stimulate technology research and development, etc.

One key issue to be addressed in the international negotiations on climate change is the extent to which developed countries like the United States ought to contribute to the solution of the climate change problem above and beyond what would be in our own direct (short run) interest. Developing countries observe that most of the greenhouse gases in the atmosphere above the natural background level was put there by developed countries. Moreover, research on the likely impacts of climate change suggest that developing countries are much more vulnerable to climate change because their economies are much more dependent on weather dependent activities like farming than those of developed economies, because they are generally located in lower latitudes where plants and animals are closer to their thermal limits, and because they have less resources and cruder institutions for adapting to any climate changes that may occur. You do not have to resolve the question of responsibility for all time with climate policy now, but you must address it in some way in formulating climate policy as it is a key issue for developing countries (witness the explicit or implicit attention paid to this issue in the UN Framework Convention on Climate Change (UNFCC) and all seven Conferences of the Parties initiated by the UNFCC). Moreover, the countries currently classified as developing will be emitting more (and probably a lot more) greenhouse gases than the currently developed countries by the end of the century, so we will definitely need their cooperation at some point to address the problem effectively.

Given these general desiderata for effective climate policy, I think it is useful to consider two paths forward – one with the US participating in a Kyoto type system and the other without the US participating in the system proposed in the Kyoto Protocol. I was not a proponent of the specific type of agreement that was reached in Kyoto as evidenced by the following quotation from a *Wall Street Journal* editorial piece entitled the 'Greenhouse Follies' that Harry Rowen and I wrote in the middle of the Kyoto negotiation process:

> The delegates to Kyoto will declare victory, but their claim will be hollow. But perhaps this meeting will be the last run of the Greenhouse Follies, followed by a process that accomplishes something useful.

Nonetheless, despite its flaws, most of the nations of the world have invested four and a half years in negotiating the details of this type of agreement so it should not be discarded without thinking through the likely reactions to that course of action. I liken this exercise to the analysis done by then President Kennedy's team during the Cuban missile crisis where do nothing, quarantine, and all-out attack options were fully developed to help guide the thinking of the President and his national security team in developing an appropriate course of action.

What might staying with the Kyoto Protocol negotiations bring? First, based on your public statements on the efficacy of this agreement, your negotiators would be in a strong position to win longstanding debates with the EU over 'open' versus 'severely restricted' use of the flexibility agreements dealing with emissions trading, trading of emission obligations over time and the use of multiple gases and sinks. They would also be in a strong position in negotiations with the developing countries to require that they be obligated to take future actions contingent on their income per capita reaching some threshold. At the same time you could pursue complementary activities on problem detection and monitoring, on supporting technology research and development (R&D) (for example, pre-competitive conservation, renewables, nuclear, and carbon sequestration R&D), technology transfer, on removing barriers to improvements in energy efficiency, the introduction of non-carbon fuels, and on institution building here and abroad.

What implications would walking away from the Kyoto Protocol have and what options might that open up? First, given the history of the negotiations, this would lead to some loss of face for the US in subsequent negotiations which could make the international cooperation that all nations desire more difficult to achieve. There might also be some retaliation in the form of less cooperation on other contemporary international policy issues or attempts at retribution by those most seriously affected by climate change such as low-lying island nations that become submerged. The other activities mentioned as possible complementary actions to a Kyoto-style agreement would also be even more crucial in this situation. In addition, it might prove useful to pursue bilateral and smaller multilateral international agreements than that being pursued in the United Nations Convention on Climate Change.

In sum, I would recommend three actions that would ease the negative reaction to the US pulling out of the Kyoto negotiations. First, I would explain why you are doing it. One explanation might be your belief that we (the international community) can achieve our objectives at much lower cost via another style of agreement. Second, I would put forward a proposal for another style of agreement, perhaps one that would initially put more weight on coordinating R&D and institution building than in focusing directly on short-term emission reductions. Finally, I would put forward a specific proposal for starting the post-Kyoto negotiations. This would seem most credible if accompanied by a tangible pledge of resources from the US, for example, in the form of $1 to 5 billion pledge to support targeted R&D and technology transfer. That might be matched by other developed countries according to some formula. There seem to be three road blocks to an international agreement on climate-change policy at present: (i) the cost to US industry and consumers might be too high, (ii) if a tax is used to ensure efficient emission reductions the tax revenues would, given political realities, be too high to recycle efficiently, and (iii) if an extensive international emissions rights trading program is used, the wealth transfers between nations would be politically unacceptable.

The main reason I favor a technology-driven approach to the climate problem is that lower-cost technology solutions can be developed that would reduce the stakes involved in the negotiations over targets and timetables along all three of the above dimensions.

A LETTER TO PRESIDENT GEORGE W. BUSH BY ROBERT L. BRADLEY, JR

Background

You President George W. Bush, inherited the Kyoto Protocol (Kyoto), an agreement signed by the Clinton administration but not submitted for ratification to the US Senate for fear of rejection. Kyoto would obligate the United States to reduce greenhouse gas (GHG) emissions 7 percent below 1990 levels between 2008 and 2012 as part of a 5.2 percent cutback among 38 developed countries. (The developing world, representing over one-third of global emissions, was not included in the agreement.) The US cutback was a tall task given a Department of Energy projection that GHG emissions would be 34 percent above 1990 levels by 2010 and 50 percent higher by 2020. The 2020 forecast represented a 1.4 percent annual increase, slightly above the 1990–2000 actual.[1]

In the face of such projections, you wisely withdrew the US from the Kyoto Protocol negotiations in March 2001. Unlike the Clinton/Gore administration (1993–2000), both Bush administrations have been careful to label CO_2 an *emission* and not a *pollutant*. CO_2 is a natural atmospheric component as well as a byproduct of the modern energy economy and an input to the Earth's biosphere. This is why in chemical and legal terms CO_2 is not classified as a criteria pollutant or toxic.

Is Climate Science Sounding an Alarm?

The third scientific assessment of the Intergovernmental Panel on Climate Change (IPCC), published in 2001, has been presented as narrowing the uncertainties and ratcheting up the climate alarm. Yet the main body of the scientific study is less alarmist than the Summary for Policymakers (SP) section, and many key issues for policy making remain unanswered. An evaluation of the IPCC report by the National Academy of Sciences (NAS), requested by the Bush administration, concluded that the SP 'could give the impression that the science of global warming is "settled," even though many uncertainties still remain'.[2] The NAS report also concluded:

- Model-estimated warming is 'tentative' due to uncertainties with the net effect of aerosols and black carbon forcing as well as future emission scenarios;
- Most of the predicted warming generated by climate models (60 percent) is due to feedback effects whose physical properties are in dispute;

- Carbon sequestration by oceans and terrestrial sinks that may offset incremental carbon emissions is not sufficiently understood;
- Regional climate change from the human influence on climate is even more uncertain than global climate change; and
- Much more research and time will be necessary to understand the past and future of natural and anthropogenic climate change.

The study also flagged the most fundamental unknown of all – 'A causal linkage between the buildup of greenhouse gases in the atmosphere and the observed climate changes during the 20th century cannot be unequivocally established.'[3]

Richard Kerr of *Science*, a journal published by the American Association for the Advancement of Science, also questioned the simplistic and consensus-driven SP. His survey of leading climate scientists found 'a growing appreciation of climate prediction's large and perhaps unresolvable uncertainties'.[4] Indeed, the error bars surrounding the predictions of climate models in the IPCC report were increased, not decreased from the prior 1995 report, and a clear link between observed warming and GHG concentrations in the atmosphere remained in doubt.[5]

The uncertain link between industrial emissions and global warming after a century of GHG buildup and decades of study points toward *lower-range, benign warming scenarios*. The 'empiricist school' of climate science weighs several key facts in place of relying on problematic model-generated long-range warming projections. The atmospheric concentration of anthropogenic GHCs has reached 65 percent of the global warming potential of a doubling of CO_2 compared to pre-industrial (1750) levels.[6] Thus we are over half way to the doubling of atmospheric GHG concentrations that the (feedback-driven) climate models estimate will eventually increase global surface temperatures between 1.4°C (3°F) and 5.8°C (10°F). *Yet how much anthropogenic warming exists given today's increase in GHG concentration?* The most recent IPCC report states, 'most of the observed warming over the last 50 years is likely to have been due to the increase in greenhouse gas concentrations'.[7] That increase would be around 0.4°C (0.7°F) of a total surface increase estimated to be 0.6°C (1.1°F). Extrapolating to a 100 percent increase – a doubling – would give an *anthropogenic* increase in surface temperature of around 0.6°C (1.1°F).[8] By point of comparison, a person cannot notice such a temperature change – one that in terms of global climate change will have taken two centuries (1850–2050) to create.

Ocean delay associated with anthropogenic warming could portend a more rapid warming over the second half of the doubling period. Equilibrium settling will also increase temperature even after the GHG forcing is stabilized. Yet a substantial 'underwarming' still remains compared to model estimates since the alleged offset cooling effect of sulfate aerosols is now recognized to have significant warming properties as well.[9] The enhanced greenhouse effect, moreover, predominantly affects minimum temperatures, which increase at twice the rate of maximum temperatures.[10] Anthropogenic warming is also disproportionately distributed toward below-freezing temperatures in the coldest air masses at the coldest times of the year.[11]

Lower-range warming suggested by the balance of evidence – a 1–1.5°C (1.8–2.7°F) increase from a doubling of GHG concentrations – is far from cataclysmic and for the US may be on balance beneficial. Robert Mendelsohn in this volume calculates *net economic benefits* for the United States and much of the world in the next half-century assuming climate sensitivity for a doubling of GHGs of up to 2.5°C (4.5°F) from pre-industrial levels. Such an extended time frame makes short-term policy activism inappropriate beyond free market no-regrets, price-neutral policies. Technological response addressing what turn out to be real problems will be profoundly different in future decades and centuries from what it is today.

A moderately warmer and wetter world from the human influence on climate has environmental and economic benefits unlike colder and drier scenarios. On the other hand, higher sea level from the human influence is a *per se* negative since populated coastal areas would be subject to more erosion and storm surges. Projected anthropogenic sea-level rise is trending downward, however. The IPCC's first estimate in 1990 was reduced by 25 percent in 1995, and the 2001 estimate was reduced by another 2 percent from 1995.[12] Yet as with temperature, the correspondence between *model-estimated* sea-level rise and *recorded* sea-level rise suggests model overestimation. The anthropogenic sea-level rise forecast for a year-2100 doubling of greenhouse gases in the atmosphere is 48 centimeters (18.5 inches), with a range of 9 to 88 centimeters (3.5 to 34 inches).[13] This climate-model forecast compares with an actual increase in the last century of 15 centimeters (5.9 inches).[14] Some of this rise occurred before mid-century when natural variability was controlling, continuing a trend from previous centuries and even millennia.[15] The anthropogenic portion of sea-level rise, like the temperature portion, suggests that the IPCC-estimated range is biased on the high side. In any case, sea-level rise has not accelerated in recent decades,[16] suggesting that factors other than GHG buildup are at work.

Kyoto and Economic/Energy Realism

President Bush, your decision to abandon Kyoto follows mainstream economic modeling studies that concluded that 'the emissions trajectory prescribed in the Kyoto protocol is neither optimal in balancing the costs and benefits of climate change mitigation, nor cost effective in leading to stabilization of the concentration of carbon dioxide at any level above about 500 ppmv'.[17] Few of the 38 developed countries that have signed the Kyoto agreement have a realistic chance of meeting their paper obligations. Inequities and a lack of enforcement mechanisms, as David Victor explains in Chapter 9 in this volume, doomed the agreement from the start. Even pro-treaty environmentalists have been concerned with the agreement's workability. Christopher Flavin of the Worldwatch Institute in a 'candid' assessment of the Protocol back in 1998 stated: 'The challenge now is to renovate the baroque structure that the Kyoto Protocol has become – or else scrap it and get ready to start over.'[18]

An accord reached in 2001 by 178 nations (sans the United States) on certain unresolved Kyoto issues cannot mask several realities. First, fundamental compliance and enforcement issues remain unresolved in the fifth year of the agreement. Second, anthropogenic climate change will not be measurably affected by full compliance with the treaty. Third, economies will be hurt to the extent that *real* instead of *paper* GHG reductions are made beyond no regrets.

The US rejection of both the Kyoto Protocol and lighter GHG reduction mandates will have a salutary effect on energy abundance and affordability at home and abroad. The alternative US framework all but ensures that a rigid international agreement will not emerge that could have as a compliance weapon restraints on international trade.[19]

A Kyoto-like energy mix is unrealistic for several reasons. First, consumers will question why more expensive and less reliable energy sources such as wind and solar power are adopted when cheaper grid electricity is available. Second, siting constraints will increasingly come into play with land-intensive alternative energy technologies. Third, environmentalists themselves are foes of many renewable projects and the two mass carbon-free energies. They have turned against the kingpin of renewable energy, hydropower, in favor of fish migration and returning rivers to their natural state. Environmentalists have blocked wind and geothermal projects in 'sensitive' areas – which is commonly the case. Their professed concern about the role of CO_2 emissions on global climate fails to square with the fact that carbon-free hydropower and nuclear power produced 175 times more grid connected electricity in the US in 2000 than wind and solar combined.[20] This reality is why both the US Department of Energy and the International Energy Agency forecast an *increasing* market share for hydrocarbon energy out to 2020.[21]

Starter Regulation: A Tyranny of Small Beginnings?

Climate policy activists use the uncertainty surrounding the human influence on climate to advocate 'modest' starter programs to regulate greenhouse gas emissions. They selectively apply risk and the precautionary principle to *climate change* but not to *climate change policy*. Yet regulatory programs intended to promote health must overcome a health loss that intrinsically occurs when private sector wealth is lost through taxation or regulatory burdens.[22] Part of this is the *seen–unseen* dichotomy where the well-intentioned aim of a specific regulatory is recognized but the diffuse, countervailing effects from the wealth transfer are not.

Unilateral cap and trade programs (suggested by Alan Manne and Paul Portney in this volume) have been pushed as an alternative to Kyoto. Yet as David Victor states in Chapter 9, unilateral programs increase the chances for global treaties and its corollary, global governance. Furthermore, proposals to price carbon domestically have difficulty passing a cost/benefit test since the direct economic climate benefits as measured by Mendelsohn appear negligible. If the climate effects of a massive carbon reduction program such as proposed by the Kyoto Protocol will be 'undetectable for many decades',[23] the climate impact of a *unilateral* US program as proposed by Manne and Portney will be much more so.

The rationale of putting the institutions in place in case of accelerated policy action is also problematic. Any regulatory program – and particularly one unleashed in a sea of scientific uncertainty – becomes a political football. Any CO_2 regulatory program will be ripe for politicization to disappoint even those economists who may now favor beginning a regulatory journey based on 'leadership' and 'insurance' analogies.[24] The appeal to 'market-based mechanisms' cannot undo the fact that efficiency toward an inefficient goal is still inefficient.

Conclusion

Your decision to withdraw from the Kyoto Protocol negotiations is a wise action. A voluntary, no-regrets approach toward GHG emissions is highly defensible given the current state of knowledge about the science and economics of climate change. A voluntary, flexible policy will allow more time for the scientific uncertainties to be addressed and for new technology strategies to emerge. Recent peer-reviewed work on feedback effects and surface temperature records seems to suggest that the alarm is moderating.[25] Better science – in particular next-generation climate models incorporating more realistic cloud and water vapor physics – will allow climate economists to better estimate the costs and benefits of climate change. In the meantime, a number of free-market 'no-regrets' policies will reduce greenhouse gas emissions in an inexpensive way.

The leading threat to energy sustainability in the new century is not resource depletion, air and water pollution, or even anthropogenic-related climate change. A strong case can be made for optimism, not pessimism, on these fronts.[26] The chief threat to energy sustainability is *climate policy activism* which interferes with energy affordability and reliability for the developed world and the 1.6 billion persons still living in energy poverty.[27]

A LETTER TO PRESIDENT GEORGE W. BUSH BY JAMES A. EDMONDS

Global climate change is one of the most complex environmental, energy, economic, and political issues confronting the international community. The impacts of climate change are likely to vary considerably by geographic region and occur over a time-scale of decades to centuries. The actions needed to manage the risks ultimately require substantial long-term commitments to technological change on the part of societies worldwide.

The Challenge

Mr President, as you have been briefed, you know that the Earth's climate is governed primarily by complex interactions among the sun, oceans, and atmosphere. The increased concentration of heat-trapping 'greenhouse gases' in the atmosphere has led to concerns that human activities could warm the Earth and fundamentally change the natural processes controlling climate.

You are also aware that carbon dioxide is the greenhouse gas contributing the majority of the projected future human influence on climate. Carbon dioxide emissions can affect the atmosphere for hundreds and even thousands of years. Some of the carbon dioxide emitted in 1800 is still in the atmosphere – and today's emissions will continue to influence climate in 2100. The total concentration of carbon dioxide in the atmosphere at any given time is much more important in determining climate than are emissions in any single year. Limiting the human impact on the climate system therefore requires that atmospheric concentrations be stabilized.

Recognizing this fact, more than 180 countries, including the United States, with the advice and consent of the United States Senate, ratified the 1992 United Nations Framework Convention on Climate Change (FCCC), and it has entered into force under international law. The *ultimate objective* of this treaty is to achieve 'stabilization of greenhouse gas concentrations in the atmosphere at a level that would prevent dangerous anthropogenic interference with the climate system' (Article 2).

The objective of the FCCC – stabilizing the concentrations of carbon dioxide and other greenhouse gases – is not the same as stabilizing emissions. Because emissions accumulate in the atmosphere, the concentration of carbon dioxide will continue to rise indefinitely even if emissions are held at current levels or slightly reduced.

The FCCC process has not yet specified a particular target concentration. But in order to stabilize concentrations at any level ranging from 450 parts per million to 750 parts per million, very large reductions of worldwide emissions (from emissions that might be anticipated were present trends to continue) would be required during the course of the present century.

Technology is Critical

Energy is central to the climate issue. Energy use appears to be the primary contributor to the global increase in carbon dioxide concentrations. Rapidly increasing world population, together with the universal desire for economic development, will lead to growing demand for the products and services that the energy system provides. The future evolution of that system – dominated today by coal, oil, and gas – is the key determinant of the magnitude of future human influence on the climate (see Figure 7.9).

Managing the risks of climate change will require a transformation in the production and consumption of energy. Technology is critical to such a transformation. Improved technology can both reduce the amount of energy needed to produce a unit of economic output and lower the carbon emissions per unit of energy used. Successful development and deployment of new and improved technologies can significantly reduce the cost of achieving any concentration target.

Recent trends in public and private spending on energy research and development suggest that the role of technology in addressing climate change may not be fully understood Total public funding of energy research in the OECD is falling. Although public investment in energy R&D has increased slightly in Japan, it has declined somewhat in the United States and dramatically in Europe, where reductions of 70 percent or more since the 1980s are the norm. Moreover, less than 3 percent of this investment is directed at a few technologies which, although not currently available commercially at an appreciable level, have the potential to lower the costs of stabilization significantly. (See Figure 10.1.)

Energy Technology Strategy

Fundamental changes in the energy system are required to stabilize concentrations of greenhouse gases in the atmosphere. Incremental improvements in technology help, but will not by themselves lead to stabilization.

A technology strategy is an essential complement to national and international policies aimed at limiting emissions, enhancing adaptation, and improving scientific understanding. A technology strategy will provide value by reducing costs under a wide range of possible futures, which is essential given the uncertainties in the science, policies, technologies, and energy resources. The lack of a technology strategy would greatly increase the difficulties of addressing the issue of climate change successfully.

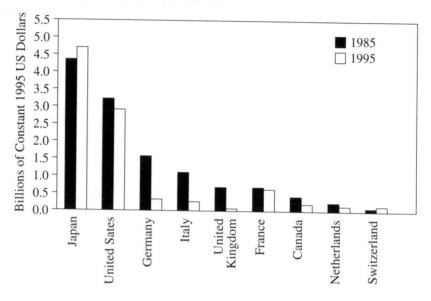

Sources: IEA (1997) and Dooley (1998).

Figure 10.1   *Total public funding of energy research and development in
selected nations in 1985 and 1995*

In the year 2000, the Global Energy Technology Strategy Program – an
international, public/private sector collaboration advised by an eminent
Steering Group – delivered these results at a special session during the
deliberations of the Conference of the Parties to the FCCC in The Hague.
The findings and recommendations of the Global Energy Technology Strategy Program, are an initial attempt at delineating the elements that will be
needed to guide the development of a technology strategy to address climate change.

These recommendations are predicated on four findings:

1. **Stabilizing concentrations of greenhouse gases in the atmosphere
   requires fundamental change in the energy system**

   - *Energy is central to the climate change issue*   Carbon dioxide emis-
     sions from the production and consumption of fossil fuels are the
     largest contributor to human emissions of greenhouse gases. Fossil-
     fuel resources are abundant, and, if used in conjunction with present
     energy technology, have the potential to increase the concentrations
     of greenhouse gases in the atmosphere substantially.

- *If present trends continue, carbon dioxide emissions from energy will continue to grow* The influences of future population growth and economic development on the demand for energy services are likely to exceed currently projected improvements in energy intensity and the ongoing transition to less carbon-intensive fuels. However, trends are not destiny – a global technology strategy could help change the present course.
- *In order to stabilize concentrations of greenhouse gases in the atmosphere, global carbon emissions must peak during the twenty-first century and then decline indefinitely* This can occur only if lower carbon-emitting technologies are deployed worldwide.

2. **Technology breakthroughs are essential both to stabilize concentrations and to control costs**

- *Although incremental technology improvements are essential, they will not lead to stabilization* Even with significant improvements in the performance of existing commercial technologies, the concentration of carbon dioxide in the atmosphere would grow to more than 2.5 times pre-industrial levels by 2100.
- *Technology breakthroughs can reduce the cost of stabilization dramatically* Technological advances can reduce the annual cost of stabilizing atmospheric concentrations of greenhouse gases by at least 1–2 percent of global world product. The savings will depend upon the concentration target and the level of technology improvement.
- *It is time to get started* The energy system is capital-intensive, and the development and deployment of new technologies can take decades. Given the lead-time necessary to develop and deploy new technologies with their associated systems and infrastructure, we must begin the process without delay.

3. **A portfolio of technologies is necessary to manage the risks of climate change and to respond to evolving conditions**

- *A diversified portfolio accommodates future uncertainties* Changing scientific knowledge and economic conditions, combined with uncertainty in the resource base, requires a diversified initial portfolio of technology investments. Portfolio investment priorities will evolve over time as these uncertainties evolve or are resolved.
- *A broad portfolio can control costs* A portfolio encompassing a broad suite of technologies can lower the costs of stabilization

significantly. However, the public and private sectors cannot fund every idea. Technology investment priorities must be established to reflect available funding.

- *A broad portfolio can meet the differing needs of key regions* Countries will need and employ different technologies based on their geography, indigenous resources, and economic, social, and political systems.
- *A flexible portfolio can accommodate alternative policy responses to the climate issue* The technology portfolio can be adapted to a diverse range of future national and international policy responses designed to address climate change.
- *A broad portfolio also can reflect the diversity of the energy system* Technologies are needed to improve the efficiency of energy use, develop non-carbon energy sources, and limit the free venting of carbon from the fossil energy that will continue to be burned.

4. **Current investments in energy research and development (R&D) are inadequate**

- *Energy R&D outlays are declining* Both public and private sector investments in energy R&D have declined significantly since the 1980s.
- *Energy R&D expenditures are unfocused and poorly coordinated* Neither public nor private sector investments are adequately focused on the technologies that could be critical for stabilizing concentrations in the long term. Among the few governments with national energy R&D programs, investments are poorly coordinated and fail to take advantage of possibilities for joint, complementary, or specialized research.
- *Terrestrial sequestration, hydrogen, and carbon capture, use, and storage technologies* potentially play an important role in stabilizing concentrations, but are currently funded at minimal levels.

These four findings in turn support four recommendations:

1. **Emissions limitations and controlling costs complement a technology strategy**

- *Emissions limits are needed to stabilize concentrations* Without such limits, individual nations have little incentive to reduce greenhouse gas emissions. It is unlikely that the required technologies to achieve stabilization will be developed and deployed if there is not any value placed on developing such technologies.

- *Controlling the costs of stabilization is necessary.* The costs of stabilizing concentrations of greenhouse gases are uncertain and are distributed unevenly across generations, nations, and sectors of the economy. Better definition and control of these costs is critical to achieving societal consensus to take action.

If the Kyoto Protocol does not represent the path forward, a suitable path is nonetheless needed. There are many options. But, without a credible commitment that cumulative emissions will be limited, important technologies will either not be developed, or be developed inappropriately.

2. Increase global investments in energy R&D

- *Increase investment in energy R&D* to improve the performance of existing technologies and to develop the next generation of technologies that are required to stabilize greenhouse gas concentrations.
- *Develop dedicated long-term funding sources* for energy R&D to support the necessary technology transformation.
- *Direct investments to specific technologies* that have significant potential to substantially reduce greenhouse gas emissions over the long term.
- *Build broad-based public support* by communicating the climate and ancillary benefits of energy R&D.

3. Improve the implementation and performance of energy R&D

- *Incorporate climate change* when revisiting current energy R&D priorities.
- *Better coordinate the roles of the public and private sectors* in the R&D process to reflect their specific strengths.
- *Fund all stages of the innovation process* from basic research to market deployment of the most promising technologies.
- *Establish long-term goals and near-term milestones* for technological performance to drive progress and to maximize returns on technology investments.
- *Design flexible R&D programs* to allow for the shifting of resources to accommodate new knowledge and conditions, particularly when sufficient technological progress is not being achieved.

4. Reflect the international nature of the research challenge

- *Develop and coordinate international and national energy technology R&D strategies* to take advantage of national scientific strengths and regional needs.
- *Provide assistance to key developing countries* to build their technical and institutional capacities for implementing energy R&D programs effectively and for deploying advanced technologies.

These findings and recommendations demonstrate the importance of technology in addressing climate change and provide general principles for moving forward.

NOTES

Letter by Lennart Hjalmarsson

* I am grateful to Henrik Hammar for useful suggestions.
1. *Enerdata Statistical Yearbook* (2000), www.enerdata.fr.
2. European Union Energy Outlook to 2020, *The Shared Analysis Project*, European Commission, 1999.
3. Russia and the former Soviet countries agreed to stabilize their emissions.
4. B. Andersson, *Essays on the Swedish Electricity Market*, Stockholm School of Economics, PhD Thesis, 1997.
5. W. Nordhaus, *The Swedish Dilemma – Nuclear Energy v. the Environment*, Stockholm SNS, 1995.

Letter by Robert L. Bradley, Jr.

1. US Energy Information Administration, *International Energy Outlook 2001* (Washington, DC: Government Printing Office, 2001), p. 185.
2. Committee on the Science of Climate Change, *Climate Change Science: An Analysis of Some Key Questions* (Washington, DC: National Academy Press, 2001), p. 22.
3. Ibid., p. 17.
4. Richard Kerr, 'Rising global temperature, rising uncertainty', *Science*, April 13, 2001, p. 192. Kerr made a similar revision to the Summary for Policymakers of the second (1995) IPCC assessment: 'An international panel has suggested that global warming has arrived, but many scientists say it will be a decade before computer models can confidently link the warming to human activities.' Richard Kerr, 'Greenhouse forecasts still cloudy', *Science*, May 16, 1997, p. 1040.
5. 'The uncertainties give some researchers pause when IPCC so confidently attributes past warming to the [enhanced] greenhouse [effect], but projecting warming into the future gives almost everyone the willies … . By all accounts, knowledge [about the human role in climate change] will be evolving for decades to come.' Kerr, 'Rising global temperature, rising uncertainty,' *Science*, pp. 192, 194. On the growing uncertainty of climate prediction and a behavioral bias of climate modeling toward conformity, see Gerald North, 'Book Review: L.D. Harvey, *Global Warming: The Hard Science*', in *Climate Change*, vol. 49, 2001, p. 496.
6. Intergovernmental Panel on Climate Change, *Climate Change 2001: The Scientific Basis* (Cambridge, UK: Cambridge University Press, 2001), pp. 350, 357.

7. Ibid., p. 10.
8. The extrapolation is not linear but logarithmic due to the properties of carbon dioxide absorptivity on infrared wavelength. E-mail communication from Gerald North, Department of Atmospheric Sciences, Texas A&M University, to author, July 6, 2001.
9. Committee on the Science of Climate Change, *Climate Change Science: An Analysis of Some Key Uncertainties*, pp. 13–14.
10. IPCC, *Climate Change 2001*, pp. 2, 4, 27, 30, 101, 104, 106, 108, and 129.
11. Ibid., pp. 13, 67, and 116–17. Higher temperatures that are still below freezing can be considered *dead warming* for purposes of ecological and economic evaluation.
12. Intergovernmental Panel on Climate Change, *Climate Change 1995 – The Science* (Cambridge, UK: Cambridge University Press, 1996), p. 6; IPCC, *Climate Change 2001*, p. 16.
13. IPCC, *Climate Change 2001*, p. 642.
14. Ibid., p. 641.
15. Ibid., p. 641.
16. Ibid., p. 31.
17. John Weyant and Jennifer Hill, 'Introduction and Overview', in *The Energy Journal*, Kyoto Special Issue, 1999, p. xliv.
18. Christopher Flavin, 'Last tango in Buenos Aires', *Worldwatch*, November/December 1998, pp. 11, 18.
19. See, for example, Duncan Brack, Michael Grubb and Craig Windram, *International Trade and Climate Change Policies* (London: Royal Institute of International Affairs, 2000).
20. US Energy Information Administration, *Annual Energy Review 2000* (Washington, DC: US Department of Energy, 2001), p. 221.
21. International Energy Agency, *World Energy Outlook* (Paris: OECD/EIA, 2000), p. 21; US Energy Information Administration, *International Energy Outlook, 2001* (Washington, DC: Department of Energy, 2001), p. 176.
22. See John Graham and Jonathan Wiener (eds), *Risk versus Risk: Tradeoffs in Protecting Health and the Environment* (Cambridge, MA: Harvard University Press, 1995) and Robert Hahn (ed.), *Risk, Costs, and Lives Saved* (Washington, DC: Oxford University Press, 1996).
23. T.M.L. Wigely, 'The Kyoto Protocol: CO_2, CH_4 and climate implications', *Geophysical Research Letters*, July 1, 1998, p. 2288.
24. The insurance rationale for beginning a small GHG regulatory program assumes that the cost of the 'policy' is cost-effective and that the redemption value is reasonably known. Neither is the case. Climate science has not defined a 'dangerous' level of anthropogenic GHG concentrations in the atmosphere. Climate economics predicts substantial benefits will accrue to offset costs from the human influence on climate many decades in the future. The 'no-regrets' action advocated below is not insurance either but a strategy to incrementally reduce GHGs in a cost-effective manner, while advancing societal wealth to adapt to climate change.
25. For new evidence on a neutral-to-negative water vapor feedback, cloud cooling from sulfate aerosols, and overestimated surface warming since the 1970s, see, respectively, Richard Lindzen, Ming-Dah Chou and Arthur Y. Hou, 'Does the Earth have an adaptive infrared iris?', *Bulletin of the American Meteorological Society*, March 2001, pp. 417–32; Robert Charleston, John H. Seinfeld, Athanasios Nenes, Markku Kulmala, Ari Laaksonen and M. Cristina Facchini, 'Reshaping the theory of cloud formation', *Science*, June 15, 2001, pp. 2025–7; and John Christy, David E. Parker, Simon J. Brown, Ian Macadam, Martin Stendel and William B. Norris, 'Differential trends in tropical sea surface and atmosphere temperatures since 1979', *Geophysical Research Letters*, January 1, 2001, pp. 183–6.
26. See, generally, Robert Bradley, *Julian Simon and the Triumph of Energy Sustainability* (Washington, DC: American Legislative Exchange Council, 2000).
27. The estimate of 1.6 billion persons is from World Energy Council, *Energy for Tomorrow's World – Acting Now* (London: World Energy Council, 2000), p. 5.

Subject index

Author index